uniquely NORMAL

Tapping the Reservoir of Normalcy To Treat Autism

BEST BOOK
AWARDS
WINNER
BestBookAwards.com

Robert J. Bernstein with Robin Cantor-Cooke

Foreword by Dr. Temple Grandin

ADVANCE PRAISE FOR

UNIQUELY NORMAL

"Bernstein has mapped out a practical path for parents to increase the skills and independence of kids on the autism spectrum while respecting their ways of experiencing the world, supporting their autonomy, and avoiding the traumatizing methods of ABA and other purely behavioral approaches."

— Steve Silberman, author, *NeuroTribes: The Legacy of Autism and the Future of Neurodiversity*

"Without exception, Rob Bernstein's work with these patients has markedly improved their ability to function effectively with others. He has a unique ability to engage with people, gently yet firmly coaxing them into the wider world, often for the first time. Once there, he guides them toward claiming their competence and channeling their untapped strengths. I stand behind Rob Bernstein's techniques without reservation."

— Ram Kairam, MD, Pediatric Neurologist, Developmental Neurology Associates (DNA); Professor of Neurology, Columbia University Medical Center

"*Uniquely Normal* provides astounding insights into the fascinating minds on the autism spectrum, and much-needed guidance to parents of neurotypical and atypical children alike."

— He Xu, PhD, Harvard University

"*Uniquely Normal* is a uniquely insightful study of human nature. Groundbreaking in what it reveals about the autism spectrum, it simultaneously speaks to the power of the great tradition of ethnographic research."

— Steven L. Strauss, MD, Neurology; PhD, Linguistics; Diplomate of the American Board of Psychiatry and Neurology; Former Professor of Neurology at the University of Maryland, currently in private practice in Baltimore, Maryland

"Rob Bernstein's book presents a groundbreaking, clear, and well-reasoned alternative approach to working with children, adolescents, and adults with autism spectrum disorders. A must-read for parents, psychologists, teachers, and those who care for and nurture individuals with ASD."

— Gloria S. Lazar, MS, MPhil, CCC, Speech-Language Pathologist

"A deeply moving account of the multi-faceted nature of autism, its course, and the power of believing in one's capacity to be—as is. Bernstein, with Cantor-Cooke, takes the reader on a tender, textured, and experience-near journey that illuminates the clinical benefits of an individualized, patient-centered approach to treating individuals who have been diagnosed with autism. A must-read for anyone who has wondered about alternatives to Applied Behavior Analysis (ABA), recognizes the multilayered experience of an individual with autism, and, most movingly, believes in the transformative nature of a core human connection."

— Lara Sheehi, PsyD, Assistant Professor of Clinical Psychology, The George Washington University

"Rob Bernstein offers a compelling and engaging model in the treatment of autism. This is an enjoyable and informative read for anyone who has a person with autism in their life."

— Mark Krakauer, MD, Pediatrician

"Bernstein's methodology, developed after years of experience in the present educational system (which clearly fails most of these individuals), demonstrates a revolutionary cognitive approach to autism that departs from current practice. It is a must-read for all parents and professionals dealing with children with autism."

— Douglas P. Hudson, MD, MPH

"Robert Bernstein is one of the smartest, most perceptive people I know. No matter where someone falls on the scale of 'normal,' Bernstein finds a way to connect."

— Will Shortz, Crossword Editor, *The New York Times*

"You're not your typical therapist, you think outside the box, which is great because John is not your typical Asperger's. He's unique in his way, and you're unique in your way."

— Coleen O'Rourke, Parent, Eastchester, NY

"You rock! You do, you rock! It's been amazing. There is no way we would have gotten this change out of him if we were not taking him to see you. He's done a lot in just the last couple months. We tried other therapy sessions and it didn't mesh. It's been unbelievable. He loves coming, he does, he loves coming here."

— N.R., Parent, Bronx, NY

"It's just amazing what you do! It's so amazing what you do that once you get it, I'm telling you, it's like I'm like on drugs—I'm in a trance now, I'm SO happy. You're so different from 99% of the people I've met. If you just disappeared I would go nuts, because I finally got it! I'm so happy. I say, 'Wake up everybody, There's a new world out there.'"

— R.T., Parent, Chappaqua, NY

"Any reader who has been drawn in by Oliver Sacks's marvelous case studies will be drawn to Rob Bernstein's new book, Uniquely Normal. Bernstein, a born storyteller, brings his experiences with children with autism to life so that any parent or caregiver will be inspired and guided to try his tested approach to effect profound change in their loved ones. His book teaches behavioral and speech strategies that shift patterns of behavior and yet honor the individuality of each child. In this extraordinary work, Bernstein employs vivid case studies—transformed into compelling stories—to revolutionize the way parents and caregivers think about and treat children with autism."

— Steve Zeitlin, Ph.D., Founding Director, City Lore

"Never in a million years did I think Mr. Bernstein would empower Jack to take the quantum leap out of 'his own world,' conceptualize everyday society, and land in our typical world. It was, and still is, the amazing breakthrough that continues to enable him to facilitate meaningful relationships with friends, family members, and acquaintances. I will never be able to repay this gift he has have given Jack, that has allowed our atypical son to soar in our everyday society. We are no longer living in 'Jack's world'."

— Jennifer Betman, Parent, Jericho, LI

"He has really helped a lot of people over the years ... every time I listen to Rob, I get so inspired because he really has made a big difference in people's lives, and has eased the stress of a lot of parents. He is always the most interesting guest; he has never disappointed me. He has done a lot of wonders for people."

— Paul Feiner, Greenburgh Town Supervisor ("The Greenburgh Report," WVOX Radio, New Rochelle, NY)

"I'm really excited. I'm totally blown away. It's fantastic. There's such hope, more than hope, already I see it working. This is unbelievable. Everything is possible. Thank you."

— Eileen Fisher (talking about her son)

UNIQUELY NORMAL:
Tapping the Reservoir of Normalcy To Treat Autism

All marketing and publishing rights guaranteed to and reserved by:

FUTURE HORIZONS INC.

721 W. Abram Street
Arlington, TX 76013
(800) 489-0727
(817) 277-0727
(817) 277-2270 (fax)
E-mail: info@fhautism.com
www.fhautism.com

Cover & interior design by John Yacio III

ISBN: 9781941765463

To my brother

CONTENTS

INTRODUCTION:

PART 1: EARLY CHILDHOOD, AGES 2–5 35

PART 2: CHILDHOOD, AGES 6–10 81

PART 3: EARLY ADOLESCENCE, AGES 11–14 161

AUTHOR'S NOTE

After years of giving talks to parents of children on the autism spectrum (including youngsters diagnosed with Asperger's syndrome, also known as high-functioning autism), I've learned that most have not come to get more information about the disorder; they have come because they want to know how they can help their children. Their deepest hope is to help their sons and daughters become functional and independent and grow up to fulfill their potential. They are committed to learning how to give their children the tools they need to live happy, rewarding lives. Adults on the spectrum who attend my talks hold the same hope for themselves.

As our knowledge of autism evolves, so does the language we use to describe it. The fifth and most recent edition of the *Diagnostic and Statistical Manual of Mental Disorders* (DSM-V), published by the American Psychiatric Association in 2013, did away with Asperger's syndrome as a discrete diagnosis, absorbing it into the category of autism spectrum disorders. Still, I have many clients who were diagnosed with Asperger's and prefer to be identified as having Asperger's than high-functioning autism, the DSM-V's preferred term. For this reason, I use both terms in the book.

The stories in these pages recount my experiences working with children and adults ranging in age from 2 to 62. My cognitive-based approach is founded on the premise that when we change the way we think, we change the way we behave and live, which is why it is effective for people of any age, at any stage of their lives. Just as I have been able to engage with and help my clients, so can you connect with your loved one and improve his or her quality of life.

To get the most out of this book, I urge you to explore the cases in every age group. The techniques I use with a 6-year-old differ from those I use with a college student, but their goal is the same: to learn how the person's mind works and retrain his or her thinking to function more productively. My hope is that you see something of your loved one in the stories that follow, and use the exercises, strategies, and techniques I describe to improve his or her ability to function in the world.

Correspondence concerning this book should be addressed to:

rjb@autismspeech.com

FOREWORD

The 27 case histories in this book cover the full range of the autism spectrum. They vary from a smart, perfectionistic student to a nonverbal child with constant stimming. Parents, teachers, and individuals on the spectrum can all find one or two case histories that they really relate to. There is no complicated jargon in this book. The prose is conversational and easy to understand.

Rob Bernstein tells the story of how he successfully worked with each individual. The ages range from a child of two years to older adults. Something I really like about this book is that busy parents and teachers can look through the cases and read only the ones that are similar to either their own child or a student at their school.

The cases include:

- Jeff, 6, who doesn't speak and bites his hand until it bleeds;
- Mitch, 11, a high-functioning perfectionist who has frequent outbursts at school;
- Harriet, 15, morose and angry with her mother;
- George, 62, who has a genius IQ but can't remember what his wife wants at the store.

Bernstein's basic principles are:

1. Look for periods of normal behavior and expand on them.
2. Use natural language and do not constantly interrupt with praise, because interruptions may block the flow of the activity.
3. Teach an individual with perfectionistic, rigid thinking different methods of solving the same problem. Doing this teaches flexible thinking.

4. Get the individual out in the real world. Recently, I talked to two teenage boys who were so overprotected that they had never bought anything by themselves in a store.

5. Teach parents and teachers not to overprotect the child. It is a big mistake when they do everything for them. This is similar to my "stretching" approaches, which get the individual to do something slightly outside their comfort zone.

I could really relate Bernstein's ideas to my own experiences. Traditional repetitive ABA training was used in speech lessons when I was two to four years old. The repetition helped strengthen faulty brain circuits, much like physical therapy. It was difficult for me to get speech out, and when people talked fast their speech turned to gibberish. Praising me after each attempt to get speech out was appropriate at this point in my life. Repetition was needed to help get my brain circuits prepared for more natural use of language. There was also a lot of time spent playing turn-taking games. By age five, when my speech was more fluent, all traditional ABA-type training was phased out; I was no longer praised for talking, and only natural language was used.

Similarly, Bernstein emphasizes the importance of providing opportunities to use words in natural situations. If a child wants something, such as juice, he or she needs to be encouraged to use words. Many kids with speech problems are like a slow computer, or a phone with only one bar. They must be given time to respond.

Recently, I visited a therapeutic horseback riding program and they asked me to be a side walker with a little girl who had limited speech. Part of her program was to learn better motor skills by tossing rings on traffic cones and tossing a ball to different people, but she had little interest in these activities. I decided to try Bernstein's methods. When she was asked to throw the ball to me, she instantly flung it hard on the ground. She was definitely not interacting with me. I responded the same way I would to a normal child. "You chucked it, and I could not catch it." After I got the ball, I faced her and said, "I am going to toss the ball gently so you can catch it." After she caught it, I said, "Toss it back gently." She responded by smiling and tossing the ball gently. I had to fight the urge to say "good job." According to Bernstein, constant or intermittent praise can sometimes interfere with the "flow" of an activity. Smiling and playing a successful game of catch was rewarding. We soon had a few successful tosses of three-person catch.

At another riding center, I met a non-verbal teenager who was learning to ride. He could not talk, so I decided to assume he had normal intelligence and communicated with gestures. When I pointed at the stall door and made a horizontal hand movement, he immediately closed the sliding door. My assumption was correct: he was intelligent.

Uniquely Normal will provide readers with lots of practical ways to work with the full spectrum of individuals with autism.

— **Temple Grandin, Ph.D.,**

author of *The Way I See It*

and *The Autistic Brain*

Introduction

STRANGER IN THE
STRANGEST LAND:
INTO THE LANDSCAPE
OF AUTISM

INTRODUCTION

On the middle finger of my right hand just above the palm, there's a gray smudge where my brother stabbed me with a pencil more than 50 years ago. I remember the pain but not the reason that Ben* attacked me, probably because it was nothing unusual. I learned early on to be wary of my older brother, whose sudden swings of mood or a Ticonderoga No. 2 garnered little attention from my parents, who had neither the time nor the psychological awareness to delve into the dark unpredictability of their first-born son. Like many first-generation Americans who came of age during the Depression, they were simple, hardworking people who never traveled anywhere other than to and from their jobs. Our modest garden apartment in Queens, New York, symbolized to them our successful assimilation into the respectable middle class. My mother in particular wanted me to grow up American, live without problems or issues in a safe, decent neighborhood, and get a good education. Parenting had not yet become a verb; mothers and fathers were nouns, and they cooked, cleaned, nurtured, scolded, and loved us until they took to their creaking bed, bone-tired, at night.

There was always something odd about Ben. He loved to mock others and had little use for me except as a target of abuse—verbal and otherwise. He became a master of the put-down, having honed his skills on me throughout our childhoods. His nickname for me was "Bee," which he would deliver with a smirk and riled me no end, not least because I didn't have a clue as to what it meant. No shortcoming of mine escaped his

---

* *My brother's real name and those of the persons whose cases are described in this book have been changed.*

3

attention: I was a shrimp, a dweeb, a pathetic weakling. He never patted my back when I was the last kid picked for a backyard ball game (which happened often); nor did he ever walk over to console me when I got hit. One winter, I got socked in the face with an icy snowball that tore open my scalp. All the kids came running except one—my brother—who stood fidgeting with his gloves watching me bleed into the snow.

Psychotherapist Jeanne Safer, who grew up with a damaged brother, writes, "No one with an abnormal sibling has a normal childhood ... their goal is to be as different from their sibling as possible."[1] I am working with two brothers now, fraternal twins, one of whom has high-functioning autism. Quinn, who is on the spectrum, will be attending community college in the fall; Connor will go to a 4-year school several hundred miles away. After 3 months of working with Quinn, I had a session with Connor for the first time last week. He spoke of his frustration with his brother, who wants to go where he goes and do what he does. "He keeps telling me to make my friends be friends with him, too," Connor said, "and he does hang out with us sometimes. But other times I just want to be with my friends, so I don't invite him. And then I feel like crap because his feelings are hurt. I mean, he's got a date for the prom, okay? And she goes to a different school, so he gets to go to her prom, too. I mean, how cool is that? I only get to go to mine, but he always thinks I've got it better than him. It pisses me off." One of my goals is to convince Quinn of his unique and valuable life and help him see that he has some good stuff his brother doesn't have. And I want to persuade Connor to make the most of these last few months at home with his brother, whom he loves, and from whom he feels compelled to distance himself.

And so it was with me, both drawn to and wary of a brother I couldn't understand. It never occurred to my parents to take Ben to a psychologist; that was for kids who started fires or stole things or ran around screaming in public. Ben didn't do any of that. Sure, he was different from other kids, but he was intelligent and got good grades and the cops never came to the house. I grew up knowing that my parents loved both of us but that Ben was the kid with problems and I was the normal one. I was expected to be a source of pride to my parents: to do well in school, be respectful, bring home nice friends, and adjust to my brother's eccentricities.

One adjustment I made was to let Ben win whatever game we were playing—Chinese Checkers, Monopoly, gin rummy—if there was going to be a winner; it was going to be him. Fiercely competitive, he needed to dominate any situation, especially if I were involved. If he were losing, he would go from peeved to hostile to angry pretty quickly, and I learned it wasn't worth it to assert my superiority at anything. Ben needed to control things and it was my role to acquiesce. By the time I was in high school and as big as he was, I had gotten really good at table tennis and chess and allowed myself to beat him now and then. But when we were kids, I lived in his shadow.

And so it was that when Ben broke his foot and wasn't allowed to play outside after school, I didn't get to go out, either. We were around 13 and 11 at the time and, like many kids growing up in the 1950s whose parents both worked, were expected to come straight home after school, let ourselves in with a key, drink a glass of milk with a couple of Oreos, and do our homework. Then, if it was still light out, we could go out to play. Except my parents had forbidden Ben to go out until the cast came off his foot, so he locked the door and told me if I tried to leave he'd kill me. I took him at his word.

I never told my parents about this, probably because I knew it wouldn't do any good. My parents couldn't deal with Ben; his moodiness and aloofness vexed them, but they were ill-equipped to respond in an effective way. I don't remember them ever demanding he do anything he didn't want to; after a while, they stopped trying. Ben was neither required to conform to norms of social behavior nor expected to exhibit conventional responses to situations or people or anything, for that matter. My wife recently pointed out the difference between our bar-mitzvah photos, each taken when we turned 13. In mine, I'm looking directly at the camera with blazing eyes and a face-splitting grin. In Ben's, he gazes beyond the lens rather than into it, and his expression is flat, distant, and disengaged. Neither my parents nor I ever remarked on how somber he looked for a bar-mitzvah boy. Ben was who he was; it was a fact of our lives.

I also think I kept quiet because I didn't want to add to my parents' worries. The last thing they needed was another kid who required extra attention. Better to put up with my brother's abuse and keep my mouth shut than undermine my status as the easy, loveable son. I may have been a glutton for punishment, but I wasn't an idiot.

Nor is my brother. Ben went to college and on to graduate school, where he earned a doctorate. Today, he is well known in his field, delivers talks across the country and the world, has published his share of articles and books, and had perhaps more than his share of marriages and divorces.

Several years ago, he proposed marriage to an accomplished woman of rare intelligence, empathy, and patience. And moxie: Before she would agree to marry him, she prodded him to go for psychological testing. She explained it to me this way: "I could marry him if he had Asperger's, but not if he was an ass." They've been married for almost 6 years now. And that's how my brother came to be diagnosed as having an autism spectrum disorder—in his mid-sixties.

This wasn't a shock for people who know Ben, but it does answer the question of why there weren't kids on the autism spectrum 50 years ago, because there were: My brother was there all along, as were thousands of others, their offbeat and sometimes off-putting behaviors branding them as eccentric, weird, or worse. They suffered the indignities of being grossly underestimated and misunderstood, and the agony of being the strange kids who refused to behave, couldn't make friends, and didn't fit in. They mystified their families, whose lack of psychological enlightenment rendered them incapable of coping with this stranger who looked like them but acted like no one they knew. They provided an irresistible target for the derision of other kids, whose own anxieties about not fitting in were eased by the spectacle of someone even more out-there than they were. They grew up accustomed to being different and more isolated than they wanted to be. Consummate outsiders, they appeared normal until you tried to shake their hand, or look them in the eye, or engage them in small talk, which is when you noticed that something was off—just off enough to make you feel uncomfortable, or look away, or find a reason to excuse yourself and seek someone else to talk to. What none of us realized at the time was that they found us as bizarre and unknowable as we found them.

As hard as it was to get along with my brother, I was getting the knack of it. I was learning what things irked him, or set him off, or pleased him. One thing he liked was living room basketball, in which we wadded aluminum foil into a small sphere and launched it toward either of two lamps on opposite sides of the room. The wire fitters of the lampshade tops formed hoops and we lobbed foul shots toward them or banked shots off the wall as we ran around giggling. I loved that game even though I never won; Ben was always better at it and, unlike some older brothers I knew, he never let me get the better of him. Still, when Ben suggested we play living room basketball or anything else, I'd run to join him because I was thrilled that he wanted to play with me. He may have been eccentric but he was still my big brother, and I basked in whatever attention he shone my way.

I was unaware of it at the time, of course, but living with Ben was educating me in the ways of autism. His unpredictable responses to predictable situations taught me to expect the unexpected. I never knew how Ben would react if I asked him to play with me, so I trained myself to wait until he approached me rather than risk rejection. When I heard him talking to himself, which he did frequently, I'd lurk nearby and listen because I could tell from his tone what kind of mood he was in. Armed with this intel, I knew whether or not to risk asking him for help with my algebra homework. Life at home provided countless opportunities to observe his mannerisms. Families ate together when I was growing up, so I must have sat at the dinner table with Ben well over 5,000 times. And afterward, we would often gather to watch TV on the big black-and-white Zenith in the living room. We didn't get to spend much time with our dad, so I loved it when he'd suggest we sit together and watch *The Jetsons*. And it would confound me when, more than once, my brother announced, "I am going away to another room so I can read." Not only was the locution awkward—I am going away to another room—but it struck me as utterly weird that he'd rather read a book by himself than watch TV with us. I didn't say anything about it when it happened, but some part of my mind was wondering why my brother was the way he was.

If some of Ben's behaviors were odd, others seemed totally normal. In addition to *The Jetsons*, my father liked watching sports on TV, so he, Ben, and I would watch together. The Yankees were nearly unbeatable back then, and Ben seemed no more unhinged than the rest of us when Roger Maris and Mickey Mantle were knocking them out of the park. Seeing him leap off the couch and shouting at the screen, he seemed like any other New York City kid (the Mets didn't hit the scene until 1962; before that, every New Yorker was a Yankees fan, period). We also loved watching *The Phil Silvers Show*, in which the comedian starred as Sergeant Bilko, a wheedling Army guy who was always trying to get his men to do his work for him and invest in his get-rich-quick schemes. Sophisticated it wasn't, but Ben and I thought it was hilarious and laughed ourselves silly for 30 minutes every week. That's when we bonded, our differences obliterated by the raucous exuberance of our young selves. To this day, I call him up at halftime during the NCAA basketball championships to ask him what he thinks of the game so far. Now I'm the one who reaches out; I always call

Ben—he never calls me—and the conversation lasts maybe a minute. But he always picks up the phone, and I always enjoy hearing his voice. It's one way I know I can connect with him.

Another way I hoped I'd connect with him was through the immortal Sergeant Bilko. Not long ago, a friend gave me a set of DVDs with maybe 60 episodes of the show. After I watched them, I packed them up and sent them to Ben via Priority Mail as a surprise. The day they were supposed to arrive, I didn't hear anything—nor the next day, nor the next. After 2 weeks, I phoned Ben and asked him if he'd gotten a package from me. There was a silence and then he spoke. "Oh, you mean the Bilko discs"—no excitement, no joy, just a flat, Ben-like tone.

"Well, yeah," I said. "They must have gotten there over 2 weeks ago."

"Yes, they did." A pause.

"And you didn't call to tell me you received them?" Another pause.

"No. I didn't." My heart sank. This was a huge deal for me; I never send Ben anything. I'd been so excited about giving him the DVDs and imagining him reliving, as I had, memories of the fun we'd had.

"Oh," I said. "I guess you didn't watch them."

"I did watch them," Ben said. "I watched all of them, one after the other. I couldn't stop. It was so much fun. Thank you."

So he had loved the gift. Yet he didn't respond. I can laugh about this sort of thing because I've grown accustomed to Ben's communication style (or lack thereof). Sixty years of continuing education will do that.

* * * *

INTRODUCTION

After graduating from college with a degree in psychology, I enrolled at Columbia University in the early 1970s to do graduate work in special education (special ed.). I wasn't sure whether I wanted to work in a school or open my own practice, but was drawn to the idea of working with kids to discover how their minds worked, especially when they worked differently.

At the time, we didn't know much about autism. The word itself hadn't even existed until 30 years earlier when Leo Kanner, a psychiatrist at Johns Hopkins, used it to describe 11 young patients of his who seemed to live in their own disconnected worlds. They were happiest when left alone, rejecting the company of both children and adults, as well as typical ways of playing and interacting. The following year, a Viennese pediatrician named Hans Asperger published a paper about four children he was treating with similar behaviors; he also used the word autism to describe their condition.[2]

Until then and for too long after, little distinction was made between what was then called mental retardation and what we now know as autism spectrum disorders. Children with symptoms of autism were often thought of as hopeless cases, their bizarre, inexplicable behaviors an indication of profound and permanent intellectual impairment. Their only salvation, it was believed, would be to develop behaviors that seemed more normal to the people around them. The techniques in vogue then were the same as those widely used today, and founded on the applied behavior analysis (ABA) system. ABA's core principle is that people can change their behaviors by undergoing a program of regulated, repeated exercises and having their progress monitored by rigorous, frequent testing. When they make progress, they receive a reward, which reinforces the newly learned behavior and motivates them to abandon their old ways and replace them with new ones. I was trained in this method, as were most special educators at the time. But it seemed wrong-headed to me in several important ways.

The first was its emphasis on repetition. I believed that rote repetition was one way—a mechanical way—to change behavioral patterns, but that it didn't address the underlying cause of the behavior and was therefore a temporary fix at best. I was convinced that many of these kids were intellectually capable of understanding why modifying some behaviors would serve them well, and that the reward of functioning competently in the wider world would mean more to them than a pizza party or any other incentive they might receive.

I learned this firsthand from 10-year-old Nathan, who attended a summer program for special needs kids that I ran many years ago. Nate's stubbornness, rigidity, and habit of walking away from his teacher and classmates and into the woods, on occasion, was infuriating the staff, who viewed these behaviors as willful antagonism. I prescribed a behavioral approach: When Nate walked away, his counselors were to address him as they would a small child, teaching him, through repetition, to stop when he heard them ask him to. If he threw a tantrum, they were to calmly explain that it wouldn't hurt him if his desires weren't immediately met. When Nate demanded the impossible, they were to explain why it couldn't be done. They were to threaten and impose negative consequences when necessary, and lavish praise whenever Nate accomplished anything.

It didn't work. Nate showed minimal and only temporary improvement; the next day, he'd revert back to his old ways and we had to start from scratch. I realized I had to unearth the roots of his behaviors, not just try to change them. To explore how his mind worked, I presented him with a pile of blocks to sort into three shoeboxes, each of which contained either a red, yellow, or blue block as a guide. He did this easily. Then I emptied the shoeboxes and changed the exercise: I placed a yellow block into one of them and a red block into each of the remaining two. Nate was confused: There was no box for the blues! Seizing a blue block but seeing no box designated to receive it, he placed it in the box that formerly held the blues—and none too happily, either. To Nate, there was one way to do the task: the way he had done it before. Nate was unable to think outside the box—literally and figuratively. His rigid thought process represented a gap in his cognitive development; he had developed neither an awareness of other people nor an ability to see things from other perspectives. This explained his inability to change his way of doing things. It also explained his insistence on exiting the classroom, which I then recognized as his way of relieving the stress he felt while inside it. Working in concert with Nate's teachers and other classroom helpers, I developed a series of actions they could take to deal with him. When Nate got up and began to wander out, the teacher would call him back while a helper would gently guide him back toward his desk. The goal was to create a new habit in concert with the old one: It was acceptable to walk away, but also fine to return upon the teacher's instruction to do so. It didn't work every time, but Nate did eventually start returning to his seat more often than not: He realized that there were options beyond those to which he'd been confining himself. His behavior improved, which was always the goal. But it improved because he changed the way he was thinking, not because he was being punished for bad behavior or rewarded for good. He improved from the inside out.

My second objection to applied behavior analysis was that it reinforced the repetitive tendencies of children with autism. ABA is based on striving for small, attainable goals—getting a barely verbal child to say car five times, for example, or recognize the same photograph after it appears repeatedly on a progression of flashcards. This process cultivates repetitive action, which in turn creates habits—unthinking performances of the same behavior, devoid of any understanding of why the behavior is desirable. In contrast, the behaviors of children who develop typically are founded on consistent patterns of thought and language that make sense to the child: If I am thirsty, a typical child will learn, I can ask daddy or mommy for a drink, and if I do it politely, they'll give me one. The thought process—I feel a certain way, I express my feelings in language that adults can understand, the adults respond in a way that makes me feel better and gets me what I want—is a mindful one that trains the child's developing brain to repeat a pattern of being aware of the self, expressing the self intelligibly to others, and receiving a satisfactory response from those others. This pattern is not only useful in negotiating countless human interactions; it is utterly necessary for conducting fulfilling relationships of every kind.

My third and perhaps most vehement objection to applied behavior analysis was that it seemed to focus on what these children could not do rather than on what they could do. Having grown up with a brother whose antisocial behaviors belied a vibrant intelligence and passionate soul, I knew better than to think that odd or even off-putting behaviors indicated limited intellectual potential. I was sure I was onto something and eager to put my theories into practice. They were teaching me methods and techniques that didn't resonate with my way of thinking and I would learn them, but I wasn't obligated to practice them. I had faith in these kids. I believed in their untapped potential. I saw things that other people didn't see, and I was determined to make the most of my insight.

Which brings me to my older son.

When he was 6 years old, his first-grade teacher called my wife and me at home. "I'm wondering if the two of you could come in for a talk," she said. "Dylan has a problem."

A problem? My kid had a problem? I was suddenly alert.

"He does things differently," the teacher said. "Whether we're working on writing or art or anything else, he insists on holding his paper vertically. Sometimes I want the children to hold it horizontally, but he challenges me, wants to know why he should do it, and when I tell him, he refuses. I've stopped asking. And that's just one thing he does." I was shaken: Some time ago, Dylan had told me his teacher had chastised him for holding his paper the wrong way. I'd been dismayed by her lack of imagination. "You're thinking for yourself—good for you," I had said, ever the supportive, forward-thinking dad. "There's no wrong way to hold your paper." Unless, of course, the teacher asked you to hold it one way and you insist on holding it another. That's wrong. Here I was, a special education professional, and I had missed a bright and shining clue into my son's psychological makeup.

There were other clues, of course, many of which escaped my wife and me until our second child arrived. Like many parents, we saw our first kid as a wonder unto himself: He was like no other baby or toddler or preschooler or kindergartner on the planet. Dylan was Dylan; that was fine with us. Until Jed was born when Dylan was almost 3, and the differences between them emerged. From his first days, Jed was an animated, energetic baby, kicking his feet and following our movements with his eyes. He'd coo and giggle and connect with Rachel and me, rewarding our attentions by kicking faster and reaching for us with his hands. We knew that Dylan was quieter and more self-absorbed than many other toddlers, but only then did we realize that he had always been quiet and serious, if there is such a thing as a serious baby. Even as a 3-year-old, Dylan had seemed less engaged with his surroundings than Jed already did, often absorbed in solitary pursuits such as arranging his toys with focused deliberation or gazing at a picture book, page by page, over and over again. I attributed this to personality: People are different, after all. Who says all kids have to be outgoing? It wasn't until Dylan's teacher pointed out his eccentricities that I was forced to see my son as others did.

I did an evaluation on Dylan, subtly subjecting him to the same challenges I would any 6-year-old whose abilities I wanted to measure. His reading skills weren't stellar, so I worked with him over the summer and by the start of second grade, he was one of the strongest readers in the class.

His report cards were good; Dylan's cognitive abilities were unimpaired. Indeed, as he grew, we saw that he possessed a determined, vigorous intelligence. His fifth-grade teacher admitted that she was flustered when he asked her what made tectonic plates move, rendering her speechless in front of the class. Her discomfort was my reassurance: Dylan was a bright kid after all.

His troubles weren't over, however. Dylan was coming home from school emotionally and physically bruised. Kids were mocking him in the lunchroom and knocking him down in the hallway. This was long before the national outcry against bullying; there were no anti-bullying programs, and if your kid had this kind of problem, you were on your own. In junior high, one kid, an athlete, was tormenting him so much that Rachel and I phoned his parents, who responded by saying that if their son was giving ours a hard time, Dylan must have it coming. We were appalled: What kind of people blame a kid for being bullied?

Rachel and I were stricken. We knew we had to protect our son but diplomacy and reason were useless. Dylan's view, however, was more optimistic as well as more perceptive: "They're not bad kids," he said, "but there's no one there like me." He realized he was different from other kids even if we didn't.

We decided to move to a different school district. It was marginally better there until Dylan's old nemesis figured out that a kid on his baseball team attended Dylan's new school, and the new kid picked up where the old one left off. Things deteriorated quickly after that. We had to get him out of there, but where could he go?

He ended up transferring to a highly competitive prep school where he was one of many kids content to think of themselves as nerds. They weren't all on the spectrum, of course, but they were comfortable being around kids with obsessive work habits, eccentric personalities, and awkward social behaviors. Dylan had finally found his people, and he flourished. He's fine now, with a college degree, an Ivy League MBA, a well-paying job in a field he loves, and a committed relationship with an accomplished young woman.

If Dylan's difficulties were hard on him, they also had a profound effect on me and galvanized my interest in autism into a passion to understand it. I knew my son was intelligent, sensitive, and capable; I also knew he needed to be taught differently so he could learn, as did the other children I worked with. My brother's challenges were now my son's, and I vowed to spend my life learning how to improve the lives of people like them. Living closely with family members on the spectrum equipped me with confidence that there was a way inside the minds of persons with autism, and an intuitive sense of how to find it. People have told me, in fact, that my intuitive ability to get inside the heads of my clients is a gift I was born with, something they can't understand and could never do.

But I disagree. I believe I learned how to get inside the minds of persons with autism first by growing up with my brother, next by rearing my son, and, for the past 35 years, by working with hundreds of children, adolescents, and adults with the disorder. I have not only seen but studied their behaviors; not only heard but listened to their utterances; not only catalogued but analyzed their responses to people, places, and situations; and observed not only their bizarre and seemingly abnormal actions, but also inferred how these actions may be interpreted as logical and uniquely normal, if not typical, responses to everyday life.

I learned to do these things, and I believe you can, too.

A COGNITIVE APPROACH

People with an autism spectrum disorder, or ASD, have traditionally been treated with the behavioral approach I learned in graduate school, which rewards them for acting more like the rest of us and less like themselves. We're so eager for them to fit in, to get by, to be normal, that we set about training them to act that way. On the surface, they seem less weird, more regular, and we are reassured: Maybe now our son will start acting more like our other kids, we tell ourselves; maybe now our daughter will be more like the other girls. But underneath, they are who they always were, as confounded by us as we are by them.

My approach is different because it is based on cognition—thinking— rather than on behavior. My goal is not for people with ASD to act more like the rest of us (although that often happens, eventually). My goal is for them to be able to live in the world and connect with the people in it as themselves, to express their unique humanity and engage more fully in the human interactions that give life meaning and make it worth the effort of getting out of bed every day. And I help them do this not by insisting that they act more like everybody else, but by entering their worlds, one person and one world at a time, and following wherever they lead me. I believe that whatever we do therapeutically must be on the terms of the person with autism: He or she must lead.

And lead they do. For over 30 years, I have been working with people on the autism spectrum—children and adults—by watching what they do; listening to what they say and hearing what they do not say; observing their actions without judgment or criticism; and waiting, however long it takes, for the moment when they do something—anything—that makes some sort of sense to me. When that moment comes and the door opens a crack, I wedge in my curiosity, look around, and venture into the unknown world that beckons with a human face, the face of the person who will show me the way inside.

You can do this, too; in fact, you're already doing it. What I will show you is how to do it in a more focused, intentional way. I will help you to not only look at what your ASD son is doing, but to see the possible logic from which it springs. I will help you resist the temptation to command your ASD daughter to stop doing that! And instead allow her to continue while you focus not on how much it's driving you crazy but rather on discovering what she's getting out of it. Because she is getting something out of it; the challenge is to figure out what it is, and then help her satisfy the need differently.

For example, many children with ASD like to distract themselves with repetitive movements or actions. This self-stimulation, or stimming, can go on for hours and entail wagging the head back and forth, or flapping the hands, or jumping repeatedly, or any of a million other actions whose logic eludes the rest of us. But think for a moment: If you're a man, have you ever stood idly by, jingling the coins in your pocket while you chatted with a colleague or waited for your double espresso (or martini) to arrive? If you're a woman, have you ever absentmindedly twirled your hair with your fingers, or played with your necklace? Those behaviors could qualify as stimming, and we all do them in one way or another.

Jingling coins and twirling hair are repetitive behaviors we perform unconsciously—as are doodling, rubbing our palms together, jiggling a knee, and clicking our tongues quietly inside our mouths—as we consciously think about something else. Why do we do these things? Probably to relieve stress, make contact with our physical selves, and heighten bodily awareness in a way we're unaware of. I believe these actions are primitive, unthinking ways of comforting ourselves, which is what I think stimming is. The main difference is that our methods of stimming are common and therefore socially acceptable, while an ASD person's methods of stimming are often not.

I am not suggesting that we persuade people with ASD to jingle change and twirl hair rather than wag their heads. I am suggesting that by ascertaining and understanding the reason for odd ASD behaviors, we can help the people doing them to express their needs in a way that works better for them and the people around them. We all have needs, some of which we manifest explicitly, some that we hide, and others that we reveal unawares. This goes for all of us, whether our behavior falls into the motley category of normal or not.

And who's to say what's normal? Those of us who are not on the autism spectrum—neurotypical folks, in other, newish* words—are thought of as normal because our eccentricities don't prevent us from interacting with others or conducting our lives effectively. But just as neurotypicals are capable of behaving oddly, so are persons with ASD capable of behaving typically.

My approach is founded on my belief that all people with ASD have reservoirs of normalcy within themselves. I also believe that the key to helping them develop more typical behaviors is to understand how to circumvent each ASD person's unique constellation of limitations and tap into those reservoirs. My approach can be duplicated by others—parents, family members, teachers, caretakers—because it calls upon not academic training but fundamental capacities we all have and can develop, if need be: the ability to watch closely and observe; to listen carefully and interpret; to explore logic different from our own; to refrain from correcting in favor of guiding; and to expand our perceptions of reality to include those that do not come naturally to us.

In the sections ahead, I will guide you toward mastering the three basic elements of my approach:

1. Recognizing that each person with ASD contains a reservoir of normalcy that he or she can tap into;
2. Believing that each person with ASD is different from every other person with ASD, tuning in to the unique psychological landscape

---

* *The words* typical *and* neurotypical *have replaced* normal *in the lexicon to describe thinking and behavior associated with people who do not have ASD. I continue to use the phrase* reservoir of normalcy *because it resonates with the parents of my young clients. Reservoir of* typicality *doesn't have quite the same ring.*

of that person, and working to see the world from his or her point of view; and

3. Creating and seizing opportunities that enable each ASD person's typical behaviors to emerge and develop.

Years of experience have taught me that every child and adult with ASD carries within him- or herself the seeds of typical development. Even those most severely involved have fleeting moments of normalcy. I once had an 11-year-old boy stomp into my office, fling himself to the floor, and shriek "baah-baah" nonstop for nearly half an hour, after which he strode about the space, acting bizarrely. Twice he dropped things and bent down to pick them up—the only logical behavior he manifested. I seized that sliver of normalcy and used it to start interacting with him. By the end of the session, Patrick was mirroring me, pursing his lips and trying to speak (for more on Patrick, see Part 3). For 11 years, his entire life, this child had not said a word; no form of treatment had induced him to connect meaningfully with anyone. How could it be that less than 90 minutes after we met, he had felt impelled to take a stumbling step toward meaningful speech?

It's not because I'm a magician. It's because the effectiveness of existing methods remains questionable at best, and for many persons with ASD, they are useless. Parents of children with ASD are often directed toward schools and therapists that propound the behavioral strategy I've described, which produces limited results and in some cases actually makes things worse by reinforcing rote, repetitive behaviors that reflect memorized actions rather than organic, thought-based ones. When a child reaches a behavioral plateau and cannot ascend to the next developmental level, parents are told that it is their child's limitations, not the therapy's, that impede his or her progress. I could not disagree more.

These children can learn; they can change their ways of interacting with the world. This brings me to the second element of my approach: understanding that no two ASD persons are alike. Persons on the spectrum don't need to be reminded of their inability to process reality the way other people do. What they do need is for someone to home in on the way they do things with an eye not on changing their ways—at least not at first—but on understanding them. When you learn to tune in to the workings of the mind that produce atypical ASD-associated behaviors, you can elicit and build upon the unique, inherent abilities of your affected child or adult and guide him or her to the next level of typical development. If you are the parent of a child with autism, you are in the best position to do this: No one knows your child as well as you do, or has as many opportunities to attend to how he or she goes about navigating everyday life. Long ago, I embraced the wisdom of following clients into their individual, inscrutable, autistic worlds rather than trying to drag them, kicking and screaming, sometimes literally, into ours.

This is the basis of my cognitive approach, whose priority is to create understanding and which embraces the notion that our brothers, sisters, and children with autism will lead us toward themselves if only we will follow. I have seen over and over that when ASD persons acquire typical behaviors, even in small increments, the new behaviors reinforce themselves.

Children and adults with autism feel better when they act more typically and are motivated to perpetuate new behavior patterns. Once they achieve a rewarding level of accomplishment, the cascade of advancements that follows surprises them.

The third element of my approach is to foster awareness of potential opportunities to enable your atypical child's typical behaviors to emerge. They are all around us, if only we would see them; and seeing them is mostly a matter of paying closer attention to the ordinary interactions that punctuate our lives. I am currently working with a high-functioning 12-year-old whose aggressive and inappropriate remarks to strangers were deterring his parents from taking him out in public. At our first session I took him to a fast food restaurant, where he went up to a man mopping the floor, sidled up to his bucket, and asked, "Do you have any tattoos?" Startled, the guy stopped, stared at Charles, and laughed. "Yeah, man," he said, and hiked up his sleeve to expose a bluish snake on his biceps. Thus emboldened, Charles smiled, turned, and strode over to a middle-aged woman sitting by herself. By the time I got over there, he'd already popped the question, and she didn't look amused (they don't call it the home of the whopper for nothing). I apologized and hustled him outside before he could offend anyone else. We walked a few blocks to a small café with outdoor seating. I chose a table near the entrance.

"Charles," I said, "when you ask people personal questions like that, they get upset. If you go up to people you don't know and ask them if they have tattoos, or if they shave, or if they wear a wig, you can make them angry. Do you want people to be angry with you?" He looked up and said that no, he didn't want that. I pressed on.

"Pretty soon, someone's going to walk by our table and go into the restaurant. Do you think you can control yourself and not say anything?" He considered this, and then nodded his head.

"This is for real, Charles. I want you to commit to not talking to the next person who walks by. Will you do that?" He wouldn't meet my gaze but said yes, he would. A few minutes later a young woman sauntered up the sidewalk and past our table into the café. Charles stared at her feet as she passed but said nothing. I told him he'd done well and asked him to do it again. And he did, over and over again, as we sat for half an hour munching nachos and sipping lemonade. He had the capacity to control his impulse to confront strangers; why had he not done it before? His parents said they had been begging, cajoling, and bribing him to stop—in other words, deploying the behavioral approach—with no success. What they had not done, I believe, was explain to Charles the consequences of his actions. All too often, we assume that persons on the spectrum are incapable of thinking rationally or understanding the consequences of their actions. But when I told Charles that his intrusive questions would not only make people angry but also make them angry with him, he connected thought with emotion, and was motivated to reconsider his behavior. Merely telling him to stop annoying strangers might have little resonance for Charles, whose powers of empathy were ill-developed. But no one, whether off the spectrum or on it, likes it when others are angry with him. By prompting Charles to consider the future consequences of his actions, I connected with him and sparked a cognitive pattern of thought—the concept that what he does in the present may affect his life in the future—and this motivated him to behave in a more typical way.

Persons with autism make real progress when they grasp concepts rather than imitate behavior. You can help your ASD person grasp concepts by helping him or her learn to think coherently. Consistent sparking of cognition kindles a glow of understanding within all thinking human beings, atypical and typical alike; that's how we all learn. By paying close attention—observing, listening, and attending to the actions, vocalizations, and behaviors of your person on the spectrum—you will eventually be able to connect intimately with him or her and help instill real and lasting change.

For almost four decades, I have been working with children and adults to help them emerge from the landscape of autism into one more like our own. In the pages to come, I will describe my encounters with a broad array of clients, ranging in age from 2 to 62. Each story will illustrate how the client and I interacted in our sessions, both in my office and outside of it. I will describe the thinking process that governed my actions and how each client responded, as well as how I adjusted my thinking in accordance with the client's responses. I will not provide a program guaranteed to work for every person with autism, because there is no such thing. Rather, I will share the principles that guide my work and have led me to meet persons with autism where they are and connect with them in ways that change us both. My hope is that you will compare my thought process and actions with your own, and use elements from my approach to enrich yours. To help accomplish this, I will close each client's story with questions about how you respond to the ASD person in your life, and offer suggestions on how you can approach with fresh eyes, ears, and heart the mysterious and frequently exasperating ways of your loved one.

Let's begin.

THINGS TO WORK ON AND THINK ABOUT.

- *Observe what your child is doing and look for patterns of behavior.*
  - When your daughter is with playmates, does she need to be in charge and require them to acquiesce to her demands? Does this trait emerge with certain playmates, or is it her standard way of interacting with peers? If the other child doesn't do what she wants, how does she respond?
  - Does your son eat foods in a certain order? Will he sip his milk, nibble his egg, sip his milk, nibble his egg, until both are gone, and only then drink his juice? At dinner, does he polish off all his mashed potatoes before starting on the carrots, then finish all of those before starting on the meat loaf? Does he eat this way all the time, no matter what is put before him?
  - Does your child want to wear the same thing all the time? Does your daughter insist on wearing the same sleeveless cotton tee shirt every day, even when it's snowing? Does your son insist on wearing the same jacket he got in kindergarten, even though the sleeves are halfway up to his elbows?
  - Does your ASD person chafe under direction? Is your daughter unwilling to brush her teeth, wash her hands, put away her toys, or

turn off the light at bedtime? Does your son insist on doing things his way, defy his teacher's instructions (as mine did), refuse his camp counselor's orders, or resent it when you ask him to do anything? (If he's a teenager, never mind: Most teenagers, atypical and typical alike, resent it when you ask them to do anything.)

• If some of these behavior patterns sound familiar, your loved one is probably manifesting inflexibility and rigidity. Many if not most people on the spectrum derive comfort, satisfaction, or reassurance by performing tasks and actions in a prescribed, orderly way. Sometimes this need manifests as bossiness, an attempt to control others' actions so that things go in a way that feels familiar and safe. Other times it shows up as a compulsion to adhere to a strict regimen that governs the order in which foods are eaten, or toys are arranged, or clothing is donned. In other cases, it shows up as a need to wear the same thing day after day, month after month. The common denominator is a quest for familiarity and order, and, I believe, a desire to exert influence over one's world when so much of it feels out of control.

• Think about why your ASD person may behave this way. Now, think about your reactions to these behaviors—do you get frustrated, annoyed, angry? If so, think about what bothers you about the behavior.

• *Observe what your child is not doing and consider it with fresh eyes.* When Dylan was about two years old, we took him to a party for another toddler in the neighborhood. When the kids sat down to play a game with the birthday boy's father, Dylan declined and instead walked around the outside of the circle, watching the group. I remember Rachel and myself murmuring about what an observant kid we had and how pleased we were that he could sustain interest in a game he wasn't involved in. But what we should have been wondering was why Dylan was the only kid who willfully kept himself aloof from an activity that had other kids rocking and giggling with delight. It was a clue to his psychological makeup that we would have done well to notice. What we should have asked ourselves was, what kind of kid doesn't want to have fun with other kids?

You'll read about a child who would climb to the top of a playground slide and then refuse to ride down. What kind of kid does that? A kid with a perseverative personality does that. In a psychological or psychiatric context, perseveration refers to the repetition of an action—a gesture, word, or other vocalization, for example—when there is no perceptible reason for the repetition. After years of working with children with autism, I inferred, after about a half-dozen trips up the ladder with this kid, that he was refusing to go down because climbing up the ladder repeatedly was the whole point of the activity for him; sliding down was beside the point. He just wanted to climb up the ladder over and over and over again. Without years of experience, I might have thought that he was afraid of sliding down, just as everyone did who had witnessed this behavior. But I had learned not only to look at such behavior but to see it differently, which is what I am urging you to do.

- *What new insights can you glean?* Instead of merely reacting to your child's atypical behavior, ask yourself why he or she might be doing it. If your child resists doing something or outright refuses—brushing her teeth, picking up his toys, shaking hands, or participating in a fun activity—don't take it personally. Or, if your child insists on doing things that mystify and maybe embarrass you—making weird noises or wagging his head back and forth—resist the temptation to berate yourself or your partner's childrearing skills. Instead, ask yourself, why is my kid doing this? What might he (or she) be getting out of it?

- *Examine how you perceive your child.* Are you biased? Are you overreacting to innocuous perseverative behaviors because they annoy you or make you feel ashamed in front of other people? Or are you doing the opposite and interpreting odd, problematic behaviors as signs of individuality? Are you congratulating yourself on rearing a rugged individualist when your son or daughter would actually love to be like other kids but can't make sense of the world the same way they do?

- *Listen to how you speak to your child.* Are you speaking in a simplistic style, the way you would to a baby? Children with autism often have trouble organizing the concepts of past, present, and future into a unified notion of time. When we talk to intelligent children with autism as if they are infants—"No, no cookie now!"—we rob them of an opportunity to learn about time through the use of language. It would be far better to speak as you would to any intelligent child: "I know you want a cookie now, but cookies are dessert, which we eat later, after dinner. First we eat dinner; then, afterward, you may have a cookie." By verbalizing the concepts of now, later, after, first, then, and afterward, you are suggesting a time sequence that every child needs to learn and that children on the spectrum need to have reinforced. If you are in the habit of addressing your ASD person in a simplistic, fragmented style, practice speaking in fuller, more descriptive sentences so he or she experiences continuity of language. The sentences can be simple, as are the two above referring to cookie consumption. Simple is good; simplistic is not.

As an autism educator and father of a son on the spectrum, I know how hard it is for families to live with the daily reality of a loved one with autism. And I know how many families like ours there are. Not long ago, I was at a dinner party chatting with a new acquaintance about the sorts of challenges facing the clients in my practice. "You know," he said, "I have a kid like that at home." This happens frequently; I am astonished at how many people tell me they have a loved one on the spectrum. Every time I hear it, I want to give them something more than friendly encouragement. I want to give them tools—insights, techniques, new ways of seeing, listening, thinking, responding, interacting—to help them engage tenderly, intuitively, empathetically, and meaningfully with the ASD person in their lives.

Uniquely Normal is that something, and I wrote it for anyone who loves someone who seems to live in a world apart from ours. That someone may seem to occupy a remote reality but is in fact here with us, struggling to make sense of what we figured out long ago. You can reach that person; you can learn to connect. I am reminded of the climactic scene near the end of *The Miracle Worker*, Arthur Penn's 1962 film based on the early life of Helen Keller. Helen (played by Patty Duke), deaf and blind since a bout of scarlet fever in infancy, lives in a state of desperation in her family's genteel Alabama home, unable to communicate with her family and subject to violent, anguished outbursts of rage and frustration. For months, teacher Anne Sullivan (Anne Bancroft) has been spelling words into Helen's open hand, trying to communicate that the movements of her fingers in Helen's palm represent letters of the alphabet, which spell words, which represent things. In the scene I'm thinking of, Helen has bolted from Sullivan to a hillside water pump. As Helen's arm furiously works the handle and water splashes into her mouth, Sullivan runs over, spells w-a-t-e-r into Helen's palm, and holds the child's hand over her own mouth as she says water for maybe the 10-thousandth time. In a moment of searing clarity, Helen's blind eyes open wide, her arm stops pumping, and everything stops—except for Helen's hoarse voice, heard for the first time, as she utters a guttural *wah–wah* sound. In this split second of cognitive connection, Helen is freed from a prison of soundless darkness and understands that she can interact intelligently with the world around her—which I believe is similar to what children with autism experience when they suddenly realize they can connect with the rest of us. Helen Keller never experienced the world the way seeing and hearing persons do, but she learned to navigate it in a way that enabled her to not only take her place fully in it, but also to deploy her sparkling wit and profound intelligence to make it a better place. So too can children on the spectrum learn to navigate the world in ways that are different from but no less effective than our own. When they realize this, they experience a life-changing moment of emancipation that is worth ten-thousand repetitions, or however many it might take to get there.

Part 1

**Nonverbal; acts startled when
other children come near her.**

When Janie's mother phoned to make an appointment, she didn't hold back. "We're desperate," she said. "My husband and I honestly don't know what to do." A reputable pediatric neurologist had diagnosed their 2½-year-old daughter with both pervasive developmental disorder and a phobic aversion to being touched. Now the mother sat in my office crying because, in addition to the medical diagnoses, the preschool psychologist had informed her that Janie had autism and would never speak normally. "My husband isn't helping matters," she said, dabbing her eyes. "He says to stop worrying, that Janie will get by on her looks." I glanced at the child, whose round face was dominated by large, dark eyes and surrounded by a halo of softly waving hair. She was indeed pretty, but no child is pretty enough to be taught that looks are enough to get her through life.

I asked the mother if Janie had friends, and she replied that she had been making up excuses when other parents invited Janie over to play. "I can't bear to see her jump every time someone comes near her," she said. "It's easier if we just play together at home." This was good: Not all parents have the patience to play with their atypical kids. On the other hand, it is important for kids on the spectrum to play with other kids, especially neurotypical kids, so they can develop awareness of how human interactions work. I ushered the mother into the waiting room and joined Janie on the floor.

First impression: inconsistent responses; unintelligible speech. As we started playing with various toys and puzzles, Janie's responses followed no discernible pattern. I handed her a wooden puzzle, the kind with pieces that fit into matching recessed areas and have little pegs to make the pieces easy to manipulate. This one had different colored circles in increasing sizes. Janie would remove circles in no particular order, willy-nilly, sometimes replacing them in random slots and other times dropping them on the floor. When I asked her repeatedly which was the biggest circle, she looked at me blankly. I brought out a set of colorful plastic rings that sat on a spindled base from largest to smallest, dumped off the rings, and invited Janie to replace them on the spindle. She dropped the biggest one on first, then added the second-smallest ring, saw it didn't belong there, removed it, and replaced it with the second-biggest one. But when it was time to add the smallest one at the top, she walked away. During her second attempt, she put the second smallest ring on the spindle too early and was astute enough to remove it, but was unable to place it correctly when its time had come. It was as if she could see each ring individually but neither the relationship between them nor how they formed a tapering tower.

I pressed on. When I placed a shape-sorting toy in her lap, she just looked at it. Later, I saw her staring at a colorful ball. "Janie, what do you want? Do you want the ball?" I kept asking. She brought her lips together and mumbled something that sounded like "buh," sat, and waited. Next I placed a toy xylophone in front of her and handed her the mallet, which she used to hit the bars from left to right, largest to smallest, lowest pitch to highest, over and over again. She never altered the order in which she struck the bars; it was always the same. I tried placing my hand over hers and directing it toward the opposite end of the instrument but she resisted; she only wanted to strike the bars from left to right.

Then something struck me: when I touched Janie's hand she didn't flinch, but continued to play with my hand atop hers. In fact, we had touched numerous times as I handed her things, but not once had she seemed to notice the contact, let alone been disturbed by it. This was odd for someone who had been diagnosed with a phobic aversion to being touched. Janie seemed comfortable with me in my office; was there something about the day care environment or the other children that made her anxious? I decided to find out.

Janie at day care. With the blessing of Janie's mother and day care teacher, I settled into a small chair at the back of the playroom. Children were milling about, including Janie's younger brother. Everyone was occupied except Janie, who stood off to the side looking disoriented. She watched the other children playing but held herself apart. She sometimes followed the teacher's instructions, as when she invited the kids to converge at a table for snack. I asked Janie if I might have one of her goldfish crackers six or seven times before she responded and gave me one. Later, I asked if I might play with a stuffed pony she wasn't using but she didn't respond. She mimed pouring herself a cup of tea from a tiny pot, but when I asked her to pour one for another child, she did not respond. It seemed that when she was playing on her own she could function at a slightly higher level, but regressed when prompted to interact with others. I watched as a small girl approached Janie, took her arm, and tried to lead her toward a pile of costumes. Janie looked momentarily startled, and then resumed her dazed expression. She didn't seem to be exhibiting panic symptoms: Her breathing didn't escalate, nor did she look frightened. This didn't look like anxiety to me but rather like profound self-absorption, as if Janie were utterly unaware of her environment, as infants are. Babies see everything as extensions of themselves, including the adults who care for them. It takes a while for them to comprehend that they are autonomous beings existing among other such beings, that they are separate from everyone and everything around them. Might it be possible that Janie's cognitive development was delayed and still in a phase where she perceived herself as unified with the objects and people around her? Was she uncomprehending of the concept that others could enter her world and make contact with her, whether she willed it or not? If so, that would explain why she was startled whenever anyone touched her. Perhaps it wasn't a phobia at all, but the response of a much younger child who is unable to see herself as an autonomous entity, neither bound to nor in control of her surroundings.

Priority: Determine if Janie can see herself as separate from her surroundings. I tested my theory when Janie came to see me the following week. There's a double-hung window in my office that looks out on a busy street. I brought out figurines of a dog and a cow and placed them on the inside sill. I then opened the window a few inches and set the cow on the outside sill. Janie stood next to me, watching the whole operation.

"Did the cow go out?" I asked.

"No," Janie replied firmly. She was mistaken, of course, but this didn't surprise me: If my theory was right and Janie saw herself as one with everything around her, she would perceive the cow as inside because she was inside. I rephrased the question.

"Who went outside, the dog or the cow?"

"Cow."

Hah! Something had changed: Janie had distinguished outside from inside. But did she really understand? I repeated the question, reversing the order of the animals to see if she would merely repeat her previous response.

"Who went outside, the cow or the dog?"

"Cow."

"Did the dog go outside, Janie?"

"No."

By answering correctly the same question posed differently, Janie had established that she understood that the cow had indeed gone outside, even though she herself had not—a small step, perhaps, but an important one on a journey of emergence from an egocentric world. And it was Janie who had to take the step: I would have done her no favors had I made it easy for her. When a child needs help understanding a concept, it is important to give her as little help as possible so she will rely on her own resources and crystalize the concept herself. If you offer your child too much help, she need not think for herself; she need only receive information by listening to you and following your lead. Had I led Janie toward a desired outcome—asked her, perhaps, "Did the cow go outside?" while nodding my head and smiling approvingly—I would have telegraphed the answer I wanted and she would have gladly provided it, learning nothing other than how to please her adult companion. Instead, she was forced to rely on her innate intelligence and think for herself, and she came up with a response that mirrored reality. My priority—and yours—is not to program your child to deliver a desired response but to elicit an authentic one, whatever it is, and to work from there.

Next goal: help Janie recognize things outside herself. I came up with activities that would introduce and reinforce Janie's perception of the boundaries between herself and others. I held my hands behind my back with a penny in one of them, presented her with both fists, and challenged her to guess which one held the coin. This forced her to understand that it was I, not she, who chose which hand held the coin; it also compelled her to interact with me in a predictable sequence: I'd present my closed hands, repeatedly ask her to choose one until she complied, unfold whichever hand she had chosen and reveal whether or not she had chosen correctly, and start again. We played this game probably two dozen times.

Another thing I did was prod her into sharing a toy with me. When she became absorbed in moving the beads on an abacus, I kept my hands in my lap and asked, "May I have a turn?" No response. Then I asked again, reaching my hand out as if expecting her to hand it to me. After repeating this four or five times, she began to hand me the toy. As before, this exercise required Janie to acknowledge my presence and interact with me, something she did not do at the beginning of our work together.

Another exercise: Every week I would hand her a half-filled watering can and ask her to water the snake plant in the corner of the room. She would take the can from me without speaking, walk over to the plant, and pour the water in. About three weeks into this activity, I handed her the can, only this time, I hadn't put any water in it. When she tipped the can and no water came out, she peered inside, turned to me, and said, "empty" (with some indignation, I might add). Developmentally, this was a huge leap: Janie had spoken a word that emanated from within, reflecting her perception that the can was empty and, I surmised from her tone, annoyance that I expected her to water a plant without water. I had set up an activity that had no connection with language, and, for weeks, Janie had participated without speaking. Now she had spontaneously uttered a coherent response, a word connected to both thought and feeling—a word, in fact, that was neither what I was expecting nor hoping to hear. When I work with children who do not speak, I don't care which words they say or how well they say them as long as the words come from within. My goal is to elicit undefined language, which means I don't know what I'm going to get. Whatever I do get, that's what I work with.

Helping Janie identify her "self." To help Janie begin to experience herself as an individual, I gave her choices. I brought a package of goldfish crackers and a small box of raisins one day and offered both as a snack (full disclosure: I already knew from Janie's mother that she did not like raisins). When Janie reached for the goldfish, I prodded her to use words: "Do you want goldfish?" "Yes." "Do you want raisins?" "No." "Do you like goldfish?" "Yes." "Do you like raisins?" "No." By choosing goldfish over raisins and verbalizing what she liked and what she didn't, Janie reinforced her growing understanding that she was an autonomous being with the ability to make choices that pleased her. And, by asking open-ended questions—"Do you want goldfish?" rather than "You like goldfish more than raisins, don't you?"—I pushed Janie to consider her preferences without being influenced by me. To help children understand how language confers power to control their lives, we must give them a reason to say no. Offered this option, Janie rejected the less appealing option in favor of the more attractive one and began to understand that words can bring pleasure, satisfaction, and control.

Until now, Janie had spoken only single words—cow, dog, yes, no. At our fifth weekly session, I held up a sealed bottle of water and asked who should open it. Over and over I asked, "Janie, who should open it? Who should open the bottle?" as she tried to wrest it from my hands. I then added a response: "Who should open the bottle? You open the bottle, Rob. Who should open the bottle? You open it, Rob." When I asked again, Janie looked at me and said, you. Was she just parroting me? Maybe. So I kept asking: "Who should open the bottle? Who do you want to open it?"—and, to my surprise, she grasped the cap with her hand. "Who should open it, Janie? Do you want to open it or should I open it?"

And she said, "I ohp bah ..."

"Okay. You open it," I said. Then Janie spoke again.

"I open the bottle," she said. The words were imprecisely pronounced but their meaning was clear. Janie had spoken her first sentence.

Janie's mother began reporting new accomplishments. In a restaurant, Janie heard a baby crying and pointed toward the infant, the first time her mother witnessed her acknowledging that a sound had meaning. In her pediatrician's waiting room, she approached another girl and joined her in play. Her day care teacher reported that Janie was becoming more sociable with the other children.

Acquainting Janie with the concept of time. I continued to meet with Janie every week, often conducting what I call window therapy: standing at the window and talking about what we saw outside. Window therapy is useful for illustrating concepts such as outside and inside, as well as the passage of time. As people, animals, and assorted vehicles approach the window, pass beneath it, and disappear, I have numerous opportunities to introduce the concepts of before, during, and after.

The first time I asked Janie what she saw outside, she said "sun," which would have been a triumph had the sky not been obscured by clouds. "Sun" was an automatic response, similar to the drawings kids produce when you ask them to draw a picture of where they live, and, 99.9% of the time, they draw a bright orange disk radiating stick-like rays in a bright blue sky. I don't think there's much data on sun-in-the-sky crayon technique, but my guess is that kids use it because that's what they think they're supposed to draw: They are pleasing adults who will be delighted to see they have created such a cheerful, pretty scene.

But pretty wasn't the goal; real was. I kept at it with Janie, asking her every week what she saw when she looked out the window. At first, she offered one-word answers; later, she began to speak about seeing a school bus, a big dog, a car going fast, birds on telephone wires. She was now stringing several words together, which was good. But after a car sped past or the birds flew away and I asked her what she had seen, she was silent: Janie was utterly flummoxed by the idea of having seen something that was no longer there. She couldn't grasp the notion that something could continue to exist when she could no longer see it: The concept of *past* was on a cognitive level she had yet to achieve.

Still at the window, I heard a siren in the distance that was growing louder. A few seconds later, a fire engine sped past, siren blaring, a streak of loud red noise that was suddenly there and then gone. Janie pointed with excitement and jumped up and down. I seized the moment.

"What was that, Janie? What did we see?" After several repetitions, Janie answered, "Fire truck." I kept at it, asking her over and over again about what we heard, what we saw when the fire truck first came into view, what color it was, what we saw, what she had seen. I talked about that fire truck until it became a fixture of the past. And when I say I talked about it, I mean I spoke of it over and over and over again, 20 or 30 times. When Janie's mother arrived half an hour later, I said, "Your mom wasn't here when we were at the window and she doesn't know what we saw. What did we see?" And Janie said, "Fire!"

Normal conversation has the past, present, and future built into it, which makes it an ideal medium to instill the concept of time. Rather than try to make the concept more accessible to Janie by using simplistic words, my strategy was to use regular conversation to spark understanding. You can do this too, of course; there are countless opportunities every day to deploy language to suggest the notion of past, present, and future. You just have to improvise on whatever the moment tosses your way.

For example, "Do you want to go outside?" is a question that not only has a built-in future—being outside—but also an implied delay. Going outside is instantaneous only on Star Trek; in earthly life, someone usually has to use the bathroom first, or find a sweater, or hunt for a cell phone. Anticipation is a critical part of understanding the future. With Janie, I worked on anticipation by asking if she would like to go outside and get some ice cream. When she expressed enthusiasm, I said, "First I have to get my keys, and then we will go outside." I didn't know if Janie understood why I had to get my keys, but I did know I had to start instilling this concept in a child who lived almost entirely in the present.

I created different exercises to help Janie anticipate and process sequences of events. I held up an uninflated balloon, talked about how wrinkly and small it was because it didn't have air in it, and said, "Now I'm going to blow up the balloon. Let's see what happens." I blew in a few puffs, squeezed the neck closed, and said, "Now the balloon has a little air in it. It's different from before. It's bigger and smoother. What do you think will happen if I blow it up some more? How about if I let some air out?" I waited for Janie to respond after each query; sometimes she did with words, other times, she would nod or shake her head. I repeated the sequence over and over again, asking, "What should I do next? What next? What next?" This way, Janie could anticipate and see the balloon get bigger and smaller. Later, to enhance the scenario, I brought in a helium tank. Now there was an added step: After tying the balloon's neck, we had to attach a string so Janie could hold onto it. She quickly learned that if she let go without attaching a string, the balloon would rise to the ceiling, out of reach. Janie had begun to understand the relationship of the past to the present to the future, and that by altering a sequence of actions she could alter their outcome.

Another time-teaching activity was feeding the goldfish. Every week I asked, "What do we have to do if the fish are hungry?" And we began: First we had to open the cabinet, find the fish food, open the tin, pinch up some flakes in our fingers, disperse them little by little into the tank, and watch Wanda and Phoebe eat it. "Well," I'd say, "the fish were hungry; now they've eaten their lunch. What's next?" We would then seal the tin, put it away, and go out to the corridor to wash our hands in the bathroom.

To reinforce the effect of what we were doing in our sessions, I asked Janie's parents and day care teachers to talk her through activities as well so she was continually receiving the message that life is a series of events that take place over time. Cooperation between a child's therapist and the other adults in his or her life is crucial for changing way the child perceives the world.

I performed these kinds of simple exercises with Janie many, many times, as did her parents and day care teacher, before she was able to consistently use language to express an understanding of why.

Expanding Janie's use of language to broach abstract thought. Janie was now able to link things together—fish and fish food, plant and water, balloon and air—which led her to link words together and begin learning syntax, which is the gateway to normal language development. She was commenting on the world now, connecting objects to actions performed in sequence: "Balloon get big; water plant; feed fish."

I believed Janie was now ready for the next level of cognitive development: grappling with abstraction, starting with the concept of why. She could now understand temporality and link words to actions, as when I would say I had to get my keys before we could go out for ice cream. In that statement there is an implicit why—why do I need to get my keys? Because I need to lock my office door. Janie's growing cognitive abilities empowered her to understand that, so it was time to prod her into using language to describe it. (My approach is based in cognition, so I tend to work toward having a client first learn a concept and then use language to define and implement the concept. I often hear from my clients' parents that their kids understand much more than they are able to verbalize. When I hear this, I am driven to teach them to not merely articulate words but to use words to express the concepts they are learning.)

I reinforced Janie's burgeoning understanding by creating obstacles that she would have to reason her way through. One way I did this was to park myself on a little stepstool I knew she needed to use to reach the coat hook in my office. When she arrived and saw me sitting there, she said, "Get up."

"Why should I get up?" I asked.

"Hang coat." I would then get up. Another day, we were filling the watering can and I turned off the spigot halfway through. "Why are we filling this can?" I asked. "Water plant," Janie replied, after which I would turn the water back on.

It was one of these obstacles that propelled Janie into a breakthrough: a real conversation. For months I had been wrapping rubber bands around the wooden puzzles she loved so the pieces were hard to remove. One day, she was engrossed with a puzzle featuring sea creatures and became frustrated because she couldn't liberate the seahorse to join its friends for a swim on the table. "He's really stuck in here," she said, trying in vain to free the poor fellow. "He needs someone's help."

"For what?"

"For he needs his friends back. He needs his friends," she said, touching the other pieces she'd managed to free. I held up a pig from a different puzzle and asked, "How about this one?" Unimpressed, Janie touched the imprisoned seahorse with her finger.

"How about this one?" she said, echoing me.

"Why does he need help?" I asked. She touched the other pieces on the table.

"Because he needs to get out and swim now. He needs to swim." She tried to free the seahorse again. "Will you help us?" she said. And then, "Will you help me, please?"

"What do you want me to do?"

"Help this fishie get out, please." I removed the rubber bands and liberated all the fishies.

Janie could now verbalize her understanding of why, so we moved on to facilitating her use of language to express a more abstract concept, namely the why of things that did not pertain directly to her. I began to ask Janie questions like "Why does the bird fly?"—to which she replied, "wings"—which was a how answer rather than a why, but no matter: I cared more about the concept of the answer than its precision. Wings was a fine response: It related to birds and the mechanics of flying, which is something else to keep in mind: Seeking perfection is not required and might even cause problems. Don't look for rightness but rather for the process that the answer reflects.

Urging Janie to venture outside her cognitive comfort zone. I began to introduce toys Janie hadn't seen before. One was an odd looking, canine-like creature. "Is it a horse? Is it a wolf?" she asked. As she never asked me to define what it was, I didn't tell her and merely shrugged instead. After many such queries, I realized that although Janie could form a percept, an impression of an object obtained by using her senses—the toy looked like a horse or a wolf—she could not grasp the concept of it belonging to a larger, abstract category—animal. Janie kept asking if it were this or that and I kept shrugging until finally, in exasperation, she said "It's an animal"—and left it at that.

So did Janie possess the concept of animal or not? Yes—somewhere inside, she did; she knew the term, after all. This exercise showed good problem solving in the face of something unfamiliar, as well as embracing an abstract concept of animal over a concrete label. Rather than getting stuck and giving up when faced with something new, Janie made a cognitive leap. In time, Janie's mind embraced conceptual thinking, categorizing things as fruit and clothes rather than merely identifying the apple in front of her or the hat on her head.

Luring Janie outside her physical comfort zone. Janie would still not play with other children, not even her younger brother. I suggested to her mother that I take Janie to a public play gym. "That's not a good idea," she said. "Janie doesn't like noise or being around lots of strangers." This may have been true, but I told her what I tell other parents: Sometimes these things stop bothering kids when they get involved in an activity. I persuaded her to let me have an hour with Janie at a local gym, and, after accompanying us there, the mother took off.

When we got there, Janie stood and gazed blankly around her. When I suggested she follow a young boy up a low slide ladder, she did so without acknowledging him. This little slide was the only equipment she wasn't afraid to try; even the ball pit made her anxious. I encouraged her to help a smaller girl who had lost her footing but she ignored her as she made her way out of the pit.

I tried to connect Janie with several other kids with varying degrees of success. A couple of kids lost interest when Janie declined to join them quickly; when I suggested Janie help a boy who was piling balls into a container, she handed him one and turned away. Eventually, I waded into the ball pit and persuaded Janie to follow me back in. It was there that we met a vivacious 5-year-old named Taylor, and that changed everything.

When Janie kept losing her balance in the pit, I asked Taylor to help her, which she did with gusto, pulling Janie's arms. The contact didn't seem to faze Janie at all. I encouraged Janie to follow Taylor to a more ambitious part of the ball pit, where Taylor helped her clamber up an incline. We were now up a level and Taylor began to crawl across a mesh bridge, beckoning Janie to follow. Janie refused and started to cry. Taylor came halfway back and bounced up and down on the bridge, reassuring Janie of its sturdiness. Slowly, on her hands and knees, Janie made her way across the bridge and then, with me behind her shouting encouragement, slid down a winding tube slide. By the time I descended, Taylor and Janie were approaching a tall octagon-like vessel just wide enough to accommodate two children, which could then be rolled, giving the kids a topsy-turvy experience. Taylor invited Janie inside with her and assigned me the job of pushing. After a few rolls, Janie was tumbling out, unafraid, and climbing back in. I suggested they hold on to each other to increase stability and then Janie put her arms around Taylor, fully engaged with another child for perhaps the first time in her life. She played with Taylor, taking her hand when invited, going where she would never otherwise have gone. The chaos of noise and lights was lost on Janie; fully engaged in joyful play with Taylor, she was unaware of everything that used to disturb her.

When Janie's mother returned and saw her playing, she was thrilled; but when Taylor went home, she turned to me. "What if this was a one-time miracle?" she asked. "You don't meet little kids like that every day." I told her that in fact, you do: Taylor was a sweet, outgoing kid, but she's far from unique; lots of kids like to help and teach. I do this a lot, taking children with autism into real-world environments and challenging them to transcend their alleged limitations. And yes, you need to find a good kid to make the experience work. But you also need to facilitate the interaction to make it successful for the child you've brought. This takes patience and persistence. I must have tried to get Janie to interact with a dozen other kids before we came upon Taylor.

My goal that day was to have a typical child engage a child with autism. Parents often feel uncomfortable doing this, but if they think their child is ready, such encounters are invaluable. Even when children are ready, their parents may feel pained by the experience: They don't want to see their kids uncomfortable or rejected, nor do they want to be embarrassed in front of other parents. To parents who have tried this and been unable to find someone with whom their child will engage, I say: If you believe your child is ready, keep trying. That's what I do. If I think a child is ready for a new experience, I may try it 87 times without success. But then, the 88th time, it works. The most valuable interactions for kids on the spectrum are those they have with typical kids. Yes, it's important for kids on the spectrum to have friends facing similar challenges, but interactions with typical kids teach atypical ones how to navigate the vast world beyond the family. Don't let your child's discomfort—or your own—dissuade you from urging your child toward connections with other kids.

CONCLUSION

I had been working with Janie for about a year; now, at 3½, she was unrecognizable as the nonverbal, disengaged child I first met. The week before Halloween she rushed in, eager to tell me about the costumes her mother had made for her and her brother. She spoke with a typical child's expressiveness, and was discussing with some detail the holiday as an eagerly anticipated future event. Her parents were excited by her use of language to communicate with them, her confidence in trying new things, and her easy interactions with other children, especially her brother. Our work ended when Janie's family moved to Pennsylvania. The last time I saw her, she was indistinguishable from a typical child her own age.

THINGS TO WORK ON AND THINK ABOUT.

- *Don't let discomfort dictate your actions.* Janie's mother didn't invite kids over because she hated seeing her daughter frequently startled. But Janie was not phobic about contact with others; in fact, contact was exactly what Janie needed to bring her out of her self-absorbed, infant-like state. Parents must not let their feelings—discomfort, self-consciousness, anxiety at the pain their child may feel, or embarrassment brought on by their child's eccentricities—dictate how they deal with their atypical child. Parents must press their child beyond everyone's comfort zones—both their child's and their own—toward the new, the challenging, the unknown.

- *Don't be too helpful.* If you do too much for your child—anticipate his desires so he doesn't have to express them, for example, or provide answers to questions she is struggling with—you interrupt the learning process. Let your child grapple with the hard stuff. Coach and encourage, but don't help too much.

- *Value authentic responses, not "right" ones.* For people to learn to think more effectively, they must forge cognitive connections that are meaningful to them. When you are working with your child to develop his or her use of language, value the word that comes from within, not the one you want to hear. Whatever the child says is ground zero. Work from there.

- *Tune in to the present moment and exploit serendipity.* When I stood at the window with Janie and heard a siren, the sound sparked the idea of how it could illustrate the concept of time. Some things you can't plan—a quarter on the sidewalk; a sparrow at your feet; a rainbow in a sun shower. Make it up as you go along.

- *Be patient. Be patient. Be patient.* Even though I knew that Janie was capable of grasping abstract concepts, it didn't happen right away. I urge you not to lose faith in the power of patient, consistent performance of cognitive exercises. You may feel as if you're repeating the process in vain, but there is almost always a moment when repetition ignites your child's understanding of the world.

Nonverbal; near constant stimming.

When meeting new young clients for the first time, I always ask their parents the same thing: What is the one thing you would like to change? Luke's mother surprised me: "The stimming," she said. "He stims constantly, and I can't stand it any more. It's driving me nuts." "But what about his lack of language?" I asked her. "Wouldn't you rather he be talking like other kids his age?" "Yes, I wish he were talking, but the stimming comes first. It's got to stop."

She said Luke would line up his toys and slowly wag his head back and forth, his eyes glued to the row, over and over again. The stimming could go on for hours, to the exclusion of everything else. It might be miniature cars, or plastic building bricks, or jars of jam on the kitchen table; Luke found them all compelling, moving his head from side to side as he gazed. Early on, his mother had tried breaking the spell by moving some objects out of position but Luke would scream so violently, she soon gave up. Luke had been seen by an early intervention specialist who would clap his hands loudly whenever the child began stimming in his office; startled, Luke would look up for a moment to find the therapist offering him a treat or a new toy. Like any kid, he'd be distracted for a few minutes with potato chips or Mr. Potato Head, but once he got home, the stimming took hold again and wouldn't let up.

Luke didn't speak but he was far from mute: whenever he didn't get what he wanted, he screamed, leaving the adults in his life clueless about what he wanted and on perpetual edge from his shrill outbursts. This behavior was wreaking havoc on his mother, who worked nights as a medical scribe in a hospital emergency room and needed to get household chores done during the day; Luke's father worked as a police officer. She said she found herself holding her breath when she brought Luke with her to the supermarket, hoping he wouldn't throw a tantrum. He almost always did, screeching and reaching toward what he wanted, which was usually sweet and displayed enticingly (and deliberately) at the eye level of a small child strapped into a shopping cart. This typically prompted Luke's mother to tear open a bag of cookies to appease him and beat a hasty retreat from the store. She said she now avoided taking him to public places lest he embarrass her.

I told Luke's mother that his stimming diminished temporarily in the early interventionist's office because the loud noise was a deterrent—a behavioral technique meant to change Luke's behavior—which it did, however briefly. Luke would eventually revert to his old, perseverative ways because the reason for the behavior had not changed: There had been no change in Luke's cognition—his thinking—to spark an ongoing diversion from the stimming. Because I believe that many stimming behaviors are manifestations of atypical children's stress at feeling isolated, I decided my immediate goal with Luke would be to help him learn to connect with others though language. The payoff would be his long-term cognitive and developmental growth.

PART 1: EARLY CHILDHOOD (Luke, 2½)

First impression: no language, no acknowledgment of my presence, lots of stimming. Luke was an example of a typical atypical kid, if there is such a thing. Entering my office, he ignored his mother's request that he greet me and headed straight for a small table piled with plastic bricks and small figures. Sitting down, he lined up the objects, lowered his head so his eyes could home in on the row, and slowly moved his head back and forth, following the changing perspective of the row with his eyes. I watched him do this for 5 or 6 minutes. When I pivoted a small police car 90 degrees, he turned it back without looking up; when I relocated a goat a few inches away, he restored it to its original position, his gaze undeterred.

I believed that once we could engage Luke in normal language development, his mind would be teeming with vital, spontaneous thoughts that would satisfy him more than stimming. But how to begin? Before we could replace Luke's bad habits with healthy ones, I needed to figure out how to disrupt the obsessive perseveration that was hijacking his mind. I had worked with obsessive kids whom I had coaxed into thinking and functioning in the moment, but Luke looked like an extreme case. Because stimming was overwhelming his ability to think, the best way to start would be to provide a stim-proof activity, one that Luke could not lock into and subvert into an obsessive target. It had to be something he had never done before, with inherent variety; something that would interest him.

Priority: Disrupt the obsessive stimming. I presented Luke with a sorting toy that made different sounds as plastic shapes were slipped into their corresponding slots. Momentarily distracted from stimming, Luke picked up an orange triangle and moved it toward a slot. But before he could sort it, I covered the slot with my hand. As with any of my benign obstructions, this one was meant to interrupt a thinking process and instigate a reaction—the opposite of the mindless repetition Luke engaged in when stimming. He tried to push my hand away but I didn't budge: I wanted him to use words, and the one that most closely described what he wanted me to do was move. "Move," I said, and waited. Nothing. So I said it again: "Move." Still nothing. Continuing to block the slot with my hand, I repeated it again and again and again. "Move. Move. Move. Move," always with the same calm but deliberate inflection. After hearing me repeat the word maybe 10 to 15 times, a tentative moo issued from Luke's mouth. I kept my hand over the slot. "Moo!" he repeated emphatically, and when I obediently withdrew my hand, he smiled.

You may be questioning the logic behind my prompting Luke with a specific word: Was that not modeling, a behavioral technique designed to get him to imitate me and say what I wanted him to say? Yes and no. Yes, I was trying to get him to say move, but—and it's a big but—my overriding intention was to get him to fuse speech to action, to connect the spoken word move with the removal of my hand from the slot he was trying to access. My goal was to acquaint Luke not so much with the act of speaking but with the purpose of speech.

Luke's language began to trickle out. Three sessions later, he was saying hand and move clearly to express his wishes but not the two words together. Luke's next word was open, which he uttered several sessions later in reference to a bag of tortilla chips he wanted. The final en sound was difficult for him, but no matter; I was looking for spontaneous, meaning-ful language, not precise pronunciation. A few weeks later, Luke picked up his cup and, swaggering across the room, announced, "Juice!" loud and clear.

Eager to accelerate Luke's progress, his parents reinforced our work at home by resisting the impulse to anticipate his desires and requiring him to verbalize them himself. When putting Luke on a swing, they would stand idly by until he said "push;" at the dinner table, they would leave his plate empty until he said "meat;" when he raised his arms with an imploring look on his face, they gazed back until he said "up." Their commitment to the process helped immeasurably. Rather than making progress 90 minutes a week in my office, Luke progressed many times each day as his parents replicated the expectations Luke had grown to expect from me.

A month or so later, he noticed a package of potato chips on my desk and ordered me to "open the bag"—his first three-word sentence. Alert to this leap, I paused a few minutes later when Luke said, "move," waiting to see if he would expand his language. Sure enough, after a 20-second stand-off, Luke came out with "move your hand," and I did.

The trickle of language now flowed as Luke began expressing himself in longer phrases. Luke's parents reported that as he was leaving preschool one day, he turned and shrieked "Bye-bye!" lest anyone be unaware of his departure—a manifestation of his awareness of others. "What do you want?" he asked his mother one day when she woke him from a nap. This showed not only progress in stringing words together, but a new way of thinking for Luke, a dawning recognition that other people had points of view and reasons for doing things. Now when he cried out in the market, his mother would ask him what he wanted. If he said "want cookie" or "want bread," she would tear open a package and give him some, which quieted Luke and enabled her to finish her shopping. Yes, she was still acceding to her child's demands, but now he was engaging in fledgling conversations rather than full-blown tantrums. The message here is to be flexible in your expectations and view your child's growth as a gradual process: It isn't going to happen all at once. In the mean time, don't expect miracles; work with what you get.

To stim or not to stim? In our sessions, Luke would now stop stimming as soon as I offered him an intriguing activity, such as playing with a pull-string helicopter or balloon-powered car. Luke's parents reported that his stimming had also decreased at home, but he still lined up his toys and wagged his head for a while when he came home from preschool. I asked if they were able to lure him away from the stimming and they said, yes, that he easily broke away when they presented him with another option. Hearing this, I told them to relax, that Luke's after-school stimming was his way of destressing, no different from the coin-jingling, hair-twirling, leg-jiggling behaviors the rest of us unconsciously engage in. We all take breaks during the day; why shouldn't someone with ASD? I told them it was nothing to worry about because Luke was now easily distracted from his stimming; it was no longer an obsession. As long as his parents lured him away after 5 to 10 minutes, I didn't see the harm in it.

Regrouping after a developmental plateau. Right in the middle of this growth spurt Luke needed eye surgery, which meant I wouldn't see him for 6 weeks. When he returned, his mother was excited to tell me that he had learned many new words during his recuperation. But by the end of the session, I saw that while his vocabulary had grown, his spontaneous and meaningful language had diminished. Whereas before he was building three- and four-word phrases to express himself, now he'd reverted to single word utterances. I had seen this before; when children with ASD are developing language, it's common for them to accumulate more words rather than more complex usage if they are not steadily encouraged to do so. Parents and teachers may unwittingly play into this by praising children when they learn lists of words, not noticing that communication is regressing. It's like the kid who's proud of being able to count to 100 but doesn't get that 9 is one less than 10: Memorizing numbers is one thing, but grasping the relationship between them is a much bigger thing. Luke's parents and I got back to working in concert, and he was back on track 6 weeks later.

Luke's expanding language and the control it gave him sometimes manifested as rebellion against his mother, who related a story in which Luke was in the basement and did not want to come upstairs to bed. A few months earlier he would have just screamed. Now he called out, "Maybe later."

"Come on, Luke," said his mother.

"Maybe later, maybe later, maybe later," Luke chanted, somewhat imperiously. It took his mother a moment to realize that this was something she said to him all the time, and had said for years. There's a lesson in this: Be careful what you say to your atypical kid, because it's going to come back and nip you in the nether regions. Not long ago, I ran into the mother of a former client who said her daughter's teacher called her in for a conference because the kid would mutter "Jesus Christ!" every time she took off her coat, which it turned out to be what this woman said every day when she came home from work. Another mother told me her 4-year-old ASD son had no sooner started speaking in two-word phrases when he began exclaiming, "Holy shit! Holy shit!" It turns out the woman's boyfriend would frequently say this around the house. When she'd ask him to stop, he'd tell her it didn't matter because the kid didn't talk anyway (wrong on both counts).

Luke's father came in and told me that for the first time, Luke hadn't had a screaming fit when told he had to have a snack before leaving on a 3-hour road trip. "He loves visiting my sister," Luke's dad said, "and was insisting, as he always does, that we leave now. But this time, when I told him 'Snack first,' Luke calmly said, 'First we get a snack and then we go to Auntie Donna's.' I was floored." Because Luke's parents, family members, and I had been speaking with him consistently about everyday matters in language that incorporated the concepts of before, now, and after, he had developed the underlying cognitive apparatus to think and respond flexibly rather than react without thinking, as he had in the past.

Helping Luke learn to interact socially. Luke and I had been working together for around ten months; I now believed it was time for him to develop skills for engaging with people outside his family. Playing catch in my office (with a Wiffle ball, very tame), I asked Luke to describe how he was going to throw the ball—underhand? Overhand? High pop? Grounder?—and how he would like me to respond: Should I throw the ball or eat the ball? Should I toss it to him or out the window? Roll it or lob it? Would he throw it hard or softly? High or low? Sometimes I would hide the ball so he would have to ask me where it was. This natural flow of language, related to an activity involving another person, teaches the social skill of taking turns, encourages creative thinking and use of language, and sparks the enjoyment of engaging with others.

His parents and I also reinforced this enjoyment by bringing Luke to outdoor playgrounds, indoor gyms, and other places that provided op-portunities for him to interact with other kids. The encounters were not uniformly idyllic. Once, in a sandbox, Luke stepped on another boy's castle. I was momentarily stricken: The action looked both intentional and playful rather than malicious. I was with his parents when it happened and his mother leapt up. "Oh, no!" she cried, "That's terrible! Why did he do that?" She was about to run to the sandbox when Luke's father said, "No, no, let it be. That's what boys do. Let's see what happens." We watched from the edge of our bench as the two boys confronted each other and in time, flat-tened the remains of the castle and built a new one.

Whenever you bring these kids into such social situations, you hold your breath to see how other kids will react. Luke's dad was right: Sand castles eventually get stomped on, especially if the architects are boys. Herein lies another lesson: Boys, neurotypical and atypical alike, like to destroy things, even after they've spent a lot of time creating them. Most men know this because they did it when they were kids and aren't distressed when they see their sons doing it. Mothers, on the other hand, are more likely to interpret the behavior as the hostile, willful destruction of a carefully engineered work of art. As the father of two sons and a former boy myself, my view is, if you've used up all your blocks building a tower, you've got to knock it down to build something else, right? Luke's sandcastle stomping may not have seemed like an auspicious beginning but it ended with the two boys patiently taking turns with the sand toys, working together to solve problems such as extricating leaves from a clogged funnel, and having fun.

I stopped working with Luke after 2 years, when he was 4½. At that point, he indulged in stimming for about ten minutes when he got home from preschool and seldom at other times. He no longer retreated into a private, isolated world but easily engaged with the people and things around him. When he started kindergarten a few months later, he was placed in a regular class; an observer would have taken him for a child who had been developing typically all along.

I attribute Luke's progress in no small part to his parents' cooperation and support. It's not unusual for parents to terminate their child's therapy when they see rudimentary signs of change. Convinced that a spell has been broken, they mistake a first leap for a cure and imagine the work is done. But this work takes consistent, relentless reinforcement, and if you ease up too soon, the child will regress, as Luke did when recuperating from surgery. Luke's parents stuck with the program and me for 2 years, long after his progress began. When the work ended, I was the one who suggested we terminate the sessions, as Luke was fully integrated into groups of kids his age.

THINGS TO WORK ON AND THINK ABOUT.

* *Mind how you speak to your nonverbal child.* He or she may start speaking up a storm one day, and when that happens, you're going to get back what you put in. Speak to your atypical child as you would any other, in coherent, mature language imbued with meaning.

* *Don't be doctrinaire.* Some stimming is acceptable once obsessive stimming is curbed. Stimming is a way of relaxing and releasing stress. Once you can interrupt your child's stimming without inciting a tantrum, allowing it for a few minutes now and then is okay. It may even be therapeutic.

* *Emphasize thinking over memorization.* Reciting the alphabet by heart is a good thing, but putting letters together to form words is a great thing. It's exciting when your child's vocabulary expands, but don't value acquisition of words over meaning-laden language use. Press your child to express him- or herself verbally in increasingly complex ways.

* *Don't ease up or quit when you start to see progress.* Frame progress as an incentive to work more, not less. If what you're doing with your child is working, congratulate yourselves and keep on going. If your child is in therapy and it's working, stick with it. (If the cost of therapy is straining your finances, talk to the therapist. He or she may

be willing to work with you. Luke's parents were in their early 30s and told me at the beginning that they weren't sure they could afford ongoing sessions. I reduced my fee a bit, which enabled them to keep Luke in therapy long after his initial burst of progress. Other therapists may be similarly inclined.)

IVAN, 4½

Nonverbal; responds to gestures and visual cues.

I 've always believed in keeping an open mind, but it was Ivan and his parents who made me a true believer. Their openness to perceiving what wasn't immediately obvious was responsible in large part for their son's progress from a nonverbal kid to a speaking one in a year.

First impression: sweet-tempered; doesn't respond to verbal prompts, yet parents insist he understands everything they say. Ivan was nearly 5 years old when I met him, a full 2 years older than Luke and Janie were when we met. I knew he wouldn't progress as quickly as they did simply because he was older, with 2 more years of bad habits to dismantle. But his amiable demeanor heartened me; upon entering my office, he immediately busied himself with toys and puzzles while I talked with his parents. They had emigrated from Eastern Europe 7 years earlier. Ivan's father was a graduate student in physics and his mother, who had a degree in music, taught piano part-time and was Ivan's primary caregiver. She had been unusually forthcoming in our initial phone conversation and described her mounting desperation. "At night in bed, I hope I not wake up in the morning," she said, "but my son needs me; he will always need me. I want to die but I must stay alive for him." When I asked them my standard question about what they would change if they could, they said they wished Ivan could talk. "It's strange he does not talk because he understand everything," his father said. His mother agreed: "Yes, yes, when we talk, he listen, he understand."

I didn't respond at first because I knew that questioning a kid's abilities is a sensitive issue for parents. I nodded, turned toward the child, and called his name. No reaction. I called his name again; again, nothing. Then his father called his name a bit gruffly, and Ivan looked up.

"Ivan," I said, looking at him, "why don't you take off your coat?" He gazed at me but didn't move. "Ivan, your coat," I continued. "It's time to take off your coat." Still no movement. Then his mother spoke.

"Ivan, *draga*,* take off your coat," she said. Then, smiling and nodding, she shrugged her jacket off her shoulders. Ivan stood up and removed his coat.

"See?" his father said. "He understands."

I didn't see it that way. I gently pointed out that Ivan didn't remove his coat until he saw his mother remove hers. He had not responded to her words but to her actions. To me, this meant he did not understand.

It's always tricky when parents apprise me of their kid's abilities. Sometimes they're right, but they're often wrong, and it can be awkward trying to reconcile our views, which is important for the work to succeed. Ivan's parents accepted my appraisal, which not only established trust but also made it possible for me to do my job. My relationship with a client's parents is important, but my first loyalty is to the child; if I were to change my techniques to accommodate parents' sensitivities, I'd be abdicating my responsibility. Some years ago, a woman brought in her 12-year-old

* *Sweetheart.*

daughter for help with reading. The child was in middle school and had what we then called Asperger's syndrome. After four sessions, the mother came in and started yelling, "What have you been doing? My daughter used to be very obedient; now she won't listen to me! She doesn't ask me for help anymore! She does whatever she wants!"

"You came to me with a reading problem," I said. "How's that going?"

"Her reading's much better," the mother said.

"Well," I said, "isn't that what you wanted?"

One of the reasons the daughter had a reading problem was that she had not been letting her mind rove freely, liberated from her mother's hovering and guidance. Now this newfound independence was carrying over into other parts of her life. She wasn't trying to provoke her mother; she was merely exploring her nascent sense of self. Nor was the mother trying to squelch her daughter's evolution; she was reacting emotionally to feeling less necessary and in charge than before. Still, her immediate response was to feel threatened by her daughter's budding autonomy, something that she needed to address. I told the woman that if her daughter kept working with me, it would continue like this. After a moment, she said she thought I was probably right and signed up for another four sessions.

First priority: surround Ivan with language. At 4½, Ivan was way behind in terms of language skills (he had none). My plan was to keep talking to him until he began to respond and then build on those responses. Ivan's mother said that after 3 years of trying to get him to converse with her, she had given up because his utter lack of response was so painful. Instead, she had learned to interpret his utterances and anticipate his needs. This assuaged her anguish but didn't do much for Ivan, who now had no motivation to speak in words. Like many parents, she was filling the gap between her mind and that of her child. This may be expedient in the moment, but in the long run, it isn't helpful.

I began to work with Ivan by instigating scenarios and talking nonstop throughout them. I picked up a Spider-Man action figure he liked and started zigzagging around the furniture and spouting a running commentary on what a great toy it was. Each time I ran by him he reached for it, but I swung it out of reach, grinning and saying, "Don't take it!" and dashing away. I did this over and over and over again, knowing that the words wouldn't mean anything to him at first. But I knew he liked the toy and hoped that his emotional connection to it might eventually forge a connection to language. The word "don't" has high emotional resonance; when you deliver it in a playful way, it adds nuance and complexity to the command. I ran around the office with many objects Ivan liked, saying, "Don't!" and eluding his grasp. This was not teasing but a game: I was smiling the whole time, as was he.

One day I handed Ivan the toy and he imitated my behavior, running around with it and giggling. As he came at me for maybe the fourth time, I reached for the toy and he scooted away and said, "Don't!" This was huge: a spontaneous, organic use of language that came from within.

"Don't?!" I replied, using the word as a question and exclamation. Every time he ran past me, I repeated "Don't?!" with exaggerated glee, saying it over and over again to reinforce the connection he'd made. "Don't" in this context was infused with emotion and fun, which is why I imagine he didn't say "Spider-Man" instead. Emotion is key to language; when a feeling outgrows the space inside us, we liberate it through speech. Kids typically acquire language by hearing and watching the people around them fuse feeling with words, but atypical kids don't do this naturally. My role—and yours—is to teach these kids what other kids get through osmosis.

Parents are my greatest allies in this venture, and Ivan's were tremendously helpful. They played the "Don't!" game at home using crayons, toys, dinner—anything Ivan might want to grab—verbalizing their actions using standard, everyday speech, over and over again. With Ivan, I might say the same thing 30 times in an hour to provide many chances for him to say something. Or I might pause in an activity and stand there, waiting quietly if it looked as if he were trying to produce language. As long as a child has an emotional connection to a situation, I try to elicit language. If I see the child is getting tired and no longer having fun, I stop.

But there's more fun in simple things than you might think. And you never know when a child will leap to the next level.

A few sessions later, Ivan was dashing around the office, Spider-Man in hand, and, when I reached out to grab it, he shouted "No spider!"—a new and original way of telling me not to take the toy. I had never spoken those words together during the game; this was Ivan expressing himself in his own words. The next development came when his mother joined us in session and we wrapped Ivan up in toilet paper. He would break out, laughing, and we would pick up the paper and do it again (get the cheaper jumbo rolls for this; the squeezingly soft stuff will set you back). After he had broken free one time, his mom scooped him up and sat him on her lap. He squirmed out of her arms, and then surprised us by commanding, "Paper on!"—a spontaneous instance of typical language development. Ivan wanted something, he used language to express it using words he had never used before, and put them together to create meaning. Moreover, he expected a response, and got the one he wanted.

I continued to put Ivan in language-provoking situations. We rolled up newspapers and played at sword fighting. I deliberately dropped my weapon and stood there, waiting; after about fifteen seconds, Ivan picked it up and tried to hand it to me but I wouldn't take it. Eventually, he said, "Take sword," and I did. Later, when he grew tired and flopped down in a chair, I said playfully, "Stand up and fight!" Thereafter, when I would randomly sit down in the middle of sword fighting, Ivan would call out, "Rob, fight!" And of course I did.

Ivan began using two-word phrases regularly: "scissors cut" when creating artwork; "garbage down" when throwing something in the trash can; "it stuck" when something didn't work. These utterances were different from his earlier ones in that they did not express desires or beg a response. Rather, Ivan was attaching language to what he was experiencing in the moment—another aspect of typical language development.

Ivan's parents accelerate his progress. I had been working with Ivan for about four months at this point and he was using language regularly, which I attributed in large part to his parents' energetic participation in the program. Perhaps their commitment to improving their English helped them empathize with their son's language struggles. Or it may have been because they often sat in on sessions (his mother was there almost all the time) and learned my techniques by watching. What is certain is that they respected Ivan's developmental process; they understood that he had his own thoughts and feelings and might be saying something that held meaning for him even if they didn't understand it at first—which led to the true-believer episode I mentioned earlier.

Ivan's mother came in one day and said she was puzzled because he had taken to exclaiming "Peeshu! Peeshu!" at home from time to time for no apparent reason. Hearing this, she would lead him to the toilet, as peeshu means "urinate" in their native language. But Ivan would just stand there, refusing to use the commode and instead pointing to his nose. This went on for weeks until one day she arrived at my office, Ivan in tow, her face aglow. "I hear him say peeshu," she said, "and then he touch his nose and say, 'Ah-choo'—you see? He not saying peeshu; he saying 'peshu'—bless you—when I sneeze!" I was as excited as she was: Ivan had tapped into his reservoir of normalcy and was uttering consistent, appropriate responses to his mother's sneezes; it just took her a while to hear them accurately. It reminded me of the millions of kids who come home from school and ask their parents about Richard Stands. "Who?" their parents ask. "You know," the kids say. "When we pledge allegiance to the flag of the United States of America, and to the republic for Richard Stands." It's both hilarious and perfectly logical: We learn the pledge by hearing it, and what a lot of kids hear is for Richard Stands, not for which it stands. You have to use your imagination as well as your ears. Ivan's mother was superb at this.

At first, she assumed he was trying to say something in her native language. But when Ivan didn't respond to her interpretation, she focused on his utterances with the expectation that he could communicate his ideas. By keeping her mind open to unforeseen possibilities, she learned that her young son was listening to and learning from the people around him and wanted to join polite society using language.

Venturing into abstract speech. The next breakthrough for both Ivan and his parents came when they told me he had gone to bed the night before saying "dinosaur," referring to a small plastic apatosaurus he was fond of. His father told him they could not play with it because it was time for bed. I then asked what they thought Ivan would have done had they relented, and they said he would probably have gotten out of bed and taken it off the shelf. I told them I had a hunch that Ivan wasn't saying he wanted to play with the dinosaur, but that he was thinking about it and sharing his thoughts with them. It was a revelation to them that their son could be thinking about something and want to communicate it in words. I then asked the father what he might now do in a similar situation and he said, "I would say something like, 'Oh, you are thinking about your dinosaur. Why not we put him on the nightstand so when you wake up, he will be right there?' " I said that would be an ideal response, as it validated a new phase in Ivan's language development: describing abstract images swirling in his head and not only concrete things happening around him.

Ivan progressed to using three-word phrases: When his mother lit a candle, he said "light fire match;" when he wanted to sword fight with me, he said, "Ivan fight Rob." After 6 months together, I deployed one of my benign obstructions and handed him a toy alligator that I had tied up with string. He looked at me as if I were nuts and handed it to his mother, saying, "Mommy cut string alligator"—his first four-word phrase. When I'd done that in the past with parents in the room, they would invariably intercede and offer to untangle the toy, but not Ivan's mother. She just sat there, waiting to see what happened next—which was the ideal response (and what I did with Janie when her seahorse was ensnared): Rather than help your child out of a tangle, be still and give him or her a reason to use words. The key is not to remedy the situation but to elicit language from the child.

One memorable encounter with Ivan happened when we were balloon fighting. Looking fierce, he said, "Fight balloon!" and, seizing mine, tossed it away, poked me with his finger, and commanded, "Die, Rob!," flopping down on a chair to show me how it's done. I died immediately, and was reminded of how interesting it is that when formerly nonverbal kids start to talk, they're sometimes not sure the rest of us understand the English they're learning to use. It's new to them and they assume it's new to us, too.

There's no magic formula for facilitating language development in a child with autism because each child is unique. The magic occurs when therapist and parents work in concert and the child is surrounded by consistent encouragement. Ivan's parents agreed that the way to get him to talk was to continually provide him with reasons to express himself, and they did this by creating activities that he enjoyed, talking to him all the while, and letting his own language emerge naturally. They were not afraid to try things that might not work: They understood that there was no failure, only patience and persistence when trying something, and if it didn't work, trying something else. They knew that pressing Ivan to say something that held no meaning for him was useless. Once Ivan's parents saw that he was capable of saying even one or two words with meaning, even if he mispronounced them, they respected his capacity to find more language within himself and trusted that it would eventually emerge.

I worked with Ivan for a year, during which time he progressed from having no language to saying four appropriate (albeit brief) sentences in a logical sequence. He was responding well to questions. Not least, he was being more affectionate with his parents. We parted ways when the family moved to Oregon.

THINGS TO WORK ON AND THINK ABOUT.

- *Are you open to seeing your child the way others do?* Thinking well of your child's accomplishments is fine, but refusing to acknowledge his or her weaknesses can sabotage the therapeutic process. Ivan's parents were convinced he understood what they said, but when I suggested otherwise, they heard me out. Acknowledging the vulnerabilities of our children, typical and atypical alike, is not a betrayal—quite the opposite; it enables us to make them stronger and more capable.

- *Are you open to hearing what your child may be trying to say?* Parents must broaden their awareness of their child's contextual vision and their perception of what he or she might be trying to express, as it may not be what it seems. In Ivan's case, Peshu! did not mean peeshu (urinate); it meant Bless you! If parents can hear and see what their atypical child is saying and doing, they will recognize breakthroughs that come on subtly rather than strong.

• *Do you reflexively rush in to spare your child discomfort?* Parents of atypical children don't have a monopoly on this one; there are legions of overprotective parents out there and they're not doing their kids any favors. Children need to figure things out on their own, and atypical kids are no different, especially when they are learning to speak. The next time your child encounters difficulty, attend to your reaction. If your impulse is to run to the rescue, stop. Wait. Watch. Listen. Make it necessary for your child to express him- or herself. The goal is not to make things easier for atypical kids, but to get them to speak, communicate, and cope.

• *Do you ever feel threatened by your child's progress?* Be honest with yourself: Are there aspects of your child's budding autonomy that make you uncomfortable? Is there a part of you that mourns the loss of your role as your child's protector and interpreter of the typical world? If so, embrace it as a normal response. Then, find a way to relax your grip so your child can learn to navigate the world without you.

Part 2

JEFF, 6

Nonverbal; bites hand to ease stress.

I heard Jeff before I saw him: shrill screams jagged through the wall from my waiting room, followed by softer, muffled speech—his mother, I imagined. She had called the week before and said her son was 6 years old, energetic, and healthy, but with such severe autism; he had never spoken a word. He seemed oblivious to his surroundings both at school and at home. His special education teachers and school therapists agreed: Jeff was beyond help; he would never speak. But his mother wasn't convinced.

I opened my office door to find an elfin, dark-haired boy wandering around, randomly grabbing anything he could get his hands on and objecting violently when his mother gently pulled him away. She guided him into my office and sat in a chair while I seated Jeff on the floor and joined him on the carpet. My eyes were immediately drawn to the back of his hand, which was raw and bleeding. "He bites it," his mother said. "He does it when he's frustrated." I was struck by how oblivious the child seemed: Despite the pain he must be feeling, Jeff stared ahead with blank eyes. How could he do such violence to himself yet appear so disengaged? I was reminded of how sometimes, when people are emotionally agitated and afraid of losing control, they get quiet and affect a coolness they do not feel: Maybe if I act calm, they tell themselves, I'll feel calm—calm enough, perhaps, to use words instead of fists. But Jeff couldn't use words; he didn't have any. The only vocabulary he possessed comprised actions, one of which was biting his hand until it bled. It was clear that the child needed language, a way of expressing himself, to relieve the corrosive frustration he must be feeling.

As you have no doubt noticed, language development is my first priority when working with nonverbal children on the spectrum. The obvious reason—that not being able to communicate in words is a monumental handicap—is like an iceberg with an unseen, larger foundation: When we cannot express ourselves in words, we will eventually find other ways to do it. Jeff was expressing his frustration by hurting himself.

I tried to engage Jeff with small stuffed animals and colorful toys: no reaction. I caught myself speaking louder than usual in an effort to break through, much as well-meaning folks sometimes pump up the volume when speaking to blind people. After half an hour of this, I changed tactics and began playing with a little red plastic car propelled by a spring-loaded gear. As I made the car go across the floor over and over, something happened: Jeff raised his eyes and looked at me instead of through me. He then shifted his gaze to the car: he was focused, engaged. For several seconds, Jeff's veil of autism lifted.

This was what I'd been waiting for: Jeff had tapped into his reservoir of normalcy. Anyone who knows a child with autism well knows what this looks like. It may be a facial expression or a gesture or an action. It may happen only rarely but it happens, and in that moment, the child is thinking, feeling, and processing typically. Whatever happens in these moments, they are crucial. The key is to know them when you see them and follow wherever the child leads. Jeff had tapped into his reservoir, and I would go with the flow.

I held the car in my hand, aimed it in Jeff's direction, and released it as I whispered, "Go." As it scooted toward him, I repeated, "Go, go, go," softly, so as not to break his focus. When the car reached him, he took it in his hand, turned it around, and silently sent it back to me. This was no small thing: Half an hour earlier, he was inert and staring, ignoring my existence. But now he was not only aware of me but focused on what I was doing, watching my hands as they scooped up the car, turned it around, and sent it back toward him. Jeff was playing with me, not just with the car. Back and forth we went, me whispering, "Go" and Jeff pivoting the car and sending it back.

Then I changed the game: The next time the car came to me, I held onto it. I looked at Jeff, who was staring at my hands, expecting them to repeat the pattern and send the car back. I paused, did nothing. Jeff stared intently at the car nestled in my hands. Thirty seconds passed, a minute; Jeff kept staring. Thirty seconds more. I watched Jeff and waited. And then:

"Go," he said. "Go." His mother gasped. "I don't believe it," she said. "He never said a word before. Never." Her eyes pooled with tears. I looked at the clock: A little less than an hour had passed.

When I tell people this story, they're incredulous. What I did seems so straightforward, so obvious; was it possible that no one had done this with Jeff during the 6 years he'd been on the planet? Probably not. But why? Because until now Jeff, like most people with an autism spectrum disorder, had been treated behaviorally. For years he had been prodded, urged, and cajoled toward replicating the sounds and actions deemed normal by therapists and counselors, only it hadn't worked. My strategy worked because it wasn't trying to get Jeff to do anything except whatever he chose to do. I knew he wouldn't follow me, so I followed him.

It didn't take Jeff long to speak that day, but I would have waited forever, as long as he was focusing his attention on the car and on me. The key was tuning in to Jeff's point of view: When nonverbal children are calmly engaged with another person, you must let them take the next step on their own terms. In this case, the step was a quantum leap: He spoke for the first time in his life. But it wouldn't have mattered if he had said car or push, or even if he had grabbed the car away from me. What mattered was that he communicated his wish for the car to come to him. I inserted a benign obstruction—pausing before sending the car back—and Jeff broke the impasse by mining gold from within himself: the word go. This process is essential for the development of meaningful language.

The car-playing scenario was a big success, but it might not have worked. I didn't know what was going to come of all the back-and-forth until it all came together. The point is to home in on what the child is doing and follow him or her wherever they go. If Jeff had lost his concentration without saying anything, I would have let him play by himself for a few minutes. If, for example, he wandered off and started rolling a ball, I would have tried to connect with him by rolling a ball the way he was doing it, mirroring his pace and rhythm. Then I would have stopped mid-roll to see if he was engaged. If he was, he might have tried to lift my hand from the ball, or he might have said move or ball, or he might just have sat there and done nothing. It all depends on what the kid is ready for. Creating an obstacle isn't enough; the kid has to be ready to want to overcome it. When

I tuned into Jeff's point of view, I saw that he was ready, so I chose to hold onto the car until something happened. If you tune into your kid's point of view, it's not hard to know when he or she is ready.

Another first: playing for its own sake. I began meeting with Jeff every week and soon learned that what engaged him one moment might not interest him the next. I stocked up on toys and games, hoping something else might catch his fancy as the little car had and spark another breakthrough. Around 3 weeks in, Jeff was playing on the floor with some colorful plastic rings, gazing intently at his hands as he spun them on his fingers. What was going on his head? I had some ideas, and decided to supply words for what I thought they might be. "They're so pretty," I said. "Look at how they shine." Jeff gathered five rings and arranged them in the shape of a pentagon. "Oh, you've made a shape," I said. "The colors look nice in that order." He admired them silently for a moment, then picked them up one at a time, and laid them down again in a circle.

These were the first deliberate, non-random actions I had seen Jeff make, and it was a big deal. Jeff was playing because it was giving him pleasure, which is not something a child with autism does naturally. Playing is a deliberate form of reflection, and crucial to a child's developing a sense both of himself and the world. For such a child, play provides a chance to reflect, to be introspective, to think, rather than be constantly moving, grabbing, disrupting, and dismantling whatever is within reach. It is intentional, not mindless action, and represents a major step in typical development.

When I told Jeff's mother that he had made a great stride, she seemed puzzled. "But he acts deliberately all the time," she said. "He pulls me over to the refrigerator when he wants something to eat. And his brother—he always gets Craig to do things for him. Just this morning, Craig helped him get dressed for school." But there's a big difference, I explained: When a child drags you toward the fridge because he's hungry or gets his big brother to tie his shoelaces, he's trying to satisfy a basic and pressing need. But when a child plays for the joy of it, he is entertaining himself, stimulating his mind and his senses strictly for the pleasure of doing it. Arranging those rings in patterns didn't involve language, but it was a breakthrough for Jeff nonetheless.

Jeff was now using words occasionally and his hand-biting had diminished. But he still hadn't grasped that speaking could reliably get his needs met and obviate the need for pushing and pulling people toward what he wanted. To address this, I started providing low-key narrations to accompany Jeff's activities, like a broadcast journalist covering a golf tournament. It was similar to what I'd done with Ivan and the Spiderman toy, only with Jeff, I would supply language that he might be hearing inside his own head, as I had done when he was playing with the rings. I had a sense that Jeff was creating an interior world and I wanted to surround him with language relevant to whatever he was doing, in hopes that he would start adding some of his own words to mine. About two months into our sessions, I handed Jeff the watering can for our weekly horticultural segment. "The plants on the windowsill look thirsty," I said. "I think they would like some water." As we approached the door, instead of pulling me toward it as he usually did, Jeff said, "door."

I was surprised and delighted and immediately complied. But I did not praise him because I did not want to interrupt his thought process. To his mind, hearing "Good job, Jeff!" would have at best delayed the flow of our activity and at worst, encouraged him to repeat the word to win my approval. The goal is not to get a child to repeat himself, but to get language to emerge from a spontaneous connection from within, no matter what word emerges. Inserting words of praise would have disrupted Jeff's evolving comprehension of the interactive nature of conversation.

Later in the session, Jeff stopped in the midst of rolling a ball, looked at me, said, "tick," and reached over to tickle me. Two minutes later, he gravitated toward a bag of uninflated balloons. "I like balloons," I said, "but they're more fun when they have air in them." I took one, blew it up to the size of an apricot, pinched it shut and said, "Should I make it bigger?"

"Yes," Jeff said. I blew into the balloon again.

"Should I make it smaller?"

"No."

"Should I keep blowing?"

"Yes. Bigger."

This happened in one session, and the tangible results of Jeff's words seemed to delight him. He wasn't fidgeting or gnawing on the back of his hand; he was sitting calmly and focusing on the balloon and our interaction. I had never seen him so relaxed.

Jeff connects words to form sentences and uses language to control his life. The following week, I suggested we water the plants again. I paused before the door and asked, "What should we do, Jeff?"

"Open the door," he said clearly. His first sentence! At almost every session thereafter, Jeff explored new verbal territory. He began to make decisions by verbally communicating what he wanted among three choices I would offer—red, yellow, or blue balloon? Potato chips, tortilla chips, or pretzels? Apple juice, grape juice, or water? Instead of darting from one thought to another, he was able to organize his environment. He realized that some of his favorite objects maintained their locations from week to week and began requesting them. I continued to improvise on ordinary happenings that might prompt Jeff to use words to communicate. I intentionally banged my shin on my desk, cried out "Ow!—I got hurt!", and grabbed my leg. Jeff came over and pulled my hand away to see if there was a bruise. Jeff's next breakthrough happened one day when I had a bandage on my finger. He looked at it and then up at me, so I answered his unspoken question and told him how I hurt myself. (I didn't remain silent to provoke a response; I don't always benignly obstruct.) His eyes remained focused on the bandage, which I interpreted as sustained curiosity. I asked him if I should remove the bandage, but he did not respond. I continued to repeat the question, changing the wording so as not to bombard him with repetitive speech. Eventually he said, "Take bandage off." I removed it and, with great seriousness, he examined the cut.

Another day soon after, Jeff noticed that one of his shirt buttons was open and tried unsuccessfully to fasten it. His school aide was with us and she went over and began to do it for him. I stopped her and asked, "What should we do? Should we button your shirt?" He answered, "Button shirt," and so she did. Another time, I asked Jeff if he wanted to water the plants. He grabbed the can and brought it to me. I handed it back to him and said, "Here; you do it." He looked in the can, looked back at me, and said, "Empty." (He wasn't quite as indignant as Janie was when I pulled this on her, but wasn't impressed with my intelligence, either.) I had no idea he even knew the word, nor did his mother.

Within 2 months of our first session together, Jeff was no longer biting his hand; within 4 months, he was speaking consistently in three-word sentences. After 6 months, his language was evolving with improved syntax and fluency.

And then something extraordinary happened: Jeff ended up on the front page of *The New York Times* in a story about how his school district was serving kids with autism.[3] The family started getting calls from experts, one of whom, a prominent therapist in the field, expressed interest in treating Jeff. And so he left my practice. About ten months later, his mother called and asked if I would consider working with Jeff again. He had not made much progress, she said, and asked if I would like to come to the house and become reacquainted with him. I agreed.

When I arrived, Jeff's mother ushered me into the family room, where a therapist sent by Jeff's school was working with him—or trying to—Jeff kept sliding off his chair and wandering around the room until his mother physically returned him to his perch. The therapist sat with a stack of flash cards emblazoned with letters of the alphabet and was holding up

"B" when I walked in (she hadn't gotten very far). "Make a 'buh' sound, Jeff," she said. He said it once, twice, then squirmed off the chair again. The therapist spoke to Jeff's mother. "Sorry, but we have to start again. He must make the sound 10 times before we can move on." Her insistence that Jeff repeat sounds, devoid of context or meaning, was, in my opinion, the worst thing she could be doing. Poor kid—talk about boring, mind-numbing activities! And worse than the boredom was the effect of the exercise: making him articulate sounds rather than express meaning. That's speech therapy—a noble endeavor—but it is not how you engender language in a newly verbal child.

I had a few more sessions with Jeff in my office, but something had changed. He had lost interest in our old ways of connecting; the momentum was gone. He was speaking in short, simple sentences, but I wasn't able to revive the energy of our old sessions. After about four sessions, his parents and I agreed that it was best to stop treatment. That was about twelve years ago.

There's a happy coda to this story. I saw Jeff several years ago at an awards ceremony at our local high school. For about a decade now, I have donated funds for an annual award for a graduating senior who has done exceptional work with kids with autism. That year, the awards committee had chosen Jeff's brother Craig to receive the honor, citing his years of work at a summer camp for special needs kids, tutoring ASD students in middle school and high school, and his plans to major in special education in college. He and his family had been invited to the ceremony without knowing about the award; seeing the look on their faces when Craig's name was announced was unforgettable. The best part was when Jeff and Craig high-fived each other, just like a couple of guys.

THINGS TO WORK ON AND THINK ABOUT.

- *Congratulating children for making progress can stymie their progress.* It's difficult to do, but parents should resist the impulse to praise their child when he speaks for the first time: The praise may disrupt the child's thought process and prompt him to parrot words rather than use them intentionally. It's a thrilling moment when your child utters her first word, but refrain from distracting her from what she may be thinking, processing, and learning. Instead, look into the child's eyes, smile warmly, and wait. Encourage; don't distract.

- *Everyday life provides an abundance of learning moments. Seize them.* When I banged my shin on the desk, I turned it into an event to involve Jeff. Such moments abound during even the most ordinary day. If you're standing on line in the supermarket or the bank or anywhere, for that matter, leave your phone in your pocket and look around instead—you will probably notice something that could spark an interaction with your child. If you're together at the mall, attend to the sights, sounds, and constant movement: Those places are designed to overload the senses and there's always something going on (those player pianos they sometimes have are fascinating to kids and terrific conversation starters). Maintain awareness and improvise.

- *... but remember not to help too much.* The aide meant well when she started to button Jeff's shirt, but that was a learning moment too good to squander. Don't leap into the breach to solve problems quickly; invite, coax, lure your child into participating in the solution. Focus on process rather than results.

ADDISON, 6

Verbal; energetic; highly distractible.

Addison was referred to me by her pediatrician, who had known her since she was born. Diagnosed at age 3 with high-functioning autism by a psychologist at the early intervention program she attended, Addison had progressed little in the 3 years she had been there. When her parents called to make the appointment, they said she wandered around, couldn't engage in conversation for more than a few seconds, and seemed lost in her own mind. She had difficulty transitioning from one place or activity to another; used unclear, repetitive language; and spoke about whatever popped into her mind, which was often irrelevant to the matter at hand. She attended a public elementary school in an inclusion classroom in which a group of neurotypical first-graders included some special needs kids, each of whom was assigned an aide—or aides, in Addison's case; she went through them quickly. An inveterate name-caller, Addison loudly let others know they were fat, creepy, and stupid; her most recent aide quit after 3 weeks of hearing Addison repeatedly tell her she was ugly and wished she would die. I phoned her teacher and learned that she grabbed other children's belongings, including lunch as they were eating it. She was intelligent and often attentive during lessons, but when asked to work quietly at her desk, would get up and walk around, knocking books, pencil cases, and papers to the floor. Addison spoke fluently but could not maintain a conversation for more than one or two exchanges. At home, she was physically destructive and directed her 3-year-old brother, who adored her, to disrupt social gatherings by yelling curse words and pulling down his pants. Her parents were still recovering from the previous weekend when Will appeared in the dining room in the midst of a sit-down dinner for 10, dropped his drawers, and shouted "Shitty! Crappy! Doody!" until his parents, who were plating entrées in the kitchen, dashed in and removed him. It sounds funny now but at the time, they were not amused.

First impression. Addison's first session was a replay of what her parents described. She grabbed a wooden truck and banged it hard on my laptop (it was closed, thank heavens), shoved papers off my desk, was about to hurl my camera to the floor when I grabbed it, and clambered onto a chair to pull a painting off the wall. I stopped her: All the paintings in my office are the work of my wife, and they are not up for grabs. This was hardly the first time a child had tried to trash my office, but I was still unnerved when Addison went for the painting. Marring my laptop case was one thing; damaging Rachel's artwork was something else. I told her no, she was not allowed to remove the painting, took a deep breath, and considered my options. One was to take the white-room approach of another treatment program I knew of, in which therapist and child meet in a barren space, devoid of objects, color, and distractions. A kid can't do much damage in a place like that, but it won't help her learn how to manage herself in the real world, either. Whereas Addison's actions could have been construed as malicious, I knew that for many kids on the spectrum, willy-nilly de-structiveness is spurred by a cognitive deficit, not ill will. Addison was a high-energy, highly distractible girl whose problems would be more apparent in a realistic environment. I determined to treat her in the office. If things got too raucous, I'd take the paintings down.

I observed Addison for the rest of the session, intervening only to keep mayhem at bay. She spoke slowly and eccentrically, using flawed grammar ("My family used to took me to Disneyland"); awkward intonations (pronouncing cookies as cook-KEYS and apple as a-POLE); and lowering her voice to a whisper for no apparent reason. She flitted from armoire to desk to sofa, grasping a toy before dropping or tossing it aside, twirling and spinning in a seeming chaos of movement. Nothing held her interest: No sooner would she focus on an object than she'd abandon it to pursue another, as with the painted wooden creature she noticed on my desk. "I want the frog!" she said, and began to walk toward it. But in the four steps it took her to get there, she became distracted by a plant sitting on the floor and a photo lying on a table, both of which she stopped to investigate. She never made it to the frog.

A light bulb went on in my head: It wasn't that Addison wasn't interested in anything; the problem was that she was internally distracted all the time, her mind leaping from one thing to another with no continuity or purpose. When a kid is attracted to something and can't maintain her concentration long enough to get there, something is wrong. Attention-deficit/hyperactivity disorder was probably part of it—many people on the spectrum suffer from ADD/ADHD—even if it weren't the cause of Addison's other inexplicable behaviors, such as when she picked up a stuffed bear she was fond of and flung it against the wall, crying, "Little bear, I want you to die!" I was thrown along with the poor bear; where did that hostility come from?

That was a question for another day. For now, I believed that if Addison could learn to focus, such outbursts would diminish on their own. She had to learn to be aware of her seemingly random flitting from one thing to another. She needed to be able to stop abandoning an initial intentional action and pursue it to the end. And at some point, she would need to understand the social consequences of her actions.

Early sessions: perpetual, lyrical motion. Addison's next visits were much like the first: darting around the office like a hummingbird, forward and backward, gliding swiftly from object to object. I had decided to observe Addison for several sessions to get an idea of what I was dealing with, and by the third I thought I might be dealing with a dancer. I began to see a lyricism in Addison's movements: She bent from the waist to pick up a ball with one hand, sweeping the other aloft while pointing the toes of her foot, ballerina style. She would sway her upper body while sashaying across the room, rhythmically bobbing her head from side to side. When I commented on her grace, she told me that she loved to dance and had in fact performed her improvisational moves at a recital. But when I asked her to repeat a combination of steps she'd just done, she couldn't do it. I waited a minute and again asked her to duplicate a combination, but she was unable to: She could not execute anything that required memorizing steps or movements in sequence. Everything she did was impulsive and rooted in the moment, never to be remembered or repeated.

Still, Addison was a natural dancer, moving gracefully if artlessly around the room. Something was motivating her to do this, even though her mind wasn't fully engaged. If I could help her tap into that energy, maybe she could learn to use it in a deliberate way. What might work? And then it came to me.

Fourth session: an experiment. Mary, a yoga instructor, was seated in a corner of my office before Addison arrived for her next session. I often invite experts in to meet clients and have hosted a video game designer, music therapist, religious leaders, a magician, athletes, a philosopher, an experimental physicist, psychotherapists, a spiritual healer, chess instructors, a business owner, even a therapy dog. Bringing hard-to-reach clients into contact with someone who knows a lot about something they like can spark engagement and sometimes, a breakthrough.

This was the first time I had thought to work with yoga, though. I had a hunch yoga might work for Addison because it is a physical and mental discipline comprising a variety of postures performed with attention to both body placement and breathing. When you're doing yoga, you're attending both to how you're holding your body, how the posture feels, and how your breath is coming in and going out. My hope was that if Addison were intrigued by yoga, she might connect with her reservoir of normalcy and learn to exert control over both her body and her mind.

Addison's parents told me that she became anxious in the presence of strangers, so I thought that having Mary's arrival precede Addison's might be less disruptive than having Mary enter the session after it had begun.

Moreover, I instructed Mary not to engage with Addison unless and until Addison showed interest in her.

When Addison entered the room and saw Mary there, she stopped, said that she did not like Mary, and did not want to talk with her. Fine, I told her; she didn't have to have anything to do with Mary. Addison came in and began cavorting about, as usual. After a few minutes, I introduced Mary as a yoga teacher. Addison seemed not to hear me and continued moving. Then, about three minutes later, Addison stopped mid-twirl and asked Mary, "What is yoga?"

In language that Addison could understand, Mary talked about integrating breath and movement for the benefit of mind and body. She stood and began executing some fluid movements while inhaling and exhaling audibly and deliberately, and Addison imitated her. Next, Mary demonstrated a sequence of postures that Addison was able to follow and reproduce. I watched silently, not wanting to betray my excitement lest I break their connection. Just as I refrain from praising young clients when they begin to talk, so I refrained from encouraging Addison now.

Then Mary asked Addison to help her create a new series of movements and postures. Addison demonstrated four different ones, ending with her feet planted hip-distance apart and her arms aloft, palms parallel to the ceiling. I spoke up then and asked if Mary would add a movement, curious to see whether Addison would accept having her combination modified. Mary adopted Addison's stance and, bringing her palms together, lowered them until they were resting, thumbs to sternum, at what is known as the heart center. I watched transfixed as Addison adopted the posture and then added a few more, resulting in a sequence of eight movements. This might have been the first time in her life that she had followed an example and done something that was expected of her. Even better, she was smiling, looked proud of herself, and said she was going to teach yoga to her friends.

This was the breakthrough I had hoped for. Until now, Addison had been defined by her destructive behaviors; but today, something had clicked. Before, her actions had evinced no purpose beyond manifesting her impulses. Now she had made a cognitive leap. Captivated by an activity that spoke to her, Addison demonstrated that she was capable of memorizing and repeating a sequence. She was confident she could do it again and teach it to friends. Her desires were no longer strictly ephemeral: Now she could imbue them with intention.

Addison names her problem. Mary returned for the next session but could stay only 20 minutes, so she and Addison got right down to doing some yoga poses. As Mary was preparing to leave, Addison began flitting around the office and doing things she knew she shouldn't—running her hand across my laptop keyboard, messing up a stack of papers, sweeping figurines off a table onto the floor—exercising the same impulse to wreak random havoc. I spoke up before the place turned into a shambles.

"Addison," I said, "it looks to me as if your mind is jumping from thing to thing." She listened, and then nodded her head.

"This thing that happens," I said, "let's call it something." Naming something puts it in a category and makes it recognizable. "Can you think of a name for it?" Addison thought again.

"Zooming," she said. "I'm zooming."

"Do you like zooming?"

"No."

"Okay. What do you think you could do to stop zooming?"

"You tell me. Or Mary can tell me." This was interesting: I asked Addison what she could do and she foisted the responsibility back on me, on Mary, on anyone other than herself. Her response was probably a result of being ordered to behave civilly by her parents, her teachers, her aides—any adult who'd had to put up with her destructive behaviors. Now, given a chance to exert control over herself in her own way, she looked to nearby adults for instructions.

"Addison," I said, "you decide. What can you do to stop zooming?"

"You tell me."

"No, I can't."

"Mary can tell me."

"No, she can't."

We went back and forth like this until I saw I wasn't going to win.

"Okay, Addison," I said, "I'm going to tell you what to do." She looked up, suddenly attentive.

"Addison, you have to tell me what you need to do to stop this." I wouldn't have tried this with a 16-year-old; she'd have told me to go to hell. But with a 6-year-old, it might work. Because I truly didn't know what this kid had to do to stop zooming around the room; only she could figure it out. Ninety-nine percent of the questions adults ask kids, they already know the answers to: Like good lawyers, they're trying to coax out the answer they need to prove their case. But when I work with these kids, I keep my mind open because I really don't know the answer.

Addison protested and I persisted. Back and forth we went until, after maybe 10 minutes, she sprang out of her chair, planted her feet about 12 inches apart, inhaled deeply while raising her arms as if to perform a swan dive, then lowered her arms slowly to her sides, exhaling slowly. "There," she said. "I stopped what I needed to stop." I was floored. Mary, stock-still and eyes wide, mouthed "yoga." And that was it. Addison sat down again; there was no more zooming that day.

I invited Mary to return for the next few sessions, each one of which began with her performing a sequence of 9 or 10 yoga postures with Addison following along. When Addison lost track of what to do next, Mary suggested that she stop and breathe. Addison would comply and usually say that she wanted to start over. Each time she did, she completed the sequence perfectly. This was a milestone: Until now, the adults in Addison's life had been trying to control her behaviors, with scant success. Now the child had a way to exert control over herself. She couldn't always remember the sequence of postures but when she was reminded, not only did she get it right but her demeanor changed: With every exhale, her face grew more relaxed and she seemed calmer.

The second, post-yoga portion of each session gave me a chance to prod Addison into talking about what was going on inside. She sometimes resorted to flitting around the room again, albeit less destructively; now, however, she was aware of how it affected her. She said that she didn't like it when she zoomed because, as she said, "I'm nowhere." I subsequently used this insight by questioning her mid-zoom: "You took a bag of pretzels from the basket, then you said you wanted to water the plant, then you went back to the pretzels and tore open the bag, then you dropped the pretzels and started playing the xylophone. What do you think is going on?" She would respond by saying she was zooming, so I would ask her if she wanted to stop. She would say yes, she did, at which point she would stop and take a breath. Over time, just becoming aware of the zooming enabled her to stop.

When I asked how Addison felt about being able to control her zooming, she said it felt good. I wasn't surprised: I have found that most people on the spectrum feel good when they gain control over behaviors that used to feel automatic and inevitable, especially when those behaviors interfered with their ability to connect with people. Most human beings, typical and atypical alike, thrive when they are part of a community. When atypical people develop mastery over behaviors that formerly alienated them from others, the dream of community becomes a reality.

Extending self-control beyond the sessions. I had spoken with Addison's teacher, who said that her aggressive actions had mostly disappeared, although she did sometimes leave her seat and walk around the classroom. I suggested that the teacher allow her this freedom: If moving around helped Addison control her aggression, I thought it was okay as long as she didn't bother other kids or disrupt the lesson. Moreover, I thought it likely that Addison would soon return to her seat if she were entrusted with this freedom. To her credit, Addison's teacher agreed.

I wanted Addison to gain perspective on how much she had accomplished. I suggested that, since she was now able to control herself, she no longer needed to shove papers onto the floor, yank down displays from the bulletin board, or take other kids' food, and she agreed. Wondering if she could expand her perspective, I took a gamble.

"Addison," I said, "I'm wondering about something. What kind of person would you like to be?"

"I dunno." Translation: I don't want to talk about this; leave me alone; go away! I tried again.

"I'm wondering how you'd like other people to see you. Remember your aide, the one who quit? And the ones before her?" She looked at me now. "What do you think other people thought about that? What do you think they might have told your new aide about you?"

"They might have said I was mean," she said quietly.

"What do you think about that?"

"I don't like it."

"You don't want people to think you're mean?"

"No, I don't."

Addison's awareness of how others might perceive her indicated cognitive growth. Not only did she grasp that others might view her differently from how she viewed herself; she also realized she wanted others to think well of her. She had a dawning awareness that her actions might give others a bad impression of her and she wanted to change that.

I began working with Addison in February. In May, her parents said things had changed radically for their daughter. Addison had abandoned her classroom aggressions. She still strolled around the room but was seldom disruptive and was doing well academically. She sometimes persuaded Will to be naughty, but the episodes were relatively harmless, and she was showing him more affection than before. We agreed that Addison still had work to do—her tendency to lose focus persisted, although she was usually able to regain it—but her parents were relieved that her future now promised more than eternal scenarios of crisis control. They were looking into summer yoga classes and had offered her ballet lessons, which she was considering. I suggested we take a break over the summer. In September, her mother called to say that Addison was adapting well to second grade. I wished them well.

THINGS TO WORK ON AND THINK ABOUT.

- *Think outside the box and beyond convention.* No amount of verbal jousting would have convinced Addison that she could control herself, but the discipline of yogic breathing did. Open your mind. Be creative. Singing, dancing, drawing, painting, sculpting, drumming, origami, gymnastics, tae kwon do, magic tricks, playing ball, music, or chess—consider them all. Try something new, something different, something out there. It might work.

- *Don't force your child to connect; let her or him decide when to do it.* I knew that Addison wasn't crazy about strangers, so I was taking a risk by bringing Mary in. When Addison announced that she didn't want to have anything to do with Mary, I let her call that shot. I had taken a liberty by inserting Mary into the session, so I granted Addison the liberty to ignore her. She didn't, though; within minutes, her curiosity won out and she engaged with Mary on her own. Many parents are so eager for their kids to connect and make friends, they push too hard and the kids withdraw even more. When bringing your child into a social situation, let him or her lead.

HANK, 6½

Verbal; energetic; provocative.

Opening my office door, I saw a blond, wiry boy cavorting around the waiting room as his mother sat watching. Ignoring my greeting, he darted past me and started grabbing things—a geode from a shelf, a pen from my desk, and a bag of potato chips from a basket—seemingly oblivious to my presence. I again greeted him several times by name and received no response until, suddenly; he spun around, ran up to me and, grinning brilliantly, crowed, "Fuck you! Get the fuck out of here!" before spinning away and going after my camera, which I'd left on the desk. I got to it a millisecond before he did, whereupon he dodged under my arm and used the pen he'd grabbed to scribble on a sheaf of papers. Barely a minute had passed.

Part of me went into self-preservation mode as I came up with lots of reasons to tell the woman in the waiting room Sorry, lady—I can't work with your kid. What in the world could I do with this boy? Hank had made me angry and I was wracked with self-righteous indignation—for a moment. Then my brain kicked in and reminded me: Hey, this is your job. Get over yourself and attend to your client. I remembered Jeff running around and grabbing things before I noticed the open wound on the back of his hand. I'd managed to reach him; maybe I could reach this boy, too.

As Hank pinballed around the room, I focused on what I knew about him. When his father called to make the appointment, he alluded to his son's "inappropriate verbalizations" (he wasn't kidding). He said Hank was in a first-grade class of more or less typical kids, but that he gave his teachers a hard time, disrupting classroom activities, and yelling and cursing without warning. The only way they knew to deal with his behavior was to tempt him with rewards or threaten him with penalties, which seldom worked, as Hank couldn't remember from one day to the next why he was being praised or punished. Traditional behavioral therapy had not worked: The shock and horrified awe that Hank's cursing produced in adults was far more rewarding to him than the kiddie treats they offered to shut him up. Theoretically, a cognitive approach seemed promising: If I could help Hank understand that his behavior had consequences not only for him but for others and attach meaning to what those consequences might be, he might be motivated to control himself. But was he capable of that level of cognition? His chaotic, aggressive actions and seeming obliviousness to my words weren't encouraging.

After 5 minutes of energetic meandering, Hank sat on the floor and started exploring a bin of plastic building bricks. I sat down next to him, showed him pictures of milk, fruit, and bread, and asked him what kind of store they belonged in. "Washing machine," he replied. When I asked, "What's a car?" he said, "blue." It seemed he had no understanding of the simplest concepts. When I asked him to stack rings on a spindle in size order, he just stared. When I held out a toy helicopter and asked him what needed to be done to make it fly, he moved his hand as if to pull the string of the wind-up mechanism. But it took more than a minute of repeatedly asking him whether I should pull the string or if he wanted to do it before he actually said, "Pull the string."

He evinced little grasp of concepts, so I decided to try to appeal to his emotions. I said I was hungry and he ignored me. I purposely banged my knee and yelped, hoping he would recognize what had happened and perhaps say something sympathetic; again, he ignored me. Toward the end of the session, he noticed that my left forefinger was bandaged, stared intently at it for nearly a minute, and asked, "What happened?" I told him I had cut myself and he said, "Let me see!" So I unwrapped my finger, explaining how I had been slicing onions and the knife slipped, so I had to go to the emergency room—but he interrupted to ask if I had any cookies, either unable or unwilling to process what I was saying. Details were inconsequential to him, as was the notion of engaging with me with even a wisp of empathy. He just wanted me to unwrap my hand so he could see the wound. Once he saw it, he lost interest.

For the rest of the session, I tried to engage Hank in conversation to observe his thinking process. When I asked what he was building with the bricks, he said, "a building," repeating the word I'd used. When I asked him to describe whether it would be big or little, he shook his head; when I asked if it was a house or a school or a store, he said, "something." He seemed to function only in the present, unable to think beyond the brick his hand was holding in that moment to where he might place it in the next. He showed few signs of continuous thinking and, when I tried to get him to talk about anything—his father's work as a paramedic, his day at school, his favorite food—he was unable to maintain a conversation. Although Hank could put words together competently, he looked troubled when pressed to consider unfamiliar scenarios. For example, he'd had no trouble asking for cookies but when I offered him either goldfish crackers or an apple instead, the prospect of choosing stumped him. He also lacked signs of aptitude for logic and self-correction. When I asked him to add three plus one, he answered "four" correctly, but when I then asked him to add three plus seven, his response was "a hundred." There was a rupture between what Hank could conceptualize and verbalize in the moment and what he could imagine. He seemed intelligent, yet the hallmarks of intelligence in a 6-year-old—the ability to think abstractly and verbalize abstract thoughts, envision events in the future, and express in words what was going on inside him—appeared inconsistently, if at all. I needed to know more.

Early sessions: assessing Hank's cognitive abilities. I went to Hank's school to meet with his teachers, who confirmed what his father had told me.* They said that no one could predict when Hank would start shouting and cursing, and that other kids had learned to keep away from him. When he behaved wildly during afternoon recess, his teachers told him he would lose recess the next day. It seemed to me that they were striking a hopeless bargain with Hank, as he was incapable of connecting past behavior to future consequences. I knew this because when he'd ask to do something in session and I responded that we'd do it later, he never came back to me with his initial request. Once something left his mind, it was gone. The only response I imagined he would have to being docked from recess would be to scream and curse, the very behavior that got him punished in the first

---

* *I always ask permission of a young client's parent or guardian before speaking with anyone about the child. No one has ever refused.*

place—which his teachers confirmed. In fairness to them, I knew they were resorting to this tactic out of desperation. They had 20-something other kids to deal with, and had neither the time nor the resources to focus all their energies on Hank's aggressiveness.

The logical result was that Hank's teachers no longer challenged his rudeness nor insisted that he think about how it affected his classmates. Teachers become so focused on keeping the peace that they lose sight of trying to pinpoint and address the underlying reasons for the aberrant behavior. Over time, the child becomes more manipulative and the behavior gets worse. Hank soon learned that if he screamed and cursed enough, he would be removed from the classroom, his mother would be called, and she would come to take him home. His teachers said this cycle had been repeating itself for months, and that they suspected he was gaming the system. They wished they could do more but, in a crowded classroom, fostering orderly behavior usually trumps learning. This was upsetting because they all were convinced that Hank was smart, that he could learn, and that he in fact knew a lot more than he was showing.

That's what I was thinking, too. Now I had to find out how much he knew.

I had noticed in session that Hank's spontaneous speech was more cogent and sophisticated than his responses to my questions. Toward the end of our second session, he said, "Hurry up and finish. I want to get home in time for *SpongeBob SquarePants.*" At the beginning of the third session, he stood in front of the video camera I use to record our time together, put his hands on his hips, and proclaimed, "Rob Bernstein, you will make a video of me so I can show my friends!" Clearly, Hank had an age-appropriate command of certain concepts, if not elegant manners; still, he seemed able to use his mind fluidly only in impulsive bursts.

But his abilities began to emerge. One day, I took Hank out for pizza, and as we walked, we encountered a child around his age whose conversation with his parents manifested lucid thinking and articulate speech on a level that exceeded anything Hank had exhibited at school. I observed Hank watching and listening to this kid and wondered what was going on in his head. I got an idea a few minutes later when we stopped in front of some old stone steps built into the side of a hill, which I pointed out to him. To my complete and utter surprise, he began to speak.

"There's two sets of three steps and that makes six all together," he said. I played it cool and confirmed that yes, there were indeed six steps. A block later, he declared, "See? Here are 12 steps: Three plus three plus three plus three. Six here, and three plus three." I think of this as my very own 12-step program.

Later, when we were waiting on line for ice cream, Hank's personality asserted itself. "I'm getting coffee," he said. "You get coffee, too."

"I think I'd rather have pistachio," I said.

"No, get coffee," he insisted.

"Hank, I don't like coffee ice cream."

"Yes, you do! I love coffee ice cream."

"You love coffee ice cream, Hank. But I don't. I don't like the taste. You know what you like, and I know what I like. You can't tell another person what they like."

This was one of those teaching moments I live for, a viscerally engaging, improvised discussion perfect for challenging a young person's ASD-enhanced egocentrism. Perhaps adults were always telling Hank that he should eat this or that because he'd love it, and he was reiterating what he'd heard. Whatever its provenance, his position was untenable and it was important that he understand why. I told Hank what I always tell these kids when there's an argument: You can't tell another person what he or she likes; that's for them to decide, not you. And if you insist on telling other people what they like, you're going to irritate them, which is something kids on the spectrum have trouble understanding. It is our responsibility as parents and educators to acquaint our young ASD friends with the ways of the typical world so they can make their way there without us. When it was our turn, we each ordered what we wanted without further debate. And then another revelation: Seated behind us were several girls, around thirteen years old, eating ice cream and chatting enthusiastically about a nail polish color called "I Can't Hear Myself Pink." They left after about ten minutes, after which time Hank recounted, in pun-laden detail, every comment the girls had made. That session was a turning point; it proved that Hank was intelligent and could think clearly when he was interested in what was going on.

Keeping Hank engaged and motivated. I realized that to help Hank evolve, I had to think of his disorganized thinking as a habit rather than a disability and engage him in highly motivating activities, such as our pizza and ice cream outing, to facilitate the cogent thinking he had manifested then. With his mind working lucidly, I could challenge him to use it to figure things out—something he had failed to do consistently at school or at home. My theory was that once Hank developed the flexible thinking needed to ponder problems and solve them, he would feel the rush of delight that comes with it and be encouraged to think creatively in everyday situations.

I came up with the idea of a field trip to the firehouse where Hank's father and uncle, both paramedics, were stationed. Hank was obsessed with everything about their unit, had visited the firehouse many times, and was excited when I suggested we go there for our session.

"There's just one thing," I said. "I know what town the firehouse is in, but I don't know where to go once we get there. How do we get there, Hank?"

"Ask my mom; she knows," he said.

"This is between you and me, Hank; it has nothing to do with your mother. Do you know how to go?" He shook his head. "Well," I said, "I guess we can't go if we don't know where it is." I began to remove my jacket.

"I think it's on Washington Avenue," he said. I put my arm back in the sleeve.

"Great! Let's go." As we walked to the car I told him that when we got to the town, he was going to have to tell me how to get to Washington Avenue. He agreed and we got into the car. A minute later, I reminded him that he would have to give me directions soon.

"I don't know how to go!" he said.

"Well, what should we do?" I asked. Hank was silent, so I pulled the car over and waited.

"We need to look it up on the computer," he said.

"Good idea. Should we go back to my office and do that?"

"Yes, we should."

"Hank, it's good that you know about computers so we can look up the directions," I said. What I didn't say was how glad I was that he was taking responsibility for finding the firehouse. Back at the office, I emphasized that I was relying on him to get us there, but his automatic reaction was to imagine his mother doing the job. Now he was acknowledging his role in the excursion. Five minutes later, we were back in the office and logged onto the Internet. I entered a few vague search words.

"Hmm," I said, "it's not coming up."

"Try 'firehouse Washington Avenue,' " Hank said. I did, and there it was.

"Way to go, Hank! How did you think of that?"

"I just did. It was easy." And back to the car we went.

On the way I told Hank I was a little nervous about going to a place I'd never been before. He told me not to worry. "Why not?" I said. "It's a new place and I'm not comfortable." He thought for a few seconds and said, "They're really nice. You'll meet Ian and Chris." I was delighted; just as he had done during the Internet search, Hank was thinking logically and using descriptive language to express his thoughts.

"How will I meet them?" I asked. "Even if they're there, I wouldn't know what they look like." "I'll introduce you," Hank said proudly. I could tell by his voice that he was unsure of what this entailed; I was pretty sure he'd never introduced anyone before. But he had expressed confidence in his abilities. Things he usually had difficulty with were receding into the background.

We arrived at the firehouse and went inside. Neither Hank's father nor uncle was there, but a firefighter he knew greeted him warmly. I asked Hank if he would introduce me to his friend, and he did. We walked around the firehouse and I asked Hank lots of questions, most of which he could answer. The visit was brief but went well: Hank was present and engaged; he spoke clearly and neither cursed nor got upset.

But those impulses returned later that week when I visited Hank at his house. I do this sometimes to get a feel for family dynamics, which happened when I observed an interaction between Hank and his mother. He saw some kids playing ball outside and said he wanted to join them but his mother insisted he put away his toys first. Hank became irate and had a tantrum, flinging himself against sofa and chairs and his colorful vocabulary against the walls at a high decibel level. I was of two minds about the episode: I thought the mother's rule was reasonable but, were I in her place, I would have let the kid go outside after suggesting that he put his toys away afterward. I kept my thoughts to myself, because it's not my place to tell a mother how to deal with a kid I live with 90 minutes a week and she has the rest of the time. Still, watching the tantrum explode, I could see Hank triggered by his mother's adamancy and believed that a more flexible approach would have lessened his rage.

When I next saw Hank in session, I suggested that he might have gone out to play had he done what his mother asked.

"You could have stopped, like we did in my car on the way to the firehouse, and you could have thought about it, instead of just getting angry and screaming and cursing. That didn't help you. You still didn't get to go out and play." I talked about how his behavior had consequences, and how bad behavior generally brought on bad consequences. He was listening, so I pressed my case.

"If you think about it, 5 minutes of doing something you didn't want to do, like putting away your toys, could have gotten you an hour of playing with your friends. Instead you threw a tantrum, which got you nowhere but stuck inside." After a while, Hank said, "I'll try stopping next time."

This was progress: Hank was having a lucid conversation about past and future, cause and effect. We talked about how Hank often got angry in school, and how stopping himself before he blew up might have good results there, too. I thought of Addison, who stopped herself from zooming when she decided she wanted to. It was possible for her; maybe it was possible for Hank, too.

Over the next few sessions, I presented Hank with challenges that required him to think logically: putting photographs in order to create a coherent story; categorizing colored objects to solve a puzzle; sorting pegs by size and color—tasks he seemed incapable of doing earlier even though it was now clear he'd had the intellectual capacity all along. Now he was persisting in his efforts, stopping and thinking, organizing his mind, and considering the potential rewards of his actions.

I met with Hank's teachers again and asked if it might be possible to assign some group projects to accustom him to working on a team. They were receptive, and Hank began working regularly with other kids. His teachers reported that his classmates were complaining less about him and that his aggressiveness had diminished. He was still having an occasional meltdown, so I asked if he might be allowed to take a break from the activity and either walk around or have a snack rather than be punished. It worked: When Hank's outbursts were greeted with compassion rather than retribution, his rage ebbed quickly, he regained control, and felt better about himself. After a month, his meltdowns stopped. After 2 months, Hank was blossoming academically. With his anger defused, he began thinking and speaking clearly and appropriately; his classmates embraced his contributions and gravitated toward him; and he felt he belonged. He no longer gave irrelevant answers; what had appeared to be cognitive deficits vanished.

Hank's evolution toward more typical behavior was unlike that of any other client I have worked with. He progressed so quickly, it was almost as if a switch were flipped. When I first met Hank, he appeared to have significant cognitive delays and emotional problems; now, he was functioning well with his peers and working on grade level. I believe that the terrible behavior he used to manifest was a result of his never having received a proper intervention to help him learn to use his mind typically—that is, to wield his power to control his thinking and his actions. Understanding that he had the power to control himself—and in so doing, the power to influence others' responses to him—was sufficient motivation for Hank to take himself in hand. After 4 months of sessions, his parents reported that Hank was no longer having problems at school. I suggested we terminate, and they agreed.

THINGS TO WORK ON AND THINK ABOUT.

* *Think beyond prizes and punishments.* Rewarding children for man-ifesting desirable behaviors or penalizing them for undesirable ones may provide short-term results, but you must attach meaning to the proceedings if you want to change behavior in the long run. Hank's attachment to the firehouse motivated him to find ways to get there: It meant something to him, and he acted accordingly. You know your child: What holds meaning for him? What is important to her? Start there.

* *Look beyond behavior.* Abominable behavior is often a symptom of a more complex problem—frustration, anger, disappointment, despair, maybe all of them at once. When Hank hurled the F-bomb at our first meeting, I took it personally. I recovered quickly, as well I should have, and remembered that there was something else going on that need-ed to be identified and addressed. Are you unhinged by your child's execrable behavior? If so, first forgive yourself, and then get past it. Practice observing your child with rapt detachment, as you might a nature documentary. It's disturbing to watch rhinos batter one another, but the bigger question is: Why are they doing it?

* *Don't indulge your child's egocentrism.* Some parents are so grateful when their ASD kid responds to them, they'll do anything the kid demands. It's a form of bribery: Yes, sweetheart! Just keep talking to me and I'll have whatever flavor ice cream you want me to! You're not helping your child by acquiescing to demands or indulging his or her delusions of omnipotence. I believe it is our obligation to break the

news to all children, typical and atypical alike, that they are not the all-powerful beings they sometimes think they are. If you're reluctant to contradict your child because you fear it may inhibit future communication, find a way to do it kindly, gently, lovingly. But do it. Your child will thank you later. Probably much later, but thank you he will.

JEREMY, 6½

Nonverbal; paces; screams; does not interact.

S ometimes my first conversation with a client's family reveals as much about the parent as about the child, as it did when Jeremy's mother called. "I just want him to be normal," she said in answer to my standard question. "I just want him to call me mommy—that's all I want." She told me that instead of speaking, Jeremy squawked, shrieked, and emitted other noises to make himself understood. His actions veered from random to repetitive, as he'd grab at objects aimlessly and then obsessively pace around a room, touching the same spot over and over again. I told her this sounded typical of many children I work with.

"Maybe so," she said, "but it drives me crazy. I tell you, I hate being around Jeremy. That's the truth. I can't stand his noises. And when he's quiet, I can't stand his pacing. He makes me insane." This woman—I'll call her Elaine—was more open in expressing her frustration than most parents. I was grateful for her frankness; it lent urgency to my mission and opened an avenue of communication for us. Caring for a child with autism—not to mention living with him, night and day—is profoundly stressful. There may be parents out there who sustain no wounds from the ordeal but I have yet to meet them. It's a fine thing to soldier on with energy and optimism, but it's also important for caregivers to acknowledge their ambivalence and forgive themselves for feeling it. Parents tell me that they are wracked by an emotional conundrum: I have to live forever ... what happens if I die? ...

I can't go on like this ... I must go on like this ... I hope I don't wake up ... who will take care of my kid if I don't? They are buckling under a terrible burden; sharing it with someone they trust—an empathetic friend, relative, or therapist—can help.

Jeremy's first session began like many others I've known. Entering my office, he ignored my greeting and walked gingerly from the armoire to the desk to the table to the chairs, looking at nothing in particular. I ushered his parents back into the waiting room, closed the door, and watched as Jeremy touched the wooden knobs on the armoire, walked across the room, flattened his palm on the tabletop, turned, walked back to the armoire, and repeated the ritual again ... and again, and again, and again. He made noises with his mouth and reached for random objects—shells on the table, pebbles on the desk, a toy truck on a chair seat—and then abandoned them as he strode. He didn't respond to me but I felt no hostility; in fact, I sensed a sweetness in Jeremy and a gentle, if remote, spirit. I could understand why he had been placed in a special needs class; he appeared to be the stereotypical child with autism: nonspeaking, disengaged, performing perseverative actions that made no sense to me but undoubtedly did something for him. Because he had no language to communicate his wishes, he screamed to get his parents' and teachers' attention, would point to whatever he wanted and, once he got it, would soon forget about it. Unless it was something he really wanted; then, his parents said, he would shriek and shout nonstop until he got it.

After an hour with Jeremy's walking, touching, and squawking, it seemed to me that, developmentally, he was in the sensorimotor phase of early childhood. As defined by psychologist Jean Piaget, this is the first of four stages of cognitive development, lasting from birth until age 2. During this time, typical infants fuse information from their senses with bodily experiences to accumulate knowledge of the world and how to interact with it. Thus, a neurotypical 8-month-old sees a strawberry on her high-chair tray, grasps it in her fist, pulls it toward her face, smells it, thrusts it in her mouth, and tastes the sweetness, learning that seeing something pretty and red that smells good and using her hand to put it in her mouth produces a pleasing sensation. She is using her senses and motor skills to both understand and wield power over her environment. But infants with autism spectrum disorders are neurologically atypical, and their ability to synthesize sensory stimuli and motor responses is compromised in ways we don't fully understand, which is how Jeremy at 6 years old was, to my eyes, behaving much in the same way a 2-year-old might. He manifested no continuity of thought or intention, and his rapid loss of interest in the things he touched suggested unawareness of time—the concept that, were he to maintain focus on something beyond its momentary attraction, it might yield future satisfaction. He seemed to exist strictly in the moment, unaware that he was separate from the objects that he patted, grasped, and relinquished with vague neutrality.

I called Jeremy's parents into the office and explained that, while the long-term goal was to help Jeremy acquire language, my priority was to help him develop two things: the ability to think continuously, and a sense of temporal constancy, the awareness that the current moment is connected to the ones that preceded it and those that are yet to come. His father shook his head.

"He gets all that," he said. "When we play board games with Ryan we always include Jeremy. He sits at the table, nice as could be, and waits his turn."

"Does he need to be reminded that it's his turn?" I asked. Jeremy's father paused.

"Yes, I guess he does."

"So, do you think he is actually waiting his turn, or is it possible he's losing continuity, getting distracted, and disengaging from the game until you bring him back?" I didn't like disillusioning his father, but Jeremy wasn't able to wait for anything because he couldn't anticipate future events. For a child to truly take his turn and wait until it comes around again, he has to pay attention when it is not his turn, observe what other players are doing, follow the progress of the game, and anticipate his next shot—that's temporal constancy. And Jeremy didn't have it.

Early sessions: establishing focus and interrupting it. At the next session, I began a two-pronged approach. First, I presented Jeremy with activities that incorporated a set sequence of steps, such as placing blocks in a box, dumping them out, sorting them by color, tossing them back one color at a time, dumping them out again, and then repeating the process over and over again. After a few repetitions, Jeremy would internalize the order of the steps and anticipate which one came next, laying the foundation of temporal constancy.

Next, when Jeremy established mastery over the sequence, I would interrupt him and entice him into doing something else. Why? Because for

Jeremy to gain and maintain continuity of thought, he needed to practice switching between two appealing activities and realizing that each would still be available to him afterward. I know it sounds counterintuitive, but Jeremy's cognitive level allowed him to enjoy an activity only in a limited way for a brief time, as was manifested by his perseverative pacing and loss of interest in objects he touched. If Jeremy were directed from one fun activity toward another and then back again, he would learn that they were not extensions of himself but existed apart from him, constant in time and space whether he was involved with them or not. Being interrupted would imbue him with a sense of the present, and returning to the activity would implant the idea of a future, especially once he perceived the pattern. Children on the autism spectrum need to learn they can go in and out of thoughts, movements, and activities so they don't revert to obsessive, perseverative behaviors. (Another example of enforced switching is when we help an ASD kid learn to take bites of different foods rather than obsessively finishing every last pea before zeroing in on the fries. More on this later.)

Over several sessions, we played a game with a retractable tape measure in which I would have Jeremy grasp the end and follow my instructions to pull, stop, pull, stop, and eventually let it go. He liked controlling the length of the tape and loved watching it snap back into its case. In the midst of this, I handed him a xylophone and mallet and took away the tape measure, putting it where he could see it. As Jeremy commenced banging on the xylophone, I watched and waited. If he reached for the tape measure again, we'd resume the pull-push game. If he became engrossed in the xylophone, I'd interrupt him after a while and say, "What about the tape measure? Want to play that game again?" He usually did, and we would, until I'd abruptly remove the tape measure and hand him another toy in its place. It sounds as if I was teasing the poor fellow, but what I was trying to do was change the way his mind worked by forcing the resumption of an anticipatory, continuous thought process after interrupting it. I would not do this with a child like Addison, who couldn't control her impulse to zip from one thing to the next. She needed to learn to focus on one thing at a time, but Jeremy needed to learn he could switch his focus without fracturing his consciousness.

One day, Jeremy took the lead by squeezing behind a large potted plant in the corner and crouching there. This signified a change in his thinking: He was hiding, intentionally playing with me, and expecting a response. I was happy to oblige. "Where's Jeremy?" I asked. He was silent. I walked around the room. "Is he under the desk? No ... is he behind the door? No ... Aha! There you are!" I pulled back the palm fronds to expose Jeremy's face, split by a huge grin. He emerged from behind the plant. "Okay," I said, turning my back to him and busying myself with some papers on my desk, "now I know where you are." I fussed for another 20 seconds and, when I turned around, he'd hidden behind the plant again, this time curling himself around the pot on the floor. "Jeremy!" I called. "Where are you? You were here just a minute ago. Now I've got to find you again!" When I eventually did, his smile showed how much fun this was for him.

For me, it signaled a breakthrough, especially when he came back the following week and, within 5 minutes, initiated the game again. Not only had he created a game in which he interacted with another person, he was giving it his full attention and maintaining continuous focus over a substantial amount of time. And he even remembered the game a week later—talk about temporal constancy!

As I hoped, his evolving thought process was sparking speech. Jeremy began saying words—toy; open; plant—pursing his lips, shaping his mouth, moving his tongue in new ways. This is what typical 1-year-olds do when they're learning to talk: They repeat a word many times, honing pronunciation, analyzing the sound. Jeremy was doing this later than usual, but it was happening. And it happened as a natural outgrowth of his discovery of the world, as happens with typical children. We were playing the tape measure game one day when I heard Jeremy quietly say what sounded like let go. He wanted me to let go of the end of the tape. He repeated it to himself uncertainly a few times, then more and more intelligibly after I gently coached him. The following week, I was holding a model car he wanted and he clearly said let go; later, he refused to relinquish a puzzle piece I reached for, again saying (with some asperity), Let go!, even though he was the one holding it. Generalizing a phrase in this way is a form of language constancy, where let go means different things depending on when you use it. Jeremy was experimenting with the phrase to determine in which contexts it would work. In so doing, he was making the critical connection between language, thinking, and speech.

Differing standards of progress. I had had around eight sessions with Jeremy when I heard him say mommy to Elaine in the waiting room. I bounded over. "Isn't that something!" I said.

"Yes, he's been saying that, but that's all he says. I thought he'd know more words by now."

I became painfully aware that Jeremy's mother was dissatisfied with the pace of his progress. First she said all she wanted was for him to call her mommy; now that he was doing it, she wanted him to have a bigger vocabulary. I explained to her that I wanted the same things for Jeremy that she did, but although I might know what his next developmental step should be and how best to guide him there, it was up to him to do the growing, however long it took. After every session, I met with Elaine to explain what we'd done and the progress we'd made, as well as what she and her family could do at home to encourage it. Still, Jeremy's progress never seemed to be enough, let alone fast enough, for his mother. I wish I had a magic formula for the Elaines of the world, for the sake of their kids. All I can do is counsel patience, which I did every week.

And I did something else: I invited Jeremy's older brother Ryan to a session, which was illuminating. We all went to the park, where I suggested to Elaine and Ryan, who was 8, ways they might best interact and play with Jeremy at this stage of his development. Ryan was a hero that day, rolling down a hill with his kid brother, chasing him and making him laugh, going down the slide with him and then coaching him until Jeremy did it alone. Jeremy needed to be instructed and helped along, and sometimes Ryan needed to repeat an instruction several times before Jeremy followed. But Ryan was patient with his brother, which was encouraging; when there's an affectionate sibling at home, it can diffuse the effects of a parent's dissatisfaction.

Elaine kept bringing Jeremy to therapy every week, even after the family moved 90 minutes away. Three months into our sessions, Jeremy began using his natural resources, including language, when confronted with an obstacle. Trying to blow bubbles one day, he was frustrated when he couldn't get one to form. Then he pivoted his wrist to blow on the wand from the other side, and, voilà! Creative problem solving! Another time, I purposely stuck my hand in front of a toy Jeremy was reaching for. Move hand! he said—more progress, as he was using language to not only express himself but to get another person to do his bidding. Afterward, I asked Elaine to invite Jeremy's teacher to join us for a session so she could see what he was capable of and help him sustain his growth in her classroom.

Jeremy began to manifest typical thinking patterns. Now when I brought out the tape measure, he'd say, You pull; when I pulled, he'd say, Let go!, anticipating the tape's snappy return. I emphasized to Elaine the progress this represented: Jeremy understood the sequence of pulling the tape and what would happen when it was let go. A session later, Jeremy flung one of my crystalline rocks to the floor and it split apart. "You broke it," I said. "That was not good." He pouted and looked close to crying. I waited. Finally, he said, "I'm sorry." Cognitively, Jeremy's apology mirrored his tape measure commands: He was understanding continuity of action from one moment to the next, a cornerstone of lucid, typical thinking. Jeremy now understood that pulling the tape would cause it to snap back when released, just as he realized that hurling something might break it. Registering my dismay and apologizing meant Jeremy was developing empathy and on his way to relating to others in a more or less typical fashion.

Then Jeremy's behavior acquired a new feature: mischief. One day, I watched him pick up a small geode and hide with it behind the floor plant, grinning slyly. It may not sound like much on the page, but it was a real-life leap: Jeremy got it in his head to be playfully naughty by taking something that didn't belong to him and hiding it from its owner, along with himself. It was behavior we might expect of a much younger child, but Jeremy had a lot of catching up to do, which is why I was heartened by the emergence of his mischievous side and strove to encourage it by stalking around the office, intoning, "Where's Jeremy? Where's my geode?" until he emerged from hiding, rock in hand.

His mother didn't always get his humor. At one of our post-session meetings, I told her that Jeremy and I had spent time looking out the window and discussing the colors of the grass and the sky and the house across the street. "Great!" she said, picking up a blue plastic cube. "Jeremy, what color is this?" she asked. He stared at her.

"Jeremy, I asked you, what color is this?" Again, no answer. Her eyes narrowed.

"You can't act like this, Jeremy! Just say 'blue' and we'll do something else!" Not only would Jeremy not say it; he stared back at her with a glint in his eye (I could see it; she couldn't). I pointed out to Elaine that Jeremy was enjoying his ability to rile her and that his provocations were a sign of engagement, if not the sort she craved. This kind of interaction was a new experience for Jeremy and he was getting a lot of practice at his mother's expense. Had she been able to reframe the event as a game rather than a challenge to her authority, she would have been able to appreciate the growth it represented.

But she could appreciate other aspects of Jeremy's progress, most notably in his interactions with his brother. When Ryan suggested they play a game, Jeremy was much more likely to say yes. He was able to focus on his brother and the course of play for 5 to 10 minutes at a stretch, and his attention span was expanding.

Eventually, the 3-hour round-trip commute became more than Elaine could tolerate and we stopped therapy. By that time, Jeremy was able to engage in brief conversations and slowly but very surely catch up to his peers.

THINGS TO WORK ON AND THINK ABOUT.

- *Refrain from expecting too much too soon.* I have known many parents whose overoptimistic expectations blind them to small, incremental gains that betoken real progress. This undermines both the child's growth and the parents' faith in the process. Examine how you are calibrating your child's achievements, and rein in your fantasies of cosmic breakthroughs. They do happen, but on the child's timetable, not the parents'.

- *Sometimes you have to do the opposite of what makes traditional sense.* By interrupting Jeremy's focus on one activity and enticing him with another, I was flouting conventional wisdom that children learn best when encouraged to focus their attention on one thing at a time. All well and good—if you're trying to teach them to focus on one thing at a time. I wanted Jeremy to learn about the constancy of time and the endurance of objects from one moment to the next, so I experimented with fracturing his focus, then repairing the break—and it worked. If it had not worked, I would have tried something else. Don't be afraid to defy logic. If you have a gut feeling about something, try it.

- *It's normal to feel ambivalent about caring for a special-needs child.* Don't berate yourself for sometimes wishing you could run away to a deserted island where you'd have only yourself to contend with. Not only is it normal to feel overwhelmed; in my experience, it's universal. Find someone you trust and talk about your feelings of frustration, anger, resentment, even despair. Fantasizing a life without the pressures of rearing a child with problems doesn't mean you don't love your kid or that you're a bad parent. It means you're human.

Nonverbal; disengaged; blank expression.

Two years ago, a woman approached me after I gave a talk at a Bronx hospital. "I live near here," she said, in a lilting accent that sounded Caribbean, "and I have a daughter who needs help." We arranged for her to bring Freya to my office the following week.

Like many children I've described, Freya seemed to inhabit a world apart from ours. She ignored my greeting, which I repeated numerous times, as well as the hand I extended. She stood by her mother in the waiting room, her expression blank, flapping her arms and jumping up and down sporadically. "She is afraid of strangers, she won't touch. Come on, Freya, let's go in," her mother said, taking the girl's hand. Freya jumped her way into the office and sat on a chair next to her mother, who told me that she had to help her daughter execute almost every aspect of daily life. Although Freya was physically capable of brushing her teeth and dressing herself, she could not learn the processes involved and had to be guided. "She doesn't like anyone to touch her but me," the mother said, "and since she needs so much help, I have to be with her almost all the time. At school, she pulls away when the teacher tries to help her button her coat or put on her backpack. She comes home in freezing weather with her coat open." At this point, Freya slid off the chair and started wandering around the room, flapping her arms and hands and jumping every once in a while. I asked Freya's mother what she liked, and one thing stood out: "Fire engines," she said. "She loves the siren. She stops and her face gets serious, like she's really listening." This was interesting. Many kids on the spectrum are agitated by high-pitched noises, but Freya liked them. I wondered if generating high-pitched sounds in the office, perhaps from a person, might engage Freya and create an atmosphere conducive to connection. Human communication requires an exchange of energy, a back-and-forth interaction between people who want to connect. Perhaps, for Freya, we could forge this connection through sound.

An experiment. I invited a young music therapist I knew to come to our next session. Sasha arrived carrying bongos, maracas, a triangle, a wood block, and a child's size guitar. Freya, oblivious to the commotion, continued to jump, flap, and stroll her way around the room. I suggested Sasha use just her voice to start with, and she began humming in a low alto register—first scales, then airy ropes of notes strung together in no discernible rhythm or melody, something she was probably making up as she went along. If Freya heard her, she didn't let on. Then Sasha started to sing a tune with open notes and lots of *la la la* and *da di da* sounds, also in an alto register. Again, no response from Freya.

Then Sasha started to sing in a high soprano voice, notes trilling in the air. This time Freya turned toward her. The child stood motionless, not only looking at Sasha but, as Sasha told me later, looking into her eyes. For a child like Freya to initiate eye contact was remarkable because it was motivated not by anyone prodding her to do it, but by her genuine desire to connect with the source of a sound she liked. Acknowledging another person was an extraordinary achievement for Freya—and for me, too. I knew we had found a way inside.

Sasha kept singing—it sounded like an operatic aria—but after a minute or so, Freya's attention flagged. I asked Sasha to stop singing. The room went silent. Freya looked up and she and Sasha gazed steadily at each other. I didn't move: If anything was going to happen, I wanted it to come from Freya. And it did. Freya walked over and pressed her fingers to Sasha's lips, trying to pry open her mouth. It was a lightning-bolt moment, something I never expected to see. Sasha obliged and resumed singing. Freya walked away, sat down, and watched her.

When she tried to open Sasha's mouth, Freya was anticipating the singing would continue. This meant that Freya understood temporal constancy: She grasped that taking action in the present could make something happen in the future. Not only that: This was a child who allegedly didn't like being touched, yet she approached a virtual stranger and touched her mouth—an intimate gesture not usually undertaken by someone averse to bodily contact.

I see this all the time. Parents tell me their children don't like loud noises, can't tolerate crowds, are anxious around strangers, disturbed by bright lights and chaotic environments, and freak out if someone tries to touch them. Over and over, I've seen these sensitivities diminish when children are focused on something that's captured their imaginations. Atypical kids are just like the rest of us: When they're engaged in something fun or exciting, they lose track of their surroundings as well as their perceived vulnerabilities. All at once, they're doing things they never did before, which is not to say that their sensitivities don't resurface. But once you know a child is capable of transcending an alleged frailty, you're more likely to urge him or her to revisit the situation that banished it, however temporarily.

I tried to think of a simple tune with a repetitive rhythmic pattern, something we could sing together that made you want to sway along. Music and movement could be a way of helping Freya connect with others until she had the words to do so. I suggested John Lennon's "Give Peace a Chance" and Sasha began singing, again in a high soprano register. Freya made no eye contact but wore a faint smile and seemed to be listening. Sasha kept singing and Freya kept listening. Then Sasha reached out and gently lifted Freya into her lap, singing and swaying all the while. I moved closer to them, started singing along, and reached out to gently touch Freya's back and squeeze her hand. Freya seemed just as comfortable with my touch as she did sitting on Sasha's lap, and I continued to make contact with her as we sang and swayed. It was as close to a genuine Kumbayah moment as I've ever come.

After about five minutes, Sasha looked Freya in the eye and said, "Now you sing." Freya remained silent. I nodded to Sasha so she'd keep singing. Even though I doubted Freya understood what the words meant, I knew that if she was to learn to speak, she needed to be exposed to language spoken in context.

"Freya, you sing now," I said. "Now you sing, Freya." No response. Then Sasha touched Freya's mouth just as Freya had touched hers. Freya was silent but looking at Sasha, so I encouraged her to keep trying. Then, after a few more minutes, we heard *ay-ay-ay*. It was quiet with no discernible rhythm but there all the same. Sasha and I played it cool and kept singing and swaying, incorporating Freya's *ay-ay-ays* into the tune.

Freya's mother asked if she could bring her in again the following day to keep up momentum. Sasha brought her guitar and started singing to Freya, who began swaying and strumming the strings while Sasha worked the fingerboard. Then Sasha brought out a drum and an electric keyboard, which they commenced pounding at the same time. Things got chaotic pretty quickly. I let it go on for a while before calling "Stop!", at which point Sasha stopped and Freya banged away a few more times before stopping as well. After 5 seconds of quiet, I shouted, "Go!" Sasha immediately resumed playing and Freya joined in a moment later. After several minutes of this, Freya was starting and stopping with Sasha in response to my direction.

Then Sasha stood up, grabbed her guitar, and began playing an up-tempo, percussive piece. Freya stood up and began jumping, but it wasn't the mindless, perseverative jumping she'd done before. There was no arm-flapping this time as, with her eyes on Sasha, she tried to leap up and down in time to the music. As I watched, I realized that Freya wasn't jumping; she was dancing.

This was the beginning of communication for Freya. When a baby learns to talk, she is motivated by knowing that there's someone there—mommy, daddy, daycare provider, whomever—who will respond to her. Starting with crooning ay-ay-ay, to strumming the guitar, to banging on the drum and keyboard, to swaying and then to jumping, Freya was motivated by the presence of another human being with whom she yearned to connect. Listening and responding to Sasha's music making, she was learning the dynamics of conversation.

Toward the end of the session, Sasha and I began banging on different drums at the same time and then, all at once, we stopped. Freya called out, "Go!" and we began banging again, until we stopped and Freya again commanded us to continue. We brought Freya's mother in to witness her daughter's first forays into speech.

"Again!" her mother cried. "Can you do it some more? I want to hear her speak!"

"I do, too," I said, "but we have to get Freya to say something different." I explained that I didn't want Freya to latch onto one utterance, as is typical of children on the spectrum, and use it perseveratively until it is drained of all meaning.

"But what if she loses it?"

"If we keep talking to her, she won't lose it."

Be careful what you hope for. When Freya came in a few days later, her mother said that when they were preparing to leave the house the day before, Freya became impatient and said, "Go." Great—she was talking at home, so I would build on it.

"Freya," I said, "shall we feed the fish?" I dropped a pellet into the tank. Freya smiled and watched.

"Tell me to feed the fish, Freya," I said. No response.

"Shall I drop another pellet in?" Again, no response.

"Should I feed them again?" Silence.

"More?" Nothing.

I wasn't looking for a specific reaction but trying to get Freya to say something, anything, relevant to the situation. And she didn't. But—and it's a big one—she watched, she listened, she was engaged. I decided to keep talking to her to see where it led.

I got the little net and scooped the fish up in it, talking all the time about what I was doing, and inviting her to come and touch it. She was wary but eventually did, and then together we gently lowered the fish back into the water. After touching the fish three times, I dangled the net in the water and waited … and waited … until Freya said, "Up." The language part of her mind was clicking in. Music forged the link to language that Freya needed; now cognitive connections were firing to use language in a natural and meaningful way.

The next time we were together, I decided to try some window therapy. Freya was sitting in a chair on the opposite side of the room. I walked over.

"Freya, shall we go to the window and look outside?" No response. I asked the question again, and again she didn't respond. I remembered her acquiescence to Sasha's lifting her and, slowly and gently, extended my arms. "Shall I pick you up and carry you to the window, Freya?" I asked. No reaction. Slowly, I bent over, slid my arms around Freya, lifted her out of the chair, and carried her to the window. She didn't resist. I set her down at the window and asked, "Shall I pick you up again?" After asking three or four times, Freya said, "Up." So I picked her up again, carried her back to the chair, set her down, and started again. We did this over and over until, after I set Freya down one time, she said, "Pick me up" and held out her arms to me. This was Freya's first three-word phrase. There were soon many more.

When formerly nonverbal children start stringing words together, it means they have begun the process of typical language acquisition. Hearing others speak, they begin to absorb nuances of language meaning and usage through context. If we surround these children with language, their natural inclination to communicate through speech will blossom.

I continued to work with Freya by instigating activities to which I provided a constant verbal soundtrack. Narrating the course of an activity, I'd insert a prompt for her to respond to—"Freya, I think I hear a fire truck. Shall we go to the window and try to see it? Is the siren getting louder? Why do you think that is? Could the fire truck be getting closer?" Because she was fond of sirens, such invitations had good odds of getting a response. I even used her dislikes to elicit language. We inflated a balloon one day and, in the midst of batting it back and forth, I took up a needle as if to pop it. "No needle, please!" Freya said—which then gave me an opening to ask her why she didn't want me to pop it, what she thought would happen if I did, and, finally, to acquiesce to her request and put the needle down. A few weeks later, I asked Freya's mother if she was talking more at home. "Oh, yes! This morning, I gave her a glass of milk and she said, 'No, I want the green cup.' Now my child is getting annoying!"

I knew Freya was on her way toward language independence when her mother reported that Freya's teacher said she'd heard her mutter, "Damn! Damn!" one day when she couldn't get her backpack on straight. Like other parents of children on the spectrum, Freya's mother realized she needed to be careful with her own language—just like parents of typical kids.

After 3 months, Freya's mother felt she no longer needed weekly therapy. I still see her every few months for a brush-up session or two, at which I continue to engage her verbally.

THINGS TO WORK ON AND THINK ABOUT.

- *There may be aspects of your child you've never seen.* Many parents tell me that their child absolutely, positively cannot tolerate this, that, or the other thing. And I believe them. But I've seen over and over again that the things these kids allegedly can't cope with lose their power when the kid is immersed in a compelling activity. No one could have imagined that Freya—a child thought to abhor physical contact with strangers—would put her hands on Sasha's face and try to open her mouth. Yet she did it. If you have persuaded yourself that your child can't cope with crowds, noise, commotion, loud music—whatever— you may be denying him or her a chance to transcend limitations that are perceived rather than real. The next time you hear yourself rejecting an opportunity for your child to have a new experience, reconsider. She or he may surprise you.

- *Follow your child and your instincts.* You don't need a step-by-step guide to help your child progress. What you need is to open your eyes, your ears, and your mind, and trust your gut responses to what you see, hear, and perceive. After Freya tried to open Sasha's mouth, I told Sasha to continue singing rather than bring out the instruments she'd brought because I had a feeling that her voice would be more compelling to Freya. It was a feeling but a strong one, based on what I had observed in Freya's response: her focus, her intention, her utter lack of anxiety as she touched Sasha's face. I trust my feelings; so can you. Anyone can develop a greater capacity to watch, to listen, to interpret signals in a new way. Nothing's stopping you. Start now.

DAVID, 7

Nonverbal; disconnected; "the kid with the straw."

Many years ago, I was hired to supervise the educational program at a sleepaway camp for special needs kids in Upstate New York. At night, I went home to a nearby bungalow that Rachel and I rented for the summer.

It was a great job for an iconoclastic guy like me. The camp's goal was to help kids maintain their budding skills rather than grow academically over the summer, so I had neither a curriculum nor the burden of grand expectations. What I did have was lots of time and latitude to do what I thought was best for the kids. I kept a composition book full of notes on each camper and would discuss with the counselors every day how I thought they should work with them, explain my thinking, and solicit their thoughts. The counselors were mostly college students majoring in special education and eager to make a difference in the kids' lives. They were spirited, idealistic, and bristling with the raw energy of unmitigated youth. We became friendly over the summer, swapping stories of the kids' triumphs, disappointments, and inscrutable behaviors.

One of the more eccentric kids was David, a sweet-tempered 7-year-old who didn't speak. His school file said he was known as "the kid with the straw," and it was easy to see why: He never went anywhere without one. The straw had to be at least 3 inches long and he held it between the thumb and forefinger of his right hand and shook it virtually all day. If he were using his right hand for something else, he'd switch it to his left hand. It could be any drinking straw as long as it was the proper length; if it were any shorter, David would reject it. It was a common sight to see David squatting on the ground or sitting in the sandbox or standing on the playground shaking his straw, sometimes watching it and sometimes not, but always, always shaking.

David's counselor was 20-year-old Artie, a good looking, intelligent, and very funny psychology major who loved to talk with me about this boy and his mysterious habit. One day, we sat and watched as David climbed up the ladder of the slide, clutching his straw. The ladder led to a platform that accommodated several kids who would wait their turns before sliding down—except for David: He never slid down. We watched, transfixed, as David stood on the platform, looking lost and shaking his straw as the other kids arrived and departed. He must have stood there for 20 minutes, never coming down until they rang the bell for dinner, at which point Artie went over, climbed up the ladder, and inched his way down the slide with David in his lap.

Artie and David headed to the dining room and I headed to my car. Driving home, I couldn't shake the image of David standing on the platform, looking bewildered. I was bewildered, too. What kind of kid climbs to the top of a slide, stands there, and doesn't come down? David didn't look frightened; if he were afraid of heights, he wouldn't have climbed the ladder in the first place. Why did he go up there if all he wanted to do was stand around and shake his straw?

And then I understood. David had a perseverative mentality: He went up the ladder because it was there, and when the steps stopped, he did, too. Had there been 30 steps instead of 10, he'd have climbed all 30; had there been 100, he'd have climbed those, too. Climbing the ladder was like shaking the straw: a mindless repetition with no purpose or goal other than the sensation of doing it over and over again in the eternal present. Like many children with autism, David had no concept of the future, no inkling that climbing a ladder now would lead to a slide down later. He just kept doing what he was doing until he was prodded into doing something else—riding down in his counselor's lap, walking to the dining room, eating dinner. Which led me to wonder whether David's perseveration manifested at meals. I asked Artie the next morning.

"Oh, yeah. At breakfast, he picks all the raisins out of his cereal and eats them first. Then he eats the flakes, and then he spoons the milk out of the bowl. At dinner, he loads up his plate with peas and mashed potatoes. Then he eats all the peas, then all the mashed potatoes. If there's a choice of vegetables, he doesn't care; he only eats peas and potatoes, in that order. He never wants any chicken or other meat. And all the time he's shaking the straw with his other hand."

How could we reach a kid like David? This was much earlier in my career, when I was leaning away from behaviorism and working toward a cognitive-based approach. I knew that it was imperative that David learn to speak, but something told me that pushing language might not be the best way to reach him. In the first place, I knew that the part of the brain that controls language is almost fully developed by the age of 6, and David was well into his 7th year. And the constant straw-shaking indicated an entrenched obsessiveness. He had three typical siblings and was surrounded by normal conversation at home. I thought it likely that he harbored language within himself. If we could break his perseveration, we might be able to create a space for words to emerge.

That night I joined David's group for dinner. We heaped his plate with peas and mashed potatoes, which we knew he liked. Then, holding his hand, we filled his spoon with peas and guided it to his mouth. When he'd swallowed and was moving back toward the peas, we guided his hand toward the potatoes, which he loaded onto his spoon. We guided his hand back and forth, alternating peas with potatoes, until his plate was empty. Then we got more food and did the same thing with French fries and carrots, and added some chicken. David did not resist the intervention; he seemed content to load up his spoon with whichever food we guided him toward. I told Artie and the other counselors to do the same thing the following day at breakfast and lunch, and then at dinner to add some different foods to his plate and alternate between them. After a few days of this, Artie reported that David pointed to a grilled cheese sandwich on another kid's plate. Artie went to the kitchen, returned with the sandwich, and began using language with David in a focused, deliberate way: Here's your grilled cheese sandwich, David. Can you say that? Can you ask for it with words? When David pointed to a popsicle the next day, Artie worked with that. David was getting the sense that he could make choices about what he did, that he could do some of this and some of that rather than feeling compelled to take every action as far as it could go. He was becoming aware of himself as an autonomous being, separate from his surroundings and free to exert his will upon them.

David's demeanor changed. He began connecting with the other kids, using a word here and there until he started linking them into phrases. He began to engage in simple cognitive tasks, such as sorting cylinders by size. Concentrating on connecting with others, he would sometimes forget to shake his straw, and even leave it behind now and then. His counselors began to gently suggest he hand it to them, which he did with increasing ease until he ceased carrying it altogether. And we all cheered the day he climbed to the top of the slide and, taking his turn, slid right down. He seemed like a different child.

Writing this jogged my memory and I began to wonder what happened to the people I worked with that summer. I went on Facebook and, miracle of miracles, found Artie, whose youthful good looks were immediately recognizable. He must be in his 40s now, lives in Israel, and, after contacting him via the Internet, heard his voice a few days later on my cell phone as clearly as if he were next door. We talked for well over an hour about how that long ago summer changed our lives—and, we hoped, those of the kids we worked with. I told him I was working on a book and had just written about David.

"Oh, yeah! The kid with the straw!" he said. "I wonder what ever happened to him."

"Me too," I said. "Do you remember how he ate all the peas on his plate before he'd eat the mashed potatoes?" Artie exploded in laughter.

"Oh, man, it was worse than that! He used to eat the peas from everyone else's plate, too! The other kids would be sitting around yakking, then they'd look at their plates, and poof! No more peas!"

I never knew that. It made me smile for the rest of the day and well into the night. I like to imagine David now as a typical guy in his late 20s, maybe with a family, who sits down to dinner and eats like everyone else. And if there's a straw in the picture, it's in his glass.

SOMETHING TO WORK ON AND THINK ABOUT.

- *Language is often but not always the way in; in David's case, it wasn't.* Parents can glean clues about how to reach their atypical children by observing them analytically. Are there any common denominators among your child's seemingly bizarre behaviors? With David, the straw wagging, climbing up the ladder but never sliding down, and polishing off one kind of food before starting on another indicated a perseverative mentality. That was the key that unlocked the door. With practice, parents can gain insight into their kids' mysterious ways. Once you have a few clues, you can intervene at their origin and not just look on in perplexity.

DAISY, 10

Wild; aggressive; never smiles.

I remember many campers from my summers in Upstate New York, but Daisy stands out even now, decades later. When I first met Daisy—Crazy Daisy, the other kids called her—her behavior was as close to that of a feral creature as anything I had ever seen. Reading her file, I learned that Daisy's teachers at a public school for special needs students had been unable to improve her behavior. Her parents were so overwhelmed by her aggressive physicality, they had created a padded enclosure in their basement where she could fling her body about without harming herself. A note from her mother startled me: I'm at the end of my rope, it said. I have three other children who don't want anything to do with her. Why should they? She screams, takes their toys and clothes and food, and when they try to get them back, she hits and bites. I am looking into another place for her to live, someplace where they know how to handle children like her. My husband doesn't want it, but he isn't home all day with her. I am, and I can't take it any more.

Daisy could understand English and speak in full sentences but mostly communicated by screaming No! and dashing away. Counselors would chase her all over the grounds and when they caught her, were bitten for their trouble. She was strong and sturdy and exceedingly difficult to control. Getting her to wash up and clean her teeth, dress, and brush her hair were daily battles; at breakfast (as at every meal), she grabbed whatever she wanted, no matter whose plate it was on, and crammed it in her mouth. In an attempt to mitigate the chaos, her counselors had begun to anticipate her needs, keeping her plate and drinking glass full, leading her around the playground, and appeasing her with toys, games, and art supplies, none of which held her interest for more than 30 seconds.

The counselors weren't Daisy's only victims. After biting several other campers, Daisy was banished from swimming, the arts and crafts cabin, and team sports. Even on those rare occasions when she'd been induced to apply herself to a solo activity such as sorting colored beads, she would quickly lose interest. The child seemed unable to maintain focus on anything for longer than a few seconds, at which point she'd run off with adults in hot pursuit. At the end of the first week, the camp director wanted to send Daisy home. But I had a gut feeling I could help her, and the director gave me permission to try. The question was, how did the mind of Daisy, an uncontrollable girl, work? What was it like to be her?

To begin an informal evaluation, I asked Daisy what she wanted to do. No response. When I suggested drawing on the blackboard, Daisy nodded vigorously, reached for the chalk, scribbled furiously for 10 seconds, dropped the chalk, and ran away. This was curious: It was one thing to lose interest in a task that had no meaning for her, but to abandon an activity she had chosen was contradictory. Still, I was encouraged: When Daisy nodded and grabbed the chalk, she had expressed interest in an activity and followed through on it. True, she stopped after a few seconds, but for those seconds she had been engaged. This illustrated a moment of neurotypical thinking and behavior on her part. If she could have one moment, she could have more.

Daisy was an enigma. Wanting to sustain pleasurable experiences is almost a law of human psychology; what was making her quit her fun? Daisy's pattern of fleeing from things she enjoyed suggested that her thinking process was disjointed, that she had developed chaotic thinking habits that needed to be dismantled and replaced with coherent ones.

I devised a way of working with Daisy that forced her to stick with one thought before flitting to another. First I would ask her what she wanted to do: "The beads? The chalk? The slide?" When she chose the slide, I'd accompany her there and, while she was climbing the ladder, I'd ask, "What do you want to do after the slide?" The first time I did this, Daisy stared at me blankly—and the 5th time, and the 25th time. Then one day I asked her for maybe the 50th time, "What do you want to do after the slide? The swing? The sandbox? The merry-go-round?"

"Swing," she said and began to descend the ladder.

"The slide first," I said firmly, blocking her descent. "We're doing the slide now. We'll do the swing after the slide."

She didn't understand the implication of now and after, but no matter: I was speaking the words while preventing her from fleeing the activity. In time, she would make the connection. Maintaining a flow of language is a crucial component of instilling concepts in children on the spectrum. Parents do this naturally with neurotypical kids because they show us they understand, which encourages us to continue talking to them. But atypical kids often don't respond, at least not in ways we recognize, which makes talking to them feel futile. But it isn't: It is a profoundly useful technique for helping these kids absorb intangible concepts that their typical sisters and brothers learned long ago.

So there we were, a torrent of language cascading from my mouth to Daisy's ears: "What do you want to do after the slide, Daisy?" Nothing. "What shall we do after the slide?" Still nothing. I expected her to mention the swing but she just looked at me. I asked the same question maybe 20 times, then rephrased it; no response. Well, that wasn't working. What next?

Hah! I tried again.

"Daisy, you just went down the slide. What do you want to do next?" She ran off toward the swings with me in her wake. As I pushed her on the swing, I said, "You're on the swing now, Daisy. What do you want to do next?" She tried to hop off but I kept her in place and reminded her, gently but firmly, that she needed to finish what she was dong before moving on. She kept swinging and I kept asking, "Okay, Daisy. What shall we do next?", again and again and again.

"Kick the ball," she eventually said.

"Good! After the swing, we'll kick the ball." But I didn't let her off the swing—not yet. I had reintroduced the concept of after because next had sunk in; now I wanted her to associate the two. Every time she swung back to me, I repeated, "What will we do after the swing? What will we do next?" If she said "merry-go-round," or "see-saw" or "sand box," I'd reply, "No, after the swing, we'll kick the ball. What will we do after the swing?"— giving her another chance to connect. Little by little, she began to say kick the ball. After she responded this way several times, we went off to kick the ball and I started the process again.

I was teaching Daisy to connect a thought with a subsequent action, and instructed her counselors to use the same technique in her bunk, at meals, and throughout the day. We were asking Daisy's mind to stretch in new ways, so we had to be gentle but firm in guiding her. And with all of us working in concert, Daisy began to change.

After a week of consistent guidance from her counselors, Daisy was able to focus on activities she chose. For the first time, she was exerting control over herself, living an ordered life where before there had been chaos. And she liked it. That was the turning point: Once she could focus on things she wanted to do, we were able to guide her toward doing things we wanted her to do. Soon she was cooperating with her counselors and brushing her teeth, getting dressed, folding her pajamas, and making her bed without incident. Daisy was engaging with her activities, her bunkmates, and the adults who cared for her. She began to smile. Instead of living in moment-to-moment disarray, Daisy was integrating a new understanding of past, present, and future into her concept of reality and realizing she could influence the way it turned out. Within 3 weeks, midway through the summer, her wild running, biting, and defiance were gone. When her family came on visiting day, her mother was overwhelmed to see her daughter, whom she'd had to confine to a padded room, seeming content and in control of herself.

To help a child like Daisy, whose speaking and comprehension are adequate but whose mind is disordered, it is crucial to identify and build upon any germ of organized thinking she displays. In Daisy's case, it was her nodding when I asked if she wanted to draw and then taking the chalk and scribbling for a few seconds. With another child, it might be when he chases after a ball you threw that he was unable to catch. You can say,

"You're getting the ball. Now, you're throwing it back to me." As the ball comes your way, you ask, "What should I do now? Should I keep the ball? Should I throw it back to you?" Keep it simple. Give him many chances. And most of all, keep it fun; you want him to enjoy himself. Hearing language he understands and associates with his actions facilitates the process of organizing his disjointed thinking.

I don't know how Daisy's teachers tried to deal with her, but in many classrooms, it's the students' behavior rather than their thinking that's addressed. Unruly children may be told that, if they hang up their coats in their cubbies and sit quietly, they will be rewarded with a sticker. This may work until stickers lose their cachet, at which point all hell breaks loose again. Rather than reward fleeting instances of good behavior, the teacher could expose the children to language to help organize their thinking. Before they enter the classroom the teacher could ask, "When you go inside, what are you going to do?" The goal is to eventually elicit a response such as, "I'm going to hang up my coat and then sit down." It may be a long time coming, but when it does, it will mean the child has undergone an internal process of intentional, self-controlled, organized thinking.

I was eager to see how Daisy's mother would react when she picked Daisy up at the end of the season. She came with her husband, who gathered his daughter in his arms while extravagantly praising the staff. Daisy's mother stood quietly, smiling but subdued.

"She's come so far, hasn't she?" I said.

"Hmm," the mother said.

"I hope you'll stay in touch and let me know how Daisy is doing at home."

"That's the thing," she said. "I wasn't bringing her home, at least not for good. I found a place, a nice place not too far from where we live. They said they'd take her. My husband doesn't want it, but I figured after a few weeks he'd remember what it's like and come around. But now…" Her voice trailed off.

I was shocked, dismayed; then I understood. For years, this woman had been hoping and praying her daughter would get better, to no avail. After 10 years of heartbreak, she resigned herself to having a child who would never function in civilized society and had made plans for her to live elsewhere. Now she was being asked to hope again, to open her heart to the possibility that things could get better. It wasn't that she didn't want to hope. She was simply exhausted, her reserves depleted.

I once heard a story about a woman who suffered from acute agoraphobia and hadn't left her house in over 20 years. One day, she decided to seek help and called a therapist, who began treating her in her home. A year later, the woman was leading a normal life, meeting friends for lunch, driving to appointments, and exercising at a local gym. She was thrilled—but her husband wasn't. No longer was she waiting for him when he came home from work, the house gleaming and dinner steaming on the table. Her expanding world shrank his sense of importance in the marriage. He felt she didn't need him any more, and she felt he wanted to stifle her newfound independence. The relationship didn't survive the wife's recovery, and the couple divorced.

Dynamics between husbands and wives and parents and children are complex even in proverbially happy families; they can be much more complicated when one of them is grappling with a disorder. A wife's growth may imperil a husband's sense of purpose, just as the progress made by a child with autism may topple a parent's defenses against more disappointment and pain. Things are seldom as straightforward as they seem. Daisy and her family taught me that.

THINGS TO WORK ON AND THINK ABOUT.

* *Don't resign yourself to your child's wild behavior.* Daisy's parents were so overwhelmed by her violent physicality, they had resorted to confining her in a padded room. They thought she needed to be prevented from harming herself, but what Daisy really needed was firmness, consistency, and a framework that required her to repeat the same process over and over again. Daisy's parents weren't cowardly, neglectful, or unloving. They were desperate, spent, and out of ideas. Unable to reach their daughter, they resigned themselves to letting her run amok and hoping for the best. Parents must dig in and find the fortitude to remain firm with a difficult atypical child. It isn't easy. It is tedious, repetitive, and frustrating. But it's the only way to enforce an environment in which the child is subjected to consistent, coherent language in the context of a repeatable action or activity. It is this process that eventually confers order on disjointed thinking.

* *Don't mistake crazy-making behavior for an intention to make you crazy.* It was easy to interpret Daisy's dashing away and biting as intentionally

malicious acts, but I believe they were manifestations of a disordered mind that knew no other way to express itself. I don't think she meant to drive her family, teachers, and counselors nuts. And that's the point: Don't take it personally or let it get to you when your child behaves badly. When you're angry, you're not in control of yourself enough to see there may be a way to use the behavior in a constructive way. When your kid is driving you up the wall, it helps to remember that he probably doesn't mean to. Try to replace your anger with curiosity. Ask yourself, What is it like to be inside his head? What is it like to be her?

- *Use a varied vocabulary, as you would with a typical child.* When an atypical child says something new that indicates she or he has grasped an elusive concept, parents often fear the child will forget it. This makes them repeatedly use the same words that elicited the growth, or prompt the child to repeat the new word or phrase over and over. But memorization isn't the goal; thinking is. That's why I started using *after* once Daisy grasped the concept of *next*. I tried using *after* first; when she didn't respond, I tried *next*. Once she understood what *next* meant, I switched to *after* so she would associate the words as meaning something similar. I was not concerned that the new concept would be forgotten, and neither should you. Keep your vocabulary direct and basic, but do vary it. Neurotypical children learn to use language by listening to the adults around them. Give your atypical child the same advantage by varying the words you use and how you use them.

Part 3

Self-absorbed; obsessive; demanding.

Hunter's parents described him on the phone as an intelligent and high-functioning boy whose monumental self-absorption and refusal to follow directions had depleted their physical and emotional reserves. Neither they nor his teachers knew how to get through to him and had been reduced to yelling and threatening him with only sporadic success. He loved playing video games and could remain so occupied for hours, but when asked to do something, he became sullen and intransigent. Highly verbal, Hunter could talk at length about whatever was obsessing him at the moment, but otherwise deployed words like torpedoes, barking demands until they were met. After a minute or two, he would then abandon whatever he had asked for and demand something else, driving the adults in his life understandably crazy. His mother was distraught about his general lack of empathy and unkindness to his younger brother, whose overtures of friendship he spurned. I observed her frustration the day we met, when Hunter's indifference to her repeated requests to put away his iPod catapulted her into a rant about how sick she was of his shenanigans.

It sounded as if Hunter had become adept at hijacking control of his environment, creating scenes and leaving the adults in his life scrambling to cope. I decided to approach Hunter with two goals: to help adults deal with him actively rather than merely reactively; and help him develop typical thinking patterns so he could engage constructively with others rather than tyrannize them with his obsessive demands.

Hunter flunks a test. Hunter walked into my office the first time and strode around, picking up objects and putting them down in rapid succession. His face sometimes creased in a smile, which I found encouraging until I saw that it did not seem to signify pleasure or a response to our interaction. But he did talk—a lot—about wrestling, his current obsession. He went on about the WWF, which turned out to stand for the World Wrestling Federation, reeled off statistics about André the Giant and others in the pantheon, and listened raptly while I reminisced about watching Haystacks Calhoun on TV as a kid. But when I tried to veer the subject away from wrestling, he walked away. I asked him to come back, said we could return to wrestling talk, even said I felt bad that he'd left, but he ignored me. He gave no indication that he cared about the connection we'd had or that he'd hurt my feelings. I decided to break out my time-honored diagnostic instrument for measuring empathy and moral development: the water-balloon test. Hunter was the only kid I ever knew who flunked it.

My office is on the second floor of a small building and has a clear view of the sidewalk in both directions. There are cars but very few pedestrians, which makes it perfect for tossing water balloons out the window (we always clean up afterward). The young clients with whom I do this are wary at first and delighted later, but never aware that the real reason for the activity is so I can gauge their response to the question I ask beforehand:

"If we make some water balloons and throw them out the window, should we try to hit someone?"

Every kid I've ever worked with has responded with some variation of no. Hunter dashed to the window and grabbed the sill. "Yeah! Cool!" he said, his face alight for the first time. "C'mon! Let's hit someone!" I hastily withdrew the option. He was disappointed, to say the least.

Hunter was unfettered by bonds of propriety, compassion, or concern for the welfare of others. It was imperative that he become aware of this, which meant he had to experience situations that held a promise of gratification if he'd change his behavior.

Socializing a self-absorbed 11-year-old. I started by taking Hunter out to eat, because real-life situations can be more effective at eliciting change than contrived ones. I wouldn't have done this with a 6-year-old, but Hunter was 11, plenty old enough. We left the office and walked a few blocks to a small Italian place whose owner, a formal fellow with a dearth of humor, was likely to be there.

We were shown to a table and handed menus, at which point Hunter bent down, removed one of his shoes, and peeled off his sock. I told him this was not a good idea because other diners would not enjoy smelling his feet while they ate; moreover, there was probably a rule requiring restaurant patrons to keep their shoes on.

"I know," he said, and proceeded to remove his other shoe.

His manner was neither sassy nor insolent; it was, I believed, an honest response from a boy unable to reconcile his urgings with his rational mind.

Within 2 minutes, the owner appeared at our table and threatened to eject us unless my young companion put on his shoes and socks. I said nothing and waited to see if Hunter would comply. When it was clear he wouldn't, I stood up and laid my napkin on the table. Now Hunter started thrusting his feet into his shoes but I turned and walked out. I heard him scrambling behind me but didn't turn around until he was beside me on the sidewalk, shoes and socks in hand.

"Do you understand what just happened, Hunter?" I asked.

"Yeah," he mumbled.

"What happened, then?"

"I had to put my shoes back on to eat in the restaurant."

"Yes, that's right. When we sat down, I told you that taking off your shoes was inconsiderate of other people and probably breaking the rules, but you took them off anyway. And you put them back on only after the owner threatened to throw us out." He was listening.

"You do this a lot with other people, you know. You're a smart guy. You know what the right thing is, but you won't do it. You keep forcing people to threaten you into doing the right thing." He looked at me, then down at his bare feet, then back at me. I saw a flicker of something in his face; understanding, maybe. I motioned for him to sit down on the curb with me and put on his shoes.

"Hunter, do you like having people yell at you and threaten to take away what you want?"

"... No, I don't." I explained that he was getting older now and, if he continued to break rules and do whatever he wanted with no regard for the rights of others, he could eventually end up in jail. We sat in silence while he finished putting his shoes on. After a while he looked up.

"What can I do to make it be different?" he asked. I told him that we would work on that together.

Next session, I took him to an arcade to play skee ball, where you roll a ball up a ramp toward rings that deflect it toward holes of differing point values. We meandered over to where a boy of five or six was playing, accompanied by his father, who was partially blocking the adjacent alley. Eager to start playing, Hunter jostled the man to get to the vacant alley. The man glanced up; I mouthed Sorry!, then took Hunter aside and asked what was going on. "I want to play," he said.

"I know you want to play," I said. "But why do you think that man is standing there?"

"I don't know."

"Think about it." To Hunter, the man was an obstacle to be shunted aside; I wanted him to perceive the man as a human being who merited courtesy and consideration. Easy for me to say, of course; for Hunter, it meant organizing his thoughts and integrating disparate aspects of the situation. This was a challenge for him. I told him to take his time.

Hunter looked at the man and the boy. "What do you think?" I asked. "Why is the man there? Is he deliberately blocking the other alley? Is he trying to keep you away on purpose?"

"He's helping his kid."

"Exactly! He's helping his kid. So what do we do now? Do you still want to push him out of the way?"

"No." I told Hunter that was a reasonable and considerate response. He smiled.

"So, how can you get to play without the dad having to leave?"

"Wait," he said. Sure enough, another alley soon opened up and Hunter ran over.

I was pleased. Would I have preferred it if Hunter had apologized? Absolutely—but an apology wasn't in his arsenal just yet. Jostling a stranger was all Hunter had to work with when we arrived, but by the time we left, he had come up with a better option: to wait until an alley became available. Under the circumstances, his option was acceptable—not because it was optimal, but because it was relevant. What mattered was that, given the chance to think things through, he came up with a better alternative to what he'd originally done.

Walking back, we talked about how Hunter had stopped and thought, and how that had helped him behave reasonably. He acknowledged that stopping and thinking made him feel good. I emphasized the concepts of stopping and thinking as we talked, assuring him he could do it again, and not be a slave to his impulses.

The next time we met, I took Hunter to play table tennis. The ball soon flew over the net, followed by Hunter's complaint that I hadn't returned his serve.

"Didn't you see I was cleaning my glasses?" He mumbled something and retrieved the ball. Again he served, and again I wasn't ready. This time I was fiddling with my cuff buttons. He slammed down his paddle, ready to quit.

"Hunter, I'm rolling up my sleeves so I can play. You can see that, can't you?" He watched as I rolled up my sleeves, took out my handkerchief, blew my nose, and made any other adjustment I could think of. This time, he waited until I looked at him before he served—and I hit it back. We played for close to an hour, and for most of it, he paid attention to what I was doing before he served. He even asked me a few times if I was ready. He looked like a typical kid having fun.

The next time we went to eat, Hunter walked right past the "please wait to be seated" sign and plunked himself down at an empty table. I asked him to come back outside, where I told him that the proper way to enter a restaurant is to stop before entering the dining room. I explained that there is often information posted there: special dishes that arc not on the menu; a sign asking patrons to wait to be seated by a greeter, as there was inside; sometimes a sign inviting patrons to seat themselves.

"Hunter, sometimes you need to just stop and look and think," I said. "This is one of those times." We went back in, Hunter leading the way. He stopped at the sign.

"Why do we have to wait? There's nobody here. There's plenty of tables."

"We have to wait because that's the restaurant's rule. Someone will come to seat us. That's their job." And someone did. At the table, I asked Hunter to describe what had just happened.

"Next time I'll follow the rules," he said.

"What do you mean?"

"Reading what the sign says."

"In order to do that, what do you have to do?" Hunter looked at me blankly. I repeated the question several times in different ways. Finally, he responded.

"I have to stop."

"And then?"

"Think. I have to stop and then to think." I knew then that Hunter really got it.

Expect more of a kid and he just may deliver. Hunter was also getting it outside of our sessions. I heard from his mother that he was softening toward his brother. Vastly helpful to the cause was Hunter's school, which offered an unusually beneficial therapeutic atmosphere. I spoke periodically with several of his teachers, one of whom was frustrated by Hunter's continuing penchant for taking other kids' belongings. Asserting my belief that he was acting on impulse rather from malice, I asked her to refrain from imposing drastic consequences until I had time to work with him on this, and she agreed.

I chose not to subject Hunter to a lecture on why it was wrong to take other people's things; nor did I ask him, "How would you feel if someone took your stuff?" knowing he was likely to say he wouldn't care. Appealing to his emotions or sense of morality would be futile. I had to give him a new perspective. When next I saw him, I asked him what he thought about his taking things that didn't belong to him, to which he replied that he just liked other people's stuff. I reminded him of when he took off his shoes in the restaurant and how he came to understand that the owner couldn't allow it, as it would cause him to lose business. "Your teacher is like that restaurant owner," I said. "It's the owner's job to make sure his customers enjoy their meal. And it's your teacher's job to make sure her students learn, which she can't do if you're taking their things and disrupting the class."

Hunter nodded. There was a glimmer of understanding as he began to see things from his teacher's point of view.

"Hunter, next time you feel like taking someone else's stuff, what can you do instead?" He pondered for a while before speaking.

"I can stop. And think."

This was a quantum leap for Hunter: His rational mind embraced the idea that not grabbing what he wanted was both desirable and possible. It didn't matter that he wasn't coming from a place of compassion; that would come later. What mattered was that, in his mind at that moment, adopting his teacher's point of view had the potential to overpower his impulses. He could use his reason to control himself. He said that he was proud when he was able to stop himself: It didn't matter if no one knew, because he knew he was doing the right thing.

About six months into my work with Hunter, the arts teacher at his school phoned to say she was considering casting him in the class play. She had noticed that his behavior had improved and thought that the demands of play production—team work, respecting the other actors, taking direction, having to hit marks onstage, waiting for cues before speaking—would be a good experience for him. It was a tiny role, she said; what did I think? I told her it was a great idea, but that a bigger role would be better. Hunter enjoyed expounding at length about what interested him; why not give him a chance to do it on stage? I urged her not to fret about the possibility that Hunter might mess up and feel bad about it. I would rather give a child a chance to rise to a challenge and fail than coddle his ego by setting his sights too low. I don't mind failure as part of the therapeutic process: Taking a glorious risk and failing can be eminently worthwhile.

You know where this is going: Hunter was given a supporting role and blossomed in the play. He ran lines at home with his mother, took direction as well as any other kid, and was focused and happy at rehearsals. I was out of town the night of the show but heard he gave a great performance.

After 8 months of working with Hunter, I told his parents that he might no longer need my intervention. He was still prey to impulses but using his newfound ability to stop and think when they seized him. His success in the play and the pleasure he took in rehearsing it made him more open to cooperating and collaborating with his peers, and his teachers reported a steady decrease in his classroom disruptions. Hunter's mother's temperament had improved along with her son's: The strident tone she took with him when we first met had softened, and, while I wouldn't describe her new approach as tender, she sounded less irritated than before. After several weeks' consideration, she agreed to suspend Hunter's therapy.

For our last session, I took Hunter out to a self-serve frozen yogurt emporium where they have every sort of topping you can imagine. He became impatient while awaiting access to the gummy worms but recovered when I suggested that he stop and think. When we got back to the office, I suggested we recognize how far he'd come by doing something fun, like tossing water balloons out the window. He followed me to the closet to get the balloons, held them open as I filled them with water, and ran to open the window. When I got there, I looked him in the eye.

"When we throw these out the window, should we try to hit someone?" He looked away for a moment, then spoke.

"No. No, we should not."

THINGS TO WORK ON AND THINK ABOUT.

• *You're not doing your child any favors by indulging his or her bad habits.* Those of us who live and work with people with ASD have an obligation to intervene when they manifest antisocial behaviors and help them replace these with socially acceptable ones. Real-world experiences offer bountiful opportunities for this; be alert for when such teaching moments occur. Yes, awkward encounters will undoubtedly arise; no one likes being stared at and criticized by strangers. Still, if you can thicken your skin a bit and risk the discomfort of public censure, the benefits to your atypical child will be worth such wince-worthy moments.

• *If you haven't already done so, enlist your child's teachers and other school personnel as partners.* Acquaint them with the techniques you are using to engage your child at home, and ask if they would be amenable to replicating them at school when possible. True, Hunter's school was unusually receptive to cooperating with his parents and me; alas, this is not the norm. Still, do try. You may meet with resistance, but you may also encounter a teacher, a psychologist, or a coach who is receptive to your methods.

- *Remember: There's always more than one option.* When Hunter re-thought his behavior in the gaming arcade, apologizing for his rude-ness didn't occur to him. I didn't press him to apologize, as that would have resulted in rote behavior at best. The option he came up with—to wait—was thoughtful and relevant, and I was satisfied. When working with your child, look for a relevant response rather than the ideal one. Give your child an opportunity to do better, and work with that. Im-provise. Fortunately for Hunter, the man he pushed didn't get angry; this sort of stuff happens in arcades, after all. If he had gotten angry, there would have been another lesson to learn. It all comes back to following the child's lead: Whatever he or she does, go with it.

- *Set the bar higher, not lower.* It's tempting to set modest goals for a child on the spectrum: Life is hard enough for these kids; why not make it easier for them to feel good about themselves? But we don't feel good about ourselves until we know we've truly been tested, and peo-ple with autism are no different. If we don't challenge atypical kids, we deprive them of the triumph of knowing, in their bones, that they've accomplished something. So what if they fail? Failure is part of ev-eryone's life, and underrated as a factor in cultivating resilience. Don't fixate on success: It's overrated when it's a sure thing.

PATRICK, 11

Severely autistic; nonverbal.

You'll recall Patrick as the fellow whose acquaintance I made when he flung himself to the floor and brayed "baah-baah" without pause for 27 minutes (I timed it). He then stood up, removed his shirt and shoes, and began biting his arms. I tried talking to him—"Patrick, would you like to play with me? What do you like to play?"—but he seemed neither to hear nor see me. Bare chested and barefoot, pacing back and forth and chanting baah-baah now and again, he began picking up objects at random and setting them down wherever he pleased. He seized a picture book from a shelf, carried it to my computer, and balanced it atop the monitor. Grabbing my coffee mug, he traipsed to the other side of the room and set it on a seat cushion. He plucked a pencil from a cup and set off with it toward the wastepaper basket. When the pencil dropped from his fingers, he bent down, picked it up, tossed in in the trash, and chose another object to move, punctuating the proceedings with baah-baahs.

One typical action. I watched Patrick, fascinated. What was going through his mind? Why was he doing this? What was he getting out of it? I recognized the baah-baahs as a form of stimming, and imagined it was Patrick's way of comforting himself. But the moving around of objects puzzled me. I didn't see the logic of his choices, nor was I sure one existed. Why choose a book, a mug, a pencil? I kept watching and listening. Approaching a vase of dried flowers, he took it in his hand, spun around, and strode to a bookcase, where he set it on a shelf next to a Rubik's cube. Snatching the cube, he pivoted quickly, lost his balance, and dropped the cube as he righted himself. He watched the cube skitter across the floor, crossed to it, bent down, picked it up, and walked to my desk, where he set it down.

I don't remember what he picked up next because something was dawning on me: When Patrick bent down to pick up an object he had dropped, he was behaving like any other kid. In fact, this was the only typical behavior he'd manifested since he entered my office. It wasn't much but it was real, a drop of normalcy in an unknowable sea. Was it possible that the neurons in Patrick's brain were firing appropriately at these moments? And if they were, might I use them to connect with him?

Patrick paced around the room, seizing objects. Here he fetched a pad of sticky notes; there he clutched a stapler. On and on it went, until he reached for a rubber ball that was too large for his hand and it fell, rolling under a chair.

"Where?" I said, before he could get out another baah-baah. "Where, Patrick? Where did it go?" He stopped for a moment as if listening, walked to the chair, bent down. "Where? Where is the ball, Patrick?" He paused again, crouching. Then he grabbed the ball with both hands, stood up, and placed it on my desk.

These pauses weren't much to go on, but they were something. Patrick had attended to my questions: He hadn't answered with words, but he had paused twice on his way to retrieving the ball, as if he had heard me and was stopping to listen. Now the ball was both on my desk and in my court, and I would run with it. I hoped that this was a precursor of fuller engagement.

For our next session, I prepared activities and devised interventions to disrupt Patrick's stimming pattern. In the first one, I presented him with a basket of cardboard blocks and asked him to put them in size order—a simple task for a typical 11-year-old, but potentially challenging for someone like Patrick. He sat down with his back to me and, baah-baahing from time to time, started sorting the blocks. He lined up five and, when he turned to the basket for the last one, I grabbed a block from the middle of the line and held it behind my back. He turned around with the sixth block and, seeing the gap, paused in confusion. Before he could get out a baah-baah, I said, "Where? Where is it, Patrick?" He looked at me and I spoke again. "Where, Patrick? Where is the block?" I was trying to verbalize what I imagined he was thinking. He didn't answer, but he had looked at me—a victory. We had connected again. His baah-baah sounds had been diverted by my one-word question, and he had listened.

We continued with activities involving a variety of objects, some of which I would hide when Patrick wasn't looking, each of whose absence he marked with a silence into which I interjected "Where?" Again and again and again we played out the routine, which was what I expected: When working with kids with severe autism, it sometimes takes 50, 60, or 100 repetitions before a connection sparks and meaning is made.

Toward the end of the session, it happened. Patrick was arranging seashells in a circle and I slid one away when he wasn't looking. When he noticed something was missing, I said "Where," in a declarative tone, and he mouthed a wh- sound after me. I was thrilled: Patrick had uttered a recognizable sound, the beginning of a word, and imbued it with meaning. Still, I resisted the urge to praise him. Instead, I smiled warmly and continued with the activity.

I did not praise Patrick because to do so might have encouraged him to imitate my words rather than attach meaning to the formation of his own. This is an occupational hazard: If you commend nonverbal children for forming words, you send the message that what counts is making sounds rather than making specific sounds—words—that hold meaning. Many children with autism parrot a parent's or teacher's language; they see the pleasure in their elders' eyes when they speak, so they imitate what they hear without attaching meaning to it. The goal, however, is not to have nonverbal children imitate our speech, but to develop their own speech, deploy it to connect with others, and make themselves understood. Might Patrick have been merely parroting me when he made the wh- sound? Yes, he might have been. But in his case, I wasn't concerned as I might have been with another child. Patrick had been so remote at his first session, his behavior so bizarre, that anything he did that suggested awareness of another person was exciting. Patrick had, for perhaps the first time in his life, tried to say a real word in a meaningful context, and connected a feeling to speech.

Now all we had to do was help Patrick expand his vocabulary. With this in mind, I phoned his father the night before his next session and asked him to bring in something Patrick didn't like. (Patrick's father was divorced from Patrick's mother and had sole custody of both Patrick and his brother.)

The next day he slipped me a small plastic bag of multicolored jellybeans and told me Patrick detested them. Perfect.

I began by offering Patrick objects to sort, organize, and arrange, which he did with ease and the occasional baah-baah. After about fifteen minutes, I announced it was time for a snack, pulled the jellybeans from my pocket, and offered him some. The boy screamed as if I'd presented him with a tarantula.

"Patrick, if you don't want jellybeans, you may say 'I don't want any' or you may say 'no.'" I then tore open a bag of pretzels and offered him some (I knew he liked those). When he'd finished swallowing the pretzels, I offered him the jellybeans again. He screamed again. Again I told him if he didn't want jellybeans, he could say either that he didn't want any or he could say no. Then I offered him pretzels again, which he ate, and started in again with the jellybeans. We went through this maybe 9 or 10 times but eventually, when I offered him the jellybeans, instead of screaming, he said "no." Progress! The next time around, I didn't show him the candy but instead asked him if he wanted any, and he said no. It took an hour and 15 minutes of repetition but by the end of the session, he was expressing his distaste with words, not screams.

Confronting Patrick with a snack he hated was a benign obstruction designed to provoke an emotional response that we could transmute into language, and it worked. Everyday life provides many such opportunities; all you have to do is pay attention to what's happening in the moment, and make it happen differently. You know your child's likes, dislikes, and expectations; the idea is to thwart them in small ways, thereby creating situations in which your child is emotionally invested. Emotion sparks language; with patience, guidance, tolerance for tedium, and a bit of improvisation, you can help your child attach words to feelings.

I continued with Patrick in this way, contriving situations in which his expectations were confounded by my manipulations, waiting for him to say something that expressed an intention, and then responding to that intention. Baah-baahs emerged now and then but were being replaced by words. Midway through our next session, I told Patrick I was thirsty and walked to the mini-fridge. When I got there, I stopped and asked him, "What should I do?" I did not prompt him because it was clear by then that Patrick harbored a reservoir of language within him and understood what people meant when they spoke to him. I waited. Sure enough, he came out with "ope." I immediately said "Open what?" to which he responded, "doh"—open door. I said, "Okay, I'll open the door," and took out a bottle of juice for him and water for me.

This was a breakthrough for Patrick but I didn't let on. Instead, I conversed in a matter-of-fact tone lest I distract him from the cognitive process his mind was undergoing. Were I to have cheered him for saying "ope" and reinforced the behavior by proffering applause, pretzels, or a hug, I would have derailed Patrick's train of language use, and he would not have gotten to "doh." Patrick was not looking for reinforcement, nor did he need it. Prolonging our conversation was the most natural and effective reinforcement possible. He knew that by using words, he had gotten something he wanted—a sip of juice—by communicating to me that he wanted it. It was typical behavior he had observed in others for a decade, and now he had done it himself.

After about a month, Patrick was saying 20 different words in a variety of contexts. He wanted to learn proper pronunciation and would take my hand and bring it to his mouth so I could help him form the sounds. Sometimes he would repeat a word several times to try to get it right. Within 3 months, Patrick had made the connection between spoken language and communicating his ideas and feelings to others. Now when he wanted to get something across, he used some form of language, however rudimentary. I continued to present him with materials and activities he would find compelling. We would blow up balloons and bop them about the office; then, as I have done with other clients, I picked up a needle one day and asked if he wanted me to pop it. "No—no needle," he said. Later, I retreated to the far end of the room with the balloon and asked if he wanted me to pop it. He clapped his hands over his ears and said, "Yes. Do it." I did, and, not only did he like it, I got him to say "break"—as in break the balloon. I looked for new and different gadgets that might capture Patrick's interest. I found a cunning little monkey that jumped around when you wound it up. The winding mechanism was a bit tricky to master and Patrick had trouble with it—another form of obstruction, as it goaded him into using words to enlist my help. After 6 months, Patrick stopped screaming and the baah-baahing disappeared.

Dismantling outdated perceptions. When Patrick began using words, I drove out to his school on Long Island and met with teachers and staff members to discuss the importance of verbal interactions to his development. They looked at me quizzically. "Oh, Patrick?" several of his teachers said. "No, we've tried. He doesn't talk." It was both discon-certing and instructive. These were dedicated professionals who cared a great deal about Patrick; still, they were in the habit of perceiving him as nonverbal. It so happened that I videotaped some of my sessions with Patrick and, with his father's permission, screened some at the meeting. Once they saw for themselves that Patrick did indeed talk, they agreed to let him know that they expected him to use words with them. I suggested ways they might coax speech out of Patrick, urging the physical therapist to take part as well. "Why don't you put him on that big exercise ball over there?" I said. "The objective isn't for him to have fun, or even to like it. The objective is to use the experience to elicit language."

After 8 months, Patrick's father told me he could no longer make the 3-hour round-trip commute to my office from their home on Long Island. I told him that I believed that Patrick's language would continue to develop as he realized how much control it was giving him over his life. About six months later, the phone rang. It was Patrick's dad calling to tell me that his son was now putting words together into sentences, expressing what he liked and disliked, and trying all sorts of new things. "Except for jelly-beans," he said with a laugh. "He still hates those."

THINGS TO WORK ON AND THINK ABOUT.

- *Seemingly bizarre behaviors may not be impenetrable.* When Patrick lay down and commenced baah-baahing for half an hour, I didn't know what to make of it. Nor did I know why he removed his shoes and shirt, bit his arms, and randomly seized objects and repositioned them elsewhere. It wasn't until he had bent down several times to re-trieve objects he'd dropped that I perceived a logic to his actions, and pursued that logic until I found a way to engage with him. Observe your child. Pay attention. Stay focused long enough to discern patterns of behavior that reveal some sort of logic, even if its meaning eludes you. It's time- and energy-consuming, but will likely yield clues to unlocking your child's mind.

- *Resist the urge to meet your child halfway when he's on the verge of a breakthrough: Push harder so he will stay the course.* When Patrick ut-tered "ope" and "doh," it was all I could do not to high-five the kid—but that would have undermined his triumph. Praise with caution: You don't want to encourage your child to mimic behavior to provoke a warm outpouring of parental approval. Your child's feelings of self-worth will proceed from her heightened sense of self-mastery and con-nection with others, not from your praise or delight.

- *Cultivate persistence and patience.* You're not a patient person? Well, very few of us are when it comes to repeating the same words and actions, day after day, week after week, month after month. Breathe deeply and commit to practicing patience and forbearance. It may take 50, 100, or 500 repetitions before a breakthrough occurs. How long should it take for your kid to speak? Respond to your voice? Acknowl-edge your existence? As long as it takes.

SAMANTHA, 11

Very intelligent; inexplicable academic decline.

Samantha's parents were very concerned that their highly intelligent 11-year-old daughter was doing poorly in school. It started the previous year, when she was in fourth grade and began having trouble with the sorts of assignments that had never stumped her before. Now, in fifth grade, she rarely finished her work at school and a one-hour homework assignment often took her 3 hours to complete, even with her mother's help. At her teachers' urging, Samantha's parents took her in for testing and had recently learned she had high-functioning autism. Now they wanted to know what they could do to keep her from falling even more behind.

I've seen this many times: A very bright kid excels in school until third or fourth grade, when the work becomes more challenging. Now the child is asked to absorb different texts and integrate information, requiring complex cognitive organization that she or he is unable to perform. Seemingly overnight, the kid goes from star student to struggling one, and motivation and self-confidence plummet. This was the case with Samantha. She sat quietly and minded her own business; it looked to the adults as if she were daydreaming or spacing out. Had things been working properly, the school system would have noticed something was amiss by the time she was 6. But because she was cooperative and well-behaved, no one picked up on her problems until she started to fail. Good behavior had trumped learning yet again.

Evidence of Samantha's autism emerged right away. She conversed easily, describing at length the drive to my office, two badly mangled cars that had collided and caused a traffic jam, the fire truck and ambulances at the scene, and the brightly colored flares the police set up, in vibrant detail. But she seemed not to notice when I asked if she thought anyone had been injured, nor did she evince any interest when I winced several times and said my knee hurt. Matters of fact were compelling and etched in her memory, but those that involved feelings seemed of no interest to her.

The first task I gave Samantha was to complete a simple electric circuit using a wooden board preassembled with a battery, wire, switch, and bulb. Instead of connecting the wires, she plied me with well-reasoned questions about how the board worked. Like other adults in Samantha's life, I was taken with her engaging manner and taken in sufficiently that I didn't notice she hadn't completed the task. Next, I gave her a picture book that was well below her reading level, with the intention of asking her questions about it afterward. Her teachers theorized that the work was too difficult for her to follow, so I wanted to see if that were true. Reading aloud, she stopped halfway through and made up a different story that was more ingenious than the one in the book. Samantha's spacing out in class wasn't due to the curriculum being too advanced; the problem was her distractibility. No sooner would she focus on one idea than her mind would spark other ones that she seemingly had no choice but to follow.

I asked Samantha if she could describe what happened when she wasn't doing what she was supposed to be doing. She said she couldn't. I asked her to think about what had happened when she read the book. She smiled, so

I asked what had made her stop reading and start making up her own story. She thought for a moment and smiled again.

"I like when I do that," she said. I asked what she meant. "When my mind goes off somewhere else. I like that." She wasn't uncomfortable with it and she didn't realize that other people didn't do it—at least not as often and unintentionally as she did. I explained to her that what she was doing wasn't bad but that she did it a lot more than most other people. I then asked if there was ever anything she wanted to focus on but couldn't.

"Yes," she said, "when I'm getting dressed to meet my friends but I'm always late and have to rush because I think about other things instead of concentrating on what I'm doing—"I was impressed; this girl was unusually perceptive about herself—"Or, like, I take a long time to do my homework so I have to finish after dinner, and then it's too late for me to do something after, like watch TV." Okay, I thought; now we're getting somewhere.

"Wouldn't you like to be able to stop your mind from jumping around, then?" Samantha didn't hesitate.

"No," she said, "because I like myself."

Touché, Samantha.

She had set me straight, and also shown me the way in. I told her that many people liked her, including me. And that she could remain who she was but make her life even better by controlling her distractibility. "Wouldn't it be great to be able to finish your homework and still have time to do something fun afterward?" She said, yes, it would be.

Samantha needed first to understand her mental process and then be convinced that no one wanted to take it away from her, nor could they.

Like Addison, the 6-year-old who used yoga to stop zooming, Samantha possessed sufficient self-awareness to stop what she needed to stop. Once Samantha understood the issue—changing her thought process, not her essence—we started working toward a goal of maintaining focus. I had her work on homework assignments in my office and made her aware of when she seemed to be spacing out. When her focus returned and I asked her how she did it, she said, "I let it go." I asked if she thought she could let it go again and she said she thought she could, so I suggested we practice. I gave her a kite to assemble, saw her space out, and waited for her to come back on her own. We practiced this several times that day.

Over a few more sessions, I talked to her about trying to let it go when she got distracted in the classroom and doing homework—"Look," I said, "You can still be yourself, just not when you do schoolwork"—and soon she was able to bring herself back quickly and almost automatically. She said she still liked to use her mind to create stories, so I encouraged her to continue to use her imagination and write them down, just not when she was doing schoolwork. I also suggested she try writing poetry: There are no rules in poetry, no prescribed structure, length, or form; neither rhyme nor reason are necessary—just imagination, which Samantha had in abundance.

After 6 weeks, Samantha's parents and I agreed that she was back on track and would stop coming in. At our last session, she told me she had written a dozen poems. She had always enjoyed writing but her distractibility had made it impossible to focus on anything. Now the energy that had powered her hyperactive imagination was being channeled into her writing, and it flowed—as did her passion for being herself, which she had found a creative way to do. Not long afterward, Samantha's mother emailed me to say that she had won first prize in a countywide poetry contest.

SOMETHING TO WORK ON
AND THINK ABOUT.

• *What parents perceive as dysfunctional behaviors may be seen by atypical children as the essence of their identity.* These children will be loath to relinquish such behaviors and refuse to capitulate, escalating conflict within the family. Those of us who do not have autism are encouraged to think of our dysfunctional behaviors as bad habits rather than immutable character traits: They're something we do, not the essence of who we are. If we neurotypicals can regard an unwanted behavior—say, smoking a pack of cigarettes every day—as separate from our essential selves, we have a shot at changing it (along with a nicotine patch, perhaps). It's no different for persons with autism: Their dysfunctional behaviors may be habits that they can change. Parents must practice looking at themselves and separating being from doing. If parents can distinguish between who they are and what they do, they can help their atypical child make the same distinction.

MITCH, 11

High-functioning; perfectionistic; has frequent tantrums at school.

Mitch's parents were emphatic when they phoned me. "We're in a crisis," they said. "Mitchell is having terrible problems at school. He's angry and has tantrums almost every day. He's on the verge of being expelled but we can't let that happen—he's in a great school and he needs to stay there."

Mitch was intelligent and perfectionistic and would explode in violent rages when he didn't live up to his high and unreasonable expectations of himself. He attended a highly funded public school that specialized in special-needs kids and embraced a zero-tolerance behavior policy that Mitch couldn't tolerate. He had a tantrum almost every day, during which he would knock over furniture and storm out of the classroom. Something had to change, and fast.

Early impressions. Mitch was polite and thoughtful at our first meeting, but when I asked about how things were going at school, his face darkened. He said he hated school—the teachers, the kids, everything about the place. Everyone bossed him around and told him what to do, no one followed the rules but him, and everyone thought he was stupid. He was especially furious about the consequences he suffered for his behavior: "They punish me! Every day! Every day I have a time-out and when they let me back in, I don't know what they're talking about."

I usually wait a few months before visiting a client's school but scheduled a visit to Mitch's right away; I needed a sense of the culture and environment that surrounded his violent behavior. A few days later, I pulled up to the most gorgeous public school I'd ever seen.

First, I met with Mitch's teacher, who said it was hard to judge his academic ability because of his refusal to work. What she said next took me aback: "We see very deliberate, well-calculated, poor behaviors on a daily basis." Her use of deliberate and well-calculated told me she had Mitch all wrong. She said that Mitch didn't like being corrected and, when shown the mistakes he'd made on a project, activity, or test, would explode in anger and hurl chairs and kick trashcans. I asked how she dealt with this.

"We have a zero-tolerance policy for violence here," she said. "When a student acts out, he's removed from the classroom."

"So Mitch is removed whenever he gets upset?"

"Yes. It's a disciplinary time-out."

"And how long before he can come back in?"

"Two periods."

"How long is a period?"

"Forty-five minutes."

"So Mitch is removed from the classroom for 90 minutes at a time?"

"Yes. Longer, if he acts out again."

"He sometimes does it again?"

"Yes, absolutely. He's always angry when he comes back after a time-out. Just yesterday, he kicked the recycling bin and we had to send him out again." So Mitch was missing at least an hour and a half of class time almost every day. No wonder he didn't know what was going on.

Next, I met with the school psychologist, who said that not only had Mitchell's behavior not improved during his 5 years at the school; it had, in fact, gotten worse. He said this was probably due to the fact that his teachers would let him do as he pleased lest they trigger an outburst.

"Not me, though," he said, producing a stack of "anecdotals," write-ups of Mitch's many outbursts. "Just last week, I caught him wandering off school property during recess."

"Did he actually leave?" I asked.

"No, I didn't let him get that far. 'Mitchell Jamison,' I said, 'if you take another step, I'm calling the police!' And that was the end of that."

But it wasn't, of course; Mitch had had two outbursts since then. I wondered what a psychologist hoped to accomplish by threatening an 11-year-old with arrest. It seemed that no one at the school was looking at why Mitch did what he did; rather, they were intent on making him conform to their behavioral protocols. The inference was clear, at least to Mitch: The school was right, and he was wrong, period. And it had been going on for 5 years. One thing was clear: The school wasn't going to change its policies for Mitch's sake. If anyone was going to have to change, it was him.

Deconstructing Mitch's behavior. This much I knew: Mitch didn't like being told what to do, so school was intolerable for him. Because he couldn't accept that he wasn't perfect, he'd get angry with himself when he couldn't complete his schoolwork flawlessly—and how could he, when he was missing so much class time? When his teachers told him what he was doing wrong, they thought they were providing information that would inspire him to change his behaviors. But to Mitch, they were pointing out his shortcomings, which provoked his wrath. Frustrated at being misunderstood and, to his mind, treated unfairly, Mitch was in a constant state of fury.

We began weekly sessions and I set about learning how Mitch's mind worked. I got some insight early on, when he arrived with a Hammacher Schlemmer catalog and began extolling the virtues of a $600 remote-controlled car pictured in its pages. "My parents won't get it for me," he said. "So maybe you could take me to the store?"

"Mitch, Hammacher Schlemmer is an hour away, so we can't go there. But there's a hobby shop nearby that might have electronic cars. "Do you want to go and take a look?" He did, and off we went. When we got to the store, a salesman showed us his selection, which topped out at $299.99. I made a point of admiring the top model and asked the salesman to explain its features, many of which duplicated those of the $600 one and a few that exceeded them. I asked Mitch what he thought about this new information and he said he didn't know, but he still thought the more expensive car was better and cooler, and now would I buy it for him? I told him I couldn't spend $300 on a toy car, let alone $600, and we left. On the drive home, I tried to get him to explain what made his choice better and cooler, but he couldn't. "It just is," he said. Despite hearing about the cheaper car's many features, Mitch remained obsessively attached to his choice.

He was also obsessive about following rules and belligerent with class-mates whom he felt were breaking them. He complained bitterly about a boy in his class who would return early from lunch and log on to the computer even though the teacher wasn't there. "I told him to turn it off because the rule is to wait for the teacher. But he said I'm not the teacher and to butt out. So I pulled out the plug. And then I got in trouble because the computer got messed up and the teacher had to reboot it." Mitch was outraged: To his mind, the teacher should have rewarded him, not punished him, for enforcing the rule.

Not satisfied with enforcing others' rules, he established arbitrary ones of his own, arguing, for instance, that 80 times 10 was still 80 because a number could contain no more than one zero. When I explained the laws of math—which he understood—and demonstrated that 80 times 10 was indeed 800, a real number, Mitch's confusion spiraled into shame and anger, which he expressed by stridently defending his position. Another time, he mentioned the conflict in the Middle East, and I asked him when he thought it would be over. "The war will end on April 17th, one month from today, " he declared. When I questioned this he dug in, assured me he was right, and became so overwrought when I questioned his clairvoyance, he nearly broke down in tears. For Mitch to admit he didn't know some-thing—even something no one on the planet knew—was tantamount to admitting he wasn't perfect, which was intolerable to him.

It's easy to write off Mitch's convictions as absurd, but in fact, we've all been there. Have you ever found yourself on the losing side of an argument and, even when you realized you were wrong, kept insisting you were right because you were too embarrassed to back down? Now imagine living that way all the time, alienating everyone with claims of your infallibility. That was Mitch's reality. Between his self-imposed perfection and random, arbitrary rules, there was no framework against which he could evaluate the coherence of his positions. Unable to think and reflect, there was no logic to his assertions, which proceeded not from an orderly process of discernment but from an impulsive need to say something, anything that might be construed as correct. His thinking never arrived at a conclusion that felt grounded and true; instead, he was perpetually flailing, unable to trust his judgment. Because he was wrong much of the time, he would become even more distraught until he melted down and lashed out.

Priority: Help Mitch see there's often more than one answer. To keep Mitch in school, we had to dismantle the mechanism that triggered his rage at feeling wrong and foolish. To do this, I set out to help him understand that there are many kinds of problems, some of which have one right answer, others of which have more than one; that there were many ways to solve problems, even those with one right answer; and, most importantly, it was not only normal but desirable to make some missteps on the way to the best choice. Here are some of the strategies I used:

- *Breaking rote behavior with spontaneous thinking.* I started by asking Mitch to work on a math problem because you can't argue with numbers. He habitually completed schoolwork in a rote manner, duplicating whatever he remembered the teacher doing and not thinking for himself. So I started by asking him to divide 80 by 2. He looked at me as if I were nuts, informed me that that was way too easy, and picked up his pencil. "No pencil," I said. "Do it in your head." He looked at me as if I were nuts again. "Come on, Mitch. You said it was easy. Figure it out in your head. You can do it." And he did. When I asked if he were sure of the answer, he did the problem a different way in his head and came up with the same result. A gleam of recognition lit his eyes: He was taking ownership of the thinking that got him to the right answer. The process was entirely his, and he could trust it. This was the dawn of Mitch taking responsibility for making sure something was indeed true.

- *Instilling flexibility through creative play.* Continuing with math, I gave Mitch a dozen small blocks and asked him to arrange them in equal piles. First he counted them out into 2 sets of 6; we multiplied 2 times 6 and got 12. I then asked him if there were another way to arrange them in equal piles, and he made 4 sets of 3, then 3 sets of 4, then 1 set of 12, then finally, 12 sets of 1. This helped Mitch understand that there are sometimes many solutions to a question, pulling him away from right-or-wrong thinking and allowing him to experiment with different possibilities without the fear of being wrong.

- *Building confidence by connecting with a peer.* On a subsequent visit to Mitch's school, I noticed a boy who looked a bit younger and was following Mitch around as if he looked up to him. His name was Carlo, and I encouraged Mitch's parents to contact his family and see if they could get the boys together. They did, twice—once on an outing to a local fair and once to the movies. Mitch was an only child and benefited from being the older, wiser part of a duo. He also learned that sometimes he had to act gracious and do what Carlo preferred to do, which his parents described to him before the outings as adult, good-hosting behavior. Eager to rise to the occasion, Mitch went along with Carlo's few requests and felt terrific about it afterward.

• *Deconstructing received wisdom to enhance understanding.* One of the biggest challenges for people with high-functioning autism is feeling ignorant of common knowledge. Mitch would become enraged when confronted with "You didn't know? Gosh, even my little brother knows that!"—because it made him feel stupid to not know what an 8-year-old did. So we started fresh. I handed Mitch the ring toy with the spindle whose diameter widens toward the base. I told him I knew he could do it with his eyes closed, but what I wanted him to do was explain the toy—why the spindle thickened, why the rings had different sized holes in the middle, why they had to be applied in a certain order for the column to narrow at the top. After a halting start, he was able to explain the toy's logic clearly. Next, we moved on to more complex constructs. Mitch liked science, so we filled a glass with water, dipped our fingers in, and talked about how water needs to be a compound of two gases, hydrogen and oxygen, to become a liquid. Later, we tasted salt crystals and discussed how they could be safely ingested as the combined form of sodium and chlorine, either one of which alone would be harmful. That night, he explained to his father that salt is a compound of two elements that, separately, are dangerous to ingest. For Mitch, this was an affirmation of his capacity to understand complex concepts and articulate them, which eased his anguish about not knowing everything other people did. Now he knew he could learn.

• *Defuse frustration and rage by taking a break.* Mitch was having trouble opening the mini-fridge one day because the latch was broken. He became frustrated, muttering and banging it with his hand. I said my phone was vibrating and told him to sit down and take a break while I took an important call. As I pretended to converse, I watched him from the corner of my eye. About a minute later, he went back to the fridge and easily found a way to open the door. I ended the faux call and pointed out that he was able to stop, think, and change his mood, all by himself. "You mean, like I pushed the reset button?" he asked. I said it was just like that. Mitch liked the idea of resetting his mood at school to avert a meltdown and time-out. As we discussed the technique, he realized he could use it anytime, anywhere, whether he was angry with a classmate or frustrated by fractions. When he came back the following week, he told me he had reset himself many times since we last met, and had shoved a chair and trashcan rather than throwing them during math class—now, that was progress! Even better, he had not been ejected from the room. As Mitch began to exert control over his emotions, he slowly gained some self-respect and a sense of his identity in the world.

Hitting a home run. Of all the strategies I deployed, Mitch's favorite was baseball therapy. He came in one day talking obsessively about a $450 bat he'd found online, so I suggested we visit a local sporting goods store (yes, the boy was drawn to the top of the line). Once there, it was a replay of the electronic car episode: The salesman explained the relative virtues of the bats in stock, even saying outright that, for a kid Mitch's age, a $50 bat was every bit as useful as one costing nine times as much. Still, Mitch was convinced that a $450 bat would be better.

"Look," I said. "You like baseball, right?"

"I love baseball. Love it, love it, love it."

"So next time, should we go out and hit some balls?" Mitch said that would be cool. The following week I took him out to a baseball diamond, handed him a mitt, and started hitting high fly balls in his direction with an ancient Louisville Slugger that probably set me back 8 bucks. I noticed that Mitch would always twist aside as the ball came his way, moving either left or right but never right under it. His catches, when he made them, were awkward and much harder to execute than they had to be. "Mitch," I said, "I can show you an easier way to catch the ball. Want to see?" I suggested he get directly under the ball and try catching it that way, then demonstrated several times. It worked: Mitch began catching fly balls with ease. In his excitement, he actually thanked me for the tip.

"Mitch," I said, "you needed help with something, I saw what the problem was, and I told you how to fix it. That's what your teacher is trying to do in school: She's trying to help you. If you can accept that you aren't perfect and that you could sometimes use some help, like today, catching fly balls, you might like school a little more, and you wouldn't need to reset so often."

"Yeah, but she's different from you. She says things in a different way."

"Well, what would you like her to say in order to help you?" He pondered this a while before speaking.

"I want her to say, 'I can show you an easier way for you to do that math problem, Mitchell.' " I told him that made sense to me. And it also made sense to his teacher, who agreed to try explaining things differently to him. I coached her in how to speak to him, avoiding phrases that wouldn't bother a typical kid but that might trigger Mitchell's shame and anger. She caught on quickly and said she'd try it and let me know what happened. She called the next day to say she'd used the exact words Mitch had quoted, and for the first time, he accepted her advice without getting riled. Their relationship was different after that.

Things calmed down at school. After 6 months of sessions, Mitch was able to tolerate the notion that he was less than perfect, and his tantrums ceased. He still got annoyed once in a while but never lost control; nor was he ever ejected from class again. I worked with Mitch for about a year and a half, at which point he was getting along well enough at school that he no longer needed my interventions. One of my fondest memories was when I asked him what kind of job he might want after college. "Do you mean a career?" he asked. I said that's exactly what I meant. "I think I want to study history, maybe be a history teacher," he said. The irony was not lost on me: Here was Mitch, planning a future that studied the past.

THINGS TO WORK ON AND THINK ABOUT.

• *How do you respond to being wrong or feeling stupid?* Do you admit your mistake (gaffe, rudeness, obtuse behavior) with humility, humor, and grace and acknowledge that you were wrong and your spouse (partner, sister, brother, father, mother, teacher, supervisor, friend, or child, even) was right? Or do you gnash your teeth and dither about, banging utensils on the kitchen counter and hissing, "I am such an idiot!" If you went with option B, imagine feeling that way almost all the time and not understanding why. If you can imagine that, then you have a sense—and only a mild one—of how a person with autism frequently feels. Those of us who live with, work with, and care about persons with ASD must learn to recognize some of their behaviors as extreme manifestations of impulses we also have but are able to understand and control. This will help us decode seemingly bizarre ASD behaviors more accurately, and respond more compassionately and effectively.

- *Don't judge a school by its playground.* Mitch's school was dedicated to educating special needs students and was housed in a new building, had state-of-the-art equipment, and beautiful grounds. Yet the administration had established behavior protocols that were, to my way of thinking, utterly inappropriate for the population they served. My first visit discouraged my hopes that we might work together effectively. Still, in time, Mitch's teacher embraced flexibility, adapted her way of speaking to accommodate his foibles, and transformed her relationship with him. (The school psychologist was another story; I don't think he ever would have come around.) Invest in establishing relationships with the people who teach and work with your child, no matter how highly rated the school may be. Get to know them so you have a sense of their personalities and educational philosophies. Their intentions may be good, but people are unpredictable: There may be a dynamic at work that is making things harder for your child than they need to be.

High-functioning; perfectionistic; inflexible.

C ory's mother described him as depressed, angry, irrational, and withdrawn. This may have been true, but the fellow I met was highly intelligent, articulate, and capable of introspection. He acknowledged early on that he was unable to allow himself to be happy, a perception I hoped betokened a sense of humor (it did). The only good thing Cory's mother had to say about him was that he was fond of his younger brother. I was glad to hear it but wondered why she hadn't mentioned any of the admirable traits I noticed right away.

Shortly after we met, Cory told me that he was very upset about getting 97 on a math test, which he saw as worse than having failed. To his way of thinking, it was okay to flunk a test if you didn't understand the material; but if you did understand the material, which Cory assured me he did, being even three points shy of perfection was unforgiveable. He wouldn't hand in his homework that day and refused to go to school the next; he said he felt so defeated and angry with himself that, even after returning to school, he stopped working altogether. What was the point in trying if you couldn't be perfect?

When I mentioned that I needed a new cell phone, Cory said he knew which one I should get and insisted we go to the store right away: "This phone will change your life and I'm going to make you get it." I got my car keys—not because I planned to buy a phone that afternoon but because I wanted to ride the wave of Cory's enthusiasm. We drove to an electronics store where Cory regaled me with the merits of the model he liked, which was about $500 more than I wanted to spend. When I extolled the virtues of other models, he was unmoved; nothing would do but the one he was fixated on. He was disappointed when we left without it, but I wasn't. Our first session had yielded insights into Cory's thinking, which was both perfectionistic and clad in absolutes. There was triumphal success and abject failure, one shimmering ideal and worthless imitators, with nothing in between. My priority would be to massage the rigidity of Cory's thinking so he could perceive and find freedom in the vast gray area between black and white where the rest of us lived. I knew he was good at math (if not perfect), so appealing to his firm grasp of numbers seemed like a logical place to start.

Weighing the odds. To address Cory's need to be right all the time, I broached the subject of chance at our second session by hiding a pebble in one of my fists and asking him to guess where it was. He guessed wrong and began to sulk.

"Cory, come on. You had a 50–50 chance of getting it right. You got it wrong. So what?"

"I should have gotten it right."

"Why? The odds were 50–50."

"Doesn't matter. With 50–50 odds, I should get it right."

"Really? Every time?"

"Yeah, every time." His math skills were a lot better than his logic.

"Well, what would the odds have to be for you not to feel bad if you guessed wrong?" He thought for a moment.

"Less than 5%." This clued me in to Cory's penchant for creating mental systems that differentiated his thinking from that of typical kids. It's not unusual for people with high-functioning autism to latch onto numbers in ways that typical thinkers don't.

"So you feel bad about yourself if you fail at something when you have a one in 20 chance of succeeding?" He agreed.

"Cory, does that seem fair?" He didn't reply so I reframed the question.

"What if it was your brother? Would it be fair if those were the odds for him? Is he supposed to feel bad if he misses something he has only a 5% chance of getting right?" A full minute passed.

"No. That wouldn't be fair."

"Okay. So, if it isn't fair for your brother, why is it fair for you?" Again, silence.

"It isn't fair for me, either."

This was the first time that Cory recognized the imperfect logic that had convinced him he had to be perfect. The irony was not lost on him, and he giggled.

Toward the end of the session, Cory told me he was angry with his family, especially his father, who insisted on turning off Cory's light as soon as he got into bed. They argued every night, which agitated Cory and kept him awake for hours. I mentioned this to his mother when she came in at the end of the session and asked what she thought might be done about it.

"You're the therapist!" she snapped. "You tell me!"

"I beg your pardon?"

"He's got it, too, you know. Asperger's. I might as well talk to a wall. The man is—" she opened her hands and held them rigid on either side of her face—"like the horses in Central Park. He sees only what's right in front of him, nothing else." That explained a lot. I asked if she thought it might help if I had a few sessions with her husband, and she said it couldn't hurt.

Cory's father embodied many of the same characteristics I saw in my young clients. He never smiled yet spoke openly and honestly about himself, his sons, and his marriage, citing himself as the source of some family problems. His candor helped me help him, as when he explained his reason for forcing Cory to turn off his light: "It satisfies my idea of what a good father is. If I let my kids make the rules, I'm abdicating my responsibility." If Cory saw things in absolute terms, he came by it honestly.

I worked with Cory's dad on letting go of some of his absolutes, suggested he let his wife handle some issues that caused him to be abrasive, and offered some less inflammatory ways to express himself (we finessed "Cory, get in your room and do your homework now!" to "So, Cory, when do you think you'll do your homework?"). Even if Cory didn't do his homework, his father would feel he had fulfilled his role, and an outburst would have been averted—not the ideal solution, perhaps, but preferable to explosive strife and very much in the gray zone I hoped father and son would learn to inhabit.

Focus off the family. Cory's anger next targeted his mother, who wanted him to attend a summer camp for kids with high-functioning autism. Cory refused. She insisted. They fought night after night until Cory stopped talking to her, moved into the basement along with his Xbox, PlayStation, and Wii, and barricaded the door with a sofa. He came out for school, dinner, and, after a visit from me, our appointments. His parents had asked if I would come to the house and lure him out of his boy-cave. I descended into the gloom of a subterranean video den, jeans draped on consoles, books and papers strewn across the floor, underwear everywhere, air suffused with the funk of pent-up adolescent boy. I nodded at Cory and took in my surroundings. "Wow," I said, "it's pretty cool down here." We talked for a while, the upshot of which was that he agreed to come to a session the next day. Which was precisely what I hoped would happen: A kid as stubborn as Cory wasn't going to emerge from the basement because I pleaded his parents' case. My best shot was to try to bond with him, which worked.

When he arrived, I opened my laptop and we researched the camp together, even getting the director on speakerphone so Cory could ask some questions (I arranged this with the director in advance). Away from parental pressure to acquiesce, Cory acknowledged that the camp offered some activities he was interested in, including workshops in video production. He ended up going to camp for 3 weeks and coming home in love with video game design.

Once again riding the wave of Cory's enthusiasm, I contacted the computer engineer who taught the workshop and hired him to come to Cory's sessions. Using equipment I brought in, Owen worked with Cory on creating a video game they'd started over the summer, and that's when things took off. For a kid who was constantly being harangued by his parents to focus on and conform to standards he didn't understand, being permitted to immerse himself in a new passion was a revelation. I don't think anyone had ever taken Cory's own ambitions seriously; now an expert was implementing his ideas about computer design. Over several weeks, I watched as Owen and Cory brainstormed ideas, tried them out, and analyzed the results. When an idea of Cory's worked, you could see the pleasure he took both in his own skill and Owen's approbation. And when one didn't work, that was even better in a way, because it taught Cory that some ideas have to fail in order for others to work; that, when it comes to inventing something new and exciting, there's no such thing as perfection—in fact, striving for perfection cramps the creative process.

My goal for this collaboration was to enable Cory to derive satisfaction from a pursuit that he, not his parents, cared about, and it succeeded. He told me he had created several video sequences that incorporated the complexity he envisioned, and that he felt proud of himself. This evolved into a fledgling capacity to tolerate other people's demands and suggestions without feeling demeaned or diminished. He also began to experience his interactions with others from a broader, more empathetic perspective. This was demonstrated in his evolving reaction to his gym teacher, whom Cory had bitterly accused of pestering him to try out for the town soccer team. Now he saw it differently: "When he kept telling me I'd be good at it and that I might like it, I see now that he was trying to be nice." I hoped that Cory's budding capacity for empathy would deepen to accommodate his parents.

An opportunity to test this soon arose. For years, Cory's mother had been singing in a chorus, and for just as long, he had refused to attend its

concerts. I broached the idea with him of attending its upcoming performance; he refused. Undaunted, I asked him to imagine that his brother and
not his mother were singing, and how much it would please his brother to
have him there. He seemed to get that, so I pressed him to imagine how
much his mother wanted the people she loved to be there, too. He nodded
slowly and eventually agreed to come. It wasn't entirely a Hallmark Channel moment: Cory agreed to attend only if he could sit with me and not
his family, which wasn't quite what they had in mind. Still, he was in the
auditorium—which, I tried to make them see, was something. What was
also something was that he noticed another kid he knew in the audience
and, with some prodding, went to sit with him. I could see them interacting
amiably during intermission—no small thing for a kid like Cory.

Facilitating a friendship. Building on Cory's foray into empathy, I arranged
an encounter between him and Jared, another highly intelligent client of
mine a year younger than Cory who I hoped would look up to him. Jared
was not as highly functional as Cory, but I believed both were developmentally ready to embark on a true friendship. Moreover, Jared liked video
games (what kid doesn't?) and I thought they'd be a good match.

I brought them together at my office, which I'd equipped with a video
console and some popular games. The boys didn't click at first; Cory would
load up a one-player game while Jared watched and asked questions that
Cory was too engrossed to answer. When he did answer, he spoke in terms
too advanced for Jared to understand. I coached from the sidelines, urging
both boys to be patient, attentive, considerate—dynamics that neurotypical

kids figure out on their own but that are devilishly elusive to kids with autism. It took some doing, but after three sessions, the boys connected; after six, they began seeing each other outside our sessions. My interventions were helpful but the key was that both boys desperately wanted a friend. The process by which they bonded could not have been forced, nor could it have happened before each boy was ready for it. I was there to facilitate, but the energy had to come from them. Happily, it did, and with unexpected benefits. Cory came to session one day and told me about having dinner at Jared's house the night before. "Jared reached right over his mother and grabbed a chicken leg from the platter," Cory told me, "and I said, 'Come on, Jared; you should ask first.' "

Cory progressed steadily over the year I worked with him. As he became better able to tolerate imperfection, his view of learning changed. The process of designing a video game expanded into understanding that not getting everything right the first time opened new avenues of exploration. He began to look forward to the future and we talked about college, which at the time of our acquaintance was still 7 years ahead. He yearned to go away to school, where he would have freedom to study what he wanted and develop his creative potential. We discussed what it would take to get that far, which he came to accept would include making his way through some things he didn't like and getting along with some people he didn't care for.

It sounds as if he did okay. I recently heard that Cory just started his freshman year at Rochester Institute of Technology, majoring in video game design.

THINGS TO WORK ON AND THINK ABOUT.

• *What looks and sounds like arrogance may be single-mindedness. Use it.*
When Cory told me he was going to make me buy a particular phone,
he was being not belligerent but single-minded: He truly believed it
would change my life. What I heard was not pushiness but pent-up
passion: This kid loved technology and wanted to introduce me to its
wonders. Try to ignore an intemperate tone of voice and respond instead to your child's enthusiasm: If he or she is excited about doing
something—especially if it includes you—go with it. You can finesse
the rest later.

• *That said, you don't have to buy the pony.* Or the Maserati, or the
700-dollar cell phone, or whatever your child is so enthused about.
The point is not to acquiesce to your child's demands but to ride the
wave of enthusiasm wherever it takes you.

• *Even a compassionate and conscientious parent may be clueless when it
comes to handling an atypical adolescent (or a typical one, for that matter).* Cory's father struggled with the same dysfunction as his son, yet
lacked insight into how to interact with him. If an ASD father isn't
factory-equipped with empathy for his atypical son, how can non-
ASD parents know what their atypical child is going through? Parents
must understand that love alone cannot create understanding: They
must accept that autism is a foreign country, commit to learning the
language, and start from there.

• *There are many ways to be a good parent.* Cory's father believed that
doing right by his sons meant making them obey the rules. But a lot of

rules are arbitrary, as was the one requiring Cory to turn off his light at nine o'clock sharp every night. It took work for this man to revise his image of what a good father was. What's your image of a good parent? Is there only one? In truth, there are many.

- *Don't fantasize perfection: Sometimes a partial victory is as good as it gets.* Cory's family was miffed when he refused to sit with them at his mother's concert but they were missing the point, which was for her to know her son was hearing her sing. That mission was accomplished despite the scattered seating arrangement. Sometimes we have an image of how things should be and are disappointed when reality diverges from it. We must adjust our expectations; satisfaction exists in small increments of progress. Not every surrender must be unconditional.

JARED, 12

High-functioning; inflexible; perseverative; yells.

Jared's interpersonal skills blossomed when he befriended Cory (p. 205), but it was a long time coming; nearly 2 years, in fact. When we first met, it was hard to imagine him getting along with anyone: His inflexibility, perseveration, and frequent tantrums were requiring his mother to pick him up early from school several times a week. (She worked full time and Jared's father was out of the picture, so this was a major problem.) The most recent incident was triggered when Jared innocently described a classmate as fat. The girl seemed unfazed by the comment but the teacher went ballistic, chastising Jared in front of the other students and reminding him that he was never, ever, ever to comment on any aspect of someone's appearance in her classroom. Deducing that he'd done something terribly wrong but clueless as to what it was, Jared started yelling, "I'm sorry, I'm sorry!" As the teacher's jeremiad continued, Jared's thundering apologies became perseverative and she called the assistant principal, who arrived moments later and urged Jared to calm down. When that didn't work, he began to physically remove Jared from the classroom and Jared kicked him in the shins. Not good.

Was the tantrum purely Jared's making, or did the adults in the room help set it off? His mother told me that he was able to discern right from wrong in many situations, but lacked the interpersonal savvy of a typical 12-year-old. We agreed that Jared did not mean to be malicious; he was just being his honest, unfiltered self. Unable to see things from viewpoints other than his own, he was clueless that such a remark might hurt someone's feelings. To my mind, by reacting as if Jared were a typical kid, the adults escalated the conflict and whipped him into an emotional frenzy he was powerless to control. They were responsible for the tantrum as much as he was—maybe more, because they should have known better. As for Jared, our discussion of the incident focused not on whether describing a classmate as fat was wrong, but on how it may have felt to the girl. I told him that, were he intentionally trying to hurt her, yes—that would be wrong, but hurting someone unintentionally was an accident, and deserved to be treated as such. As for kicking the principal, Jared did agree that that was wrong.

To help Jared develop typical age-level thinking and behaviors, I and the other adults in his life needed to help him become more flexible, see situations from other people's viewpoints, follow directions, concentrate on tasks, speak without yelling, reflect and think before acting, and be less perseverative and anxious. I kept his mother, teachers, camp counselors, and even his parish priest, who was preparing him for his First Communion, updated on the work I was doing with Jared so we could interact consistently with him.

Broaching independence. Jared was unusually attached to and dependent on his mother, so I addressed this by exiling him to the waiting room at the end of each session while she and I spoke privately in my office. This was a challenge for him: When I said we needed 5 minutes, he timed 5 minutes exactly and then banged on the door. Next session, he managed to wait 7 minutes before banging (I timed it); the next time, 10. Over 2 months of waiting outside until he couldn't take it any more and then being invited in, he began to use the pads, colored pencils, pens, crayons, magazines, and puzzles in the waiting room to occupy himself for up to 45 minutes—as a typical 12-year-old would. This reflected a profound internal change on his part, overcoming the perseverative, obsessional thought of having to be in the same room as his mother.

Massaging Jared's inflexible psyche. Jared's mother had described his perseverative behavior as ubiquitous: His speech was repetitive, he got stuck in thought loops, and had even elongated one of his ear lobes by constantly pulling on it. When I met Jared, I could tell he was very rigid. He would do only what he wanted to do when he wanted to do it, and when he didn't get his way or get it soon enough, he whined and screamed. I began working on this by asking him what he wanted to do and, when he answered, presenting what I would like to do as another option (I made sure that my alleged preference was also something he enjoyed). If he wanted to open a bag of pretzels, I would say I'd prefer popcorn, which I knew he liked; if he wanted a helium balloon, I suggested making water balloons, which I knew he loved. If he balked at my suggestion, I would persist in saying I wanted it, reminding him that I was allowed to have desires different from his. After haggling back and forth, he would often let me prevail (when he felt strongly about his choice, I let him have it). I made this a component of every session to entrench in his mind the process of compromising. After a month, the frequency and intensity of Jared's tantrums had diminished slightly; after 3 months, they had noticeably decreased; and after 6 months, the tantrums were gone, with Jared referring to that era as "the old Jared."

Implicit in being flexible is a capacity for seeing beyond one's immediate wants and needs, so I took advantage of situations that would require Jared to do this. One day he came in 15 minutes late and immediately said he wanted to eat a bag of chips. I reminded him that the plan was for us to go out and play ball and, if he took time to eat chips, we would not have time to do this. I repeated it several times, emphasizing the concept that what you choose in the present affects what happens in the future. Still, he insisted on eating the chips, and when he was done, headed toward the door. I explained that because he had come late and eaten a snack, now there wasn't enough time to go out.

"Let's just go," he said. "Let's leave now!"

"If we leave now, I'll be late for my next client." I wanted to acquaint Jared with the idea that the world did not revolve around him, that I had responsibilities to other people, and that there were natural consequences for the decisions we make—concepts that parents need to enforce as well. I knew he was ready to be pushed a bit and was unlikely to pitch a fit. He wasn't happy about it, but not playing ball that day marked the beginning of the end of his demands for instant gratification and obliviousness to other people's needs. After several episodes like this, he eventually asked if we could go out next time, and when the next time came, he decided against a snack.

At the time, I had a part-time assistant named Kelsey, a recent college graduate who wanted some experience in special education while she looked for a teaching job. I arranged with her to accompany Jared and me to the park for a session but asked her to come around ten minutes late. When Jared arrived and saw that Kelsey wasn't there, he became impatient.

"Let's go," he said.

"Jared, the plan was for Kelsey to come with us. What should we do?"

"Let's leave without her!" I was ready for this: It was a response typical of kids with high-functioning autism and consistent with Jared's center-of-the-universe thinking. I pressed him.

"What happens if she arrives right after we leave? What's she supposed to do then? Kelsey's never been late before. I'm a little concerned about her. I'd like to know she's okay. What do you think we might do?" Jared had a brooding look on his face. He thought and thought and thought.

"We should call her," he eventually said. We did, and she picked up as she pulled up to the building. A critical element in this exercise was to focus on the situation, not a person. Rather than home in on Kelsey's feelings, I expanded the view to include factors over which she had no control: What if she were stranded with engine trouble or had been in an accident? What if she were ill? The plan for the session was for the three of us to go to the park; how could she join us if we left without her? These scenarios were possibilities that an egocentric person like Jared would never consider. Presenting them reminded him that a knee-jerk response—let's leave without her!—might be far from the best one.

As I write this, I realize it may sound as if every session heralded a new era in Jared's development, but it didn't happen that way (it rarely does). These interactions took place over nearly two years of weekly sessions, and, while Jared's progress was steady and undeniable, there were times when he suffered setbacks and reverted to old behaviors.

One occurred about seven months into our relationship, when we were driving to a hole-in-the-wall pizza joint. I reminded Jared of an incident that happened the last time we'd eaten there—or almost eaten there: When we arrived and asked where the bathroom was, the owner said there wasn't any and suggested we use one in the Mexican restaurant next door. Jared's mother was with us and, upon entering the Mexican place, she commented on how good it smelled and asked if we might not want to eat there instead. Jared agreed and we had a good meal and cordial conversation. The brouhaha happened after we left, when Jared got upset because we weren't going into the pizza place for a second meal. It took a while for him to calm down and acknowledge that he'd enjoyed the Mexican dinner, was too full to eat pizza, and that we could come back another time.

Now it was 5 weeks later and we were driving back to the pizza place for lunch. I reminded him of what happened last time, expecting a strong reaction. And I got one: Jared started shouting and gesticulating wildly and became so overwrought he shoved me while I was driving, jolting the steering wheel and causing the car to veer slightly. He began apologizing obsessively and begging me not to tell his mother. Despite my reassurances, the apologies and begging escalated into a perseverative spiral until I pulled over and cut the engine. "Look," I said, "do you want to keep apologizing for the rest of the afternoon or do you want to eat pizza?" The whining stopped. "Pizza," he said. While we were eating, we talked about what he might do instead of obsessively apologizing when he started to lose control. Bringing up the classroom incident, I suggested that, instead of apologizing louder and louder, he might have said, "I'm sorry. I don't understand what I did wrong." And so on.

It's a big and so on, of course: I worked with Jared for long time, both in the office and out in public, challenging him to speak instead of yell, ask instead of demand, consider others as well as himself. I continued to contrive varied situations that would set him off, and then worked with him through his ensuing agitation.

Toning down Jared's tone of voice. Situations frequently arose on their own, especially when it came to Jared's penchant for yelling, which seemed connected to his generally anxious state. Asking him to lower his voice was useless. Because of his limited social skills he was often misunderstood, and, anticipating this, he'd raise his voice. This often got him what he wanted, so he'd had little inducement to stop.

I noticed that when we finished an activity and I'd ask Jared what he wanted to do next, he'd usually answer by yelling. One day he yelled that he wanted to play Battleship, even though I was sitting right next to him. A reasonable response would have been to chastise him but I didn't want to interrupt the logical flow of conversation as we prepared to play. I ignored his outsized delivery and delayed fetching the game to prolong the conversation. I told him I didn't think I remembered how to play and asked if he could remind me of the rules. He could, of course, but did so in a normal tone of voice, which broke the shouting cycle. As we faced each other and Jared went through the rules, I asked questions, looking him in the eye so he would know I was focused on him and his words. I then got up, fetched the game, set up the pieces and, in a casual tone of voice, broached the issue of the day.

"So before, when you said you wanted to play Battleship, why were you yelling? Did you think you needed to raise your voice for me to pay attention?"

"I don't know."

"Well, I did ask you what you wanted to do, so I was listening. I'm listening now. Do you think that maybe next time you could try just saying it instead?" Jared said he would try. This was the awakening of his self-awareness.

There are many reasons why this intervention worked, but of paramount importance was not interrupting Jared's pre-game cognitive flow to criticize him for yelling. Just as I decline to praise young clients when they manifest new, improved behaviors, so I decline to chastise them when they revert to old, undesirable ones. I want their minds to develop new ways of thinking that more closely follow neurotypical cognitive patterns, and interrupting the flow derails the process. There are always ample opportunities to praise and correct later.

Continuing flexibility training. Now that Jared was comfortable being separated from his mother, I occasionally involved her in sessions without fear of enforcing his attachment to her. One day, I took them both to a gaming arcade to play air hockey. My plan was to improvise several problematic situations and ask Jared to work his way through them.

First, I needed to know if he could deal with defeat, so the two of us played a game and I purposely won. Jared seemed fine with it, so I told him I thought his mother wanted to play. He said fine, he'd play with his mom. Then I created a dilemma for him: I told him I wanted to play too, and charged him with coming up with a way to accommodate both his mother and me. And he did: He and I would start playing and when I scored a goal, I would bow out and his mom would take my place; then, when she scored, I would take her place, and we'd continue alternating, she and I sharing our side of the table. I was encouraged: Jared had come up with a feasible solution that accommodated the needs of people other than himself—this was good. Then I made it harder.

There's a hitch, I told him; under that scenario, his mom would have to share her playing time with me: "She shouldn't have to sit down, Jared; she hasn't played yet. Why should she have to sit out half the time?" Six months earlier, he would have exploded and walked out. Now he seemed merely perplexed. And he came up with another creative solution: This time, it would be he and I who traded off when either of us scored a goal, enabling his mom to play full time. It was remarkable that Jared suggested this, because it halved both his playing time and potential score—a sacrifice that revealed his growing empathy for other people's viewpoints. So we played and it went well, with Jared keeping track of when each of us was due to sit out. Best of all, when I asked afterward if he could explain the reasoning behind the solution, he could.

Growing independence. Around this time, I gave Jared a challenging project to do on his own: a model airplane kit. We discussed that he'd have to open the package carefully so nothing broke or got lost, and figure out how to put the many pieces together, either by trial and error or by reading the instructions. I sat and watched as Jared picked up pieces, held them together, put them down, tried again, and eventually looked for the instruction booklet. Frowning, squinting, and occasionally grinning, he followed the directions one at a time, slowly and deliberately, each small success augmenting his growing sense of mastery. It was extraordinary to behold: Over the weeks he worked on the kit, never once did he lose focus or ask me for help, which was unusual for him. When he finished and I asked him how he'd done it, he said, "I just followed the instructions," as if that were an everyday occurrence for him. This happens all the time with my high-functioning clients with autism: Once they blossom into freer ways of thinking, they forget their former inflexibility.

Friendship. About eighteen months into our relationship, I had the idea of introducing Jared to Cory, another client who was a year older than Jared and also desperate for a real friend (for more on Cory, see p. 205). I knew Jared played video games at home and, although Cory's skill was greater, hoped that gaming would provide common ground on which they could connect. I arranged for them to meet at my office the following week.

I suggested that Cory start with a one-player game and explain what he was doing while Jared watched, which worked better in theory than in practice. Cory got involved in playing and ignored most of Jared's questions; when he did answer, he used jargon that Jared didn't understand. After observing Jared's growing discomfort I gently intervened, reminding Cory that he needed to be more responsive and limit the jargon. Jared liked the arrangement: Because he did not yet have the skills to readily articulate what he was thinking, he was relieved to have me intercede on his behalf. I did as little as necessary to facilitate the boys' interactions and then receded into the background until communication broke down again, at which point I'd amble over, break down the obstacle, and recede once more.

I convened these gaming sessions for 6 weeks (the boys continued to come separately to weekly sessions as well). By the third week, they took control over what they wanted to play; by the last session, they were interacting well without my help. After that, they began to go bowling and to the movies together and to visit each other's homes.

Still, Jared needed some coaching in the friendship department. At the reception following his First Communion, his mother took me aside and told me he was upstairs in his bedroom playing a video game. I went up and sat down next to him on the bed.

"Jared, there are a lot of people downstairs who came to celebrate your Communion today." No answer.

"Cory's down there, too. He's sitting by himself on the couch in the living room, not talking to anyone. What should we do about it?" Still no answer.

"You know, his parents drove him all the way over here so he could be with you. I know you saw him in church; you two were talking after the ceremony. I think he feels lonely downstairs. What do you think we should do?" It took about ten minutes of gentle, insistent prodding, but then Jared put down the controller and went downstairs, where he spent the rest of the afternoon hanging out with Cory and the rest of the guests—a remarkable feat for both of them.

As the friendship deepened, Jared's self-confidence grew. When making plans with Cory, he would sometimes have to call the house and speak to Cory's mother first (this was before every man, woman, and infant had a cell phone). Making plans at all was a big deal for a kid like Jared, and having to speak politely to an adult on the phone was stressful for him at first. But, like a typical kid, he rose to the occasion after multiple tries.

And he kept rising to new occasions, as I heard from Jared's mother when she recounted the story of when Cory came over for dinner and admonished Jared for grabbing a piece of chicken without asking first. "That was over week ago," she said. "He's been asking ever since."

THINGS TO WORK ON AND THINK ABOUT.

- *Don't underestimate the normalizing influence of friendship.* Typical teenagers often defy their parents' wishes but may heed those of their peers; atypical teens are no different. By encouraging a wholesome friendship, you may find your atypical teen upgrading his or her behavior to please a friend.

- *When an ASD child has a tantrum, there may be more going on than mere belligerence.* In Jared's case, his agitation at having broken a classroom taboo and being publicly reprimanded sparked an uncontrollable urge to apologize with unsettling, escalating vehemence. It looked like belligerence, but it was actually humiliation and remorse. His teacher could have averted the episode by grasping an underlying truth: Jared's inability to understand the logic of her rule against commenting on a classmate's appearance. (I was just as confounded as Jared: Would it be a punishable offense to say someone looked good in a new pair of running shoes or hoodie, for instance?)

- *And speaking of rules ...* Parents and other adults in an ASD child's life must consider their audience when establishing rules. Can the child comprehend the logic governing the rule? And, most importantly, does the rule make sense? I would argue that prohibiting comments about a person's appearance is an artificial construct: People make those kinds of comments all the time. The goal is to teach children that other people have feelings, that certain kinds of remarks can hurt them, and to refrain from saying such things. That goes for all children, not just those with autism.

- *Don't interrupt cognitive flow to chastise or praise.* Just as I refrain from pausing to praise a young client, so do I refrain from pausing to chastise. Had I drawn attention to Jared's yelling during the prologue to our Battleship match, the issue would have become about his yelling rather than our conversing. There's always time to (gently, casually, kindly) discuss undesirable traits later.

Part 4

MAX, 15

Repetitive, antisocial behaviors; disjointed thinking;
minimal language.

Max's parents were distressed by his eccentric traits: Not only did he get locked into repetitive behaviors, he was also highly distractible, abandoning one activity to flit to another. They weren't crazy about his antisocial behaviors either, which included running away from social situations and religious services, hitting other kids, and pulling down his pants in public. "He's impossible. He won't do anything we ask him to. The only one he'll listen to is Eli," his mother said, pointing to her older son, who had accompanied them to the session. She then turned to Max. "Max, sit," she said, "Sit, Max. Now." She was smiling expectantly, nodding, and gesturing at the chairs in the room. Max stood, unmoving. She began cajoling in a singsong voice. "Come, Maxie, come, come. Sit, chair—" she sat down ceremoniously and patted the seat next to her—"come now, this for you, by mama." Max stared ahead, immobile. Then Eli piped up. "Max, sit down already. We've got to get out of here in an hour so I can get to class. Come on, it's enough already. Sit down." Eli plopped down in a chair and Max did, too. I noticed that Eli spoke to Max much like any 18-year-old would speak to a pain-in-the-neck kid brother—quite a departure from their mother's approach.

While their sons busied themselves around the office, Max's parents told me that he could express himself in sentences of three or four words and absorb simple instructions, but beyond this there was nothing. Watching the boys, I saw that on several occasions Eli prevailed on Max to break out of repetitive behaviors—banging a geode against his leg, running a toy car back and forth on the same 4 inches of carpet—by speaking plainly and emphatically, as he had earlier. "See," his father said, "he listens to his brother—but to his mother, never. She's so good to him, so patient, but he ignores her."

I had my own thoughts about that. Hearing Max's mother speak to him as if he were a young child, I wondered if his ignoring her were a form of protest. He'd responded right away when his brother told him what to do; the difference was that Eli spoke to him as a peer, without patronizing him. I see this all the time: Well-meaning parents address their autistic children as if they are intellectually disabled, which most of them are not.* The parents think that by oversimplifying their speaking style they're getting through to their children; instead, they're preventing them from hearing how typical speech sounds and works, and may even alienate their kids by sounding condescending. I don't know if this was happening with Max, but it was possible. There was another possibility, too. Max was the second eldest of 10 children growing up in a religious family. Inundated by a flood of younger siblings, he'd no doubt observed them dropping their pants and perhaps witnessed family members laughing about it. He might be doing the same thing in hopes of amusing them, finding himself in hot

---

* *According to a study published by the Centers for Disease Control, 62% of children identified as having an autism spectrum disorder were not intellectually disabled: https://www.cdc. gov/ncbddd/autism/documents/addm-2012-community-report.pdf, accessed September 20, 2017.*

water when he'd expected to be showered with smiles. Or perhaps pulling down his pants was another form of protest: You want to talk to me like I'm a 2-year-old? Fine! I'll act like one! Anything was possible. What was certain was that Max's parents wanted him to become more flexible in his thinking, which I believed would lead to better behavior in general. We would start there.

A possible culprit. My theory was that Max's obsessiveness and mental rigidity were preventing him from breaking out of his unwanted behaviors. Perhaps a cognitive malfunction was causing the rigidity, but I wanted to observe him before I drew any conclusions. I also invited Eli to attend Max's next few sessions so I might further observe their relationship, and he agreed to come.

I have a wooden toy comprising a rectangular base with five shafts on which red, blue, green, yellow, and orange discs can be placed. I presented Max with a heap of discs and the base, on whose shafts I'd already placed one red, one green, one orange, and two yellow discs, and asked him to sort the remaining discs on the shafts according to color. He did fine until he picked up a blue disc and saw there was no shaft designated for it. He sat staring at the disc and then at the base, then placed the blue disc atop one of the other colors. "Max, those discs aren't blue," I said. "I'd like each shaft to have only one color on it." I tried to show him that we needed to make room for the blue by removing one of the yellows; still, whenever he had a blue disc in his hand, he kept trying to sort it onto the wrong shaft. We did this six times; then, the seventh time, he stopped and said, "No blue." Eli was as surprised as I was. Max had tapped into his reservoir of normalcy, noted what was happening in the present moment, and derailed his obsessive, automatic behavior.

"Right—there is no blue. What should you do?" Max pointed to a yellow disc, indicating it should be removed to make room for a blue one. For the first time, he did not reflexively try to place a blue disc on top of a different colored one. Max had indeed switched gears; his bad habits could be broken.

I gave Max another task, this time sorting hollow wooden cubes and discs onto a base with square- and cylindrical-shaped shafts. Eli held out a disc and said, "Max, what is this—a circle?" Max said, "Circle," took it from his brother, and placed it on the corresponding shaft—perfect. Eli did the same thing again, proffering a disc and asking Max to identify its shape, which he did. Only this time, midway through sliding it onto the proper shaft, Max removed it and began trying to jam it onto a square-shaped shaft—a reverse take on trying to put a square peg in a round hole. Something had distracted him from his original, accurate impulse—what, I didn't know—but I could see that his fluency of thought had been broken. There wasn't even a flicker of change in his eyes; it just happened. Even when Max was content and cooperative, his thinking could be disrupted. Later, the three of us stood at the window and I asked Eli what he saw.

"I see cars," Eli said. He then asked his brother. "Max, what do you see?" Max was silent. Eli and I asked him, "Do you see people? Cars? Trees? Telephone wires? A building?" Max said nothing. About ten minutes later, we were working on a puzzle when Max said, "Trees." So information could enter his mind and register, but sometimes the process of verbalizing what he saw got derailed, getting back on track much later on. My mission would be to help him develop fluent thinking.

Building cognitive fluency. Next session, I handed Max a bottle of bubble stuff whose lid I'd tightened beforehand. I watched as he struggled with it, struggled some more, and then, finally, said, "Open the bubbles!" His eyes were flashing, his arm outstretched. Another spark of normalcy: Max's mind and body were united in a fluent moment of desiring something and trying to get it fulfilled. Pressing him to use more language, I asked Max what he wanted me to do (another benign obstruction). This time he pursed his lips and blew a puff of air, which was an appropriate, spontaneous response, even if it didn't use words. I held up the bottle and Max mimed blowing again. I opened it, he extracted the wand, and happily filled the office with bubbles.

This was as much of a conversation as Max had ever had, and what insight it gave me! The exchange was more than several minutes of continuous, connected thought: It embodied a way I could help Max learn to speak for himself. His mother's verbal coddling obviated Max's need to do this. By prodding Max in staccato, one-word bursts, she was unwittingly echoing his fragmented thought process and stymieing his ability to sustain a thought long enough to act on it. But when Eli spoke in full, expressive sentences, Max tended to respond. Max had no incentive to try to organize his thoughts enough to express himself. But by questioning him repeatedly, even when I knew what he wanted, I was forcing Max to channel his thinking into verbal and nonverbal expressiveness. My job now was to get him to return to this fluent state again and again. Eventually, the pleasure of realizing he could communicate his desires and get them met would triumph over his disjointed thinking habits.

When much of my office was moist with bubble residue, I asked Max what he wanted to do next—my trusty technique for establishing a sense of time. Bubble wand in hand, he stood looking at Eli and me. I tried again. "Would you like to have a snack? Have a drink? What would you like to do next, Max?" He looked at me and said, "Go to the bathroom."

Hah! He'd derailed my thinking and found a way to escape the exercise. I had no idea he was capable of this level of planning. But I didn't let him off right away: "Okay, Max. Now you need to put the wand back in the bottle and put the cover on. After you do that, then you can go to the bathroom." When Max heard he could do what he wanted after he finished doing something now, it did more to build a sense of temporal constancy than any artificial exercise I might have come up with. He closed the bottle and went down the hall.

When Max returned, he pointed to a Wiffle ball and said, "Throw." I pretended not to hear so he'd speak again. He repeated the command and I looked up.

"Oh! You want something, Max?"

"Throw."

"You want to throw the ball?"

"No. You."

"Me? What do you want me to do?"

"Throw ball."

"You want me to throw the ball? Where? To Eli? Out the window?" He smiled.

"No. You throw ball—" he pointed to himself—"me."

Following this thought to its conclusion was a significant accomplishment for Max, who at the time had little temporal constancy. This was one of many interactions in which I coaxed Max into focusing on an intention and articulating it in language. In this way, little by little, he began to understand the concept of before, now, and after.

Max's remediation program. To help fortify Max's evolving fluency of thought, I devised a program of techniques, several of which I incorporated into our weekly sessions.

- *Window therapy.* Max's variety focused on getting him to gather visual information into a unified context. Standing at the window with Max, I would mention things I saw: "Look at the tree and the leaves. There's a woman wearing a red coat with a dog on a leash. The cars are going fast." These may sound like random observations but they're actually elements of a unified reality: things you can see from my office window. The next time you look out a window, notice how your mind naturally jumps from one object to the next, creating an image of what's outside. This is a form of facilitated assimilation, a process whereby new, discrete bits of information enter the brain and unite to form a lucid concept. Six weeks earlier, Max had looked out the window but not articulated what he saw until later because his brain was not registering the information in an organized way. Now I worked with him on verbalizing, on the spot, what he saw, forcing him to participate in a typical way of thinking. The goal was for him to experience what you and I do when we say, "It's a gorgeous day!"—implicit for us are a bright sun, blue sky, fluffy clouds, sparkling water, leaves, and flowers (or skyscrapers, depending). These images unite in our minds to form a gorgeous day, something that I wanted Max to learn to do.

• *Instigating spontaneous speech.* Whenever Max expressed a desire for something—he might say thirsty, for example—I'd cajole him into talking more about it before fulfilling the request. First I'd ask if he wanted something to drink; when he said yes, I'd ask him if he wanted juice or water, knowing he loved orange soda. If he said he wanted soda, I'd ask him if he wanted orange or root beer, knowing full well what the answer would be. And I'd purposely mention orange first because he was in the habit of choosing the last thing he heard; now, to get his preferred flavor, he'd have to think rather than mindlessly repeat the last one I'd offered.

I did this consistently, offering Max choices so he'd have to think about what he wanted, and always mentioning the preferred option before the others. And I took pains to make the extended question-and-answer process sound as casual and normal as possible; the last thing I wanted was for Max to think I was teasing him.

• *Sparking anticipation to develop Max's concept of time.* As I did with Daisy, whom I prevented from abandoning the slide for the swings until after she'd slid down, I worked with Max to develop the concept of anticipating what was coming next by focusing on the present. I would ask him to think about two things he liked to do—drawing and juggling were favorites—and hold them in his mind at the same time. Then we would draw together, while I brought up juggling—"When we're done drawing, then we'll juggle. Do you want me to teach you?" When we finished our artwork, I'd get the juggling balls and teach Max some basic techniques, chatting about what we might do next. We might go back to drawing or do something else; whatever Max wanted was fine with me. This ongoing process trained Max to organize his thoughts and orient himself in the present while anticipating the future. Key to the success of this technique was asking him to think about activities he was enthusiastic about, so he would look forward to switching off.

- *Differentiating Max's bad behavior from an underlying learning issue and acting accordingly.* The teaching assistant in Max's class was convinced he had it in for her: When I visited the school, she recounted stories of how he'd pester her for a cookie or a drink and then, when she brought it to him, evince no interest in it. I explained that this was probably not manipulation but a result of Max's disrupted thinking, and urged her to try to talk to him about it whenever it happened, encouraging his language use. She seemed skeptical and then told me about how he often lagged behind when the class left for lunch, making her lose precious time from her own break while she coaxed him toward the cafeteria. And when the bell rang I observed him do just that, gathering his belongings in slo-mo and dawdling in the doorway despite her entreaties to get moving. This wasn't disrupted thinking but a 15-year-old being a royal pain, and he deserved to be called out on it. At his next session, I talked to Max about it, pointing out that his dawdling inconvenienced others.

• *Getting Max to speak as much as possible.* Translating Max's thoughts into words would help organize them, so I pressed him to verbalize in every way I could. When he was drawing, I'd ask, "What color do you want?" If he said brown, I'd ask if he wanted sepia, bronze, or burnt sienna to expand his awareness of the diversity around him (thanks, Crayola). I would also introduce different ways of expressing the same idea, suggesting he either take another crayon, switch colors, try a darker shade of blue, or choose a different color. No matter the activity, I would ask Max to tell me what he was doing in that moment. Early on, I got monosyllabic responses—"puzzle;" after 6 months, he could provide a lucid narration of his actions: "I am doing a puzzle with a goat and a cow and a pig."

I worked with Max every week for about seven months, at which point his parents secured a place for him in a residential home in Upstate New York. By the time he moved away, he had stopped running away from gatherings and was consistently keeping his pants up. He was able to converse in simple sentences and express himself.

THINGS TO WORK ON AND THINK ABOUT.

- *Resist the impulse to speak simplistically.* Max's mother was unwittingly exacerbating his problems by speaking in curt, staccato utterances that further entrenched his disjointed thinking. The goal is not merely to dismantle a dysfunctional thought process but to replace it with a new, functional one. By speaking to your atypical child as you would to any other person, you are demonstrating how to use language in a fluid, cogent way. And speaking that way means thinking that way, after all.

- *Choose process over expediency.* When Max asked me for something, I could have saved time by giving him what he wanted, but I'd have sacrificed the verbal interaction that formed the foundation of his newly fluent thinking. Drawing him out, asking him which snack or drink he preferred, improvising an exchange about which crayon to use—these one- to two-minute interactions can lay the foundation of lucid, cogent thinking. When you find yourself just wanting to get something done quickly with your child, ask yourself if you might be able to invest 3 extra minutes in enforced conversation. If you can't, you can't. But every once in a while, you'll find you have a few minutes to spare. They make a difference.

HARRIET, 15

| Nonverbal; disengaged; blank expression. |

Sitting opposite Harriet with two slices of pizza and a dense silence between us, I thought about what to say next. I'd brought her here because the pizza was good and the homemade ice cream was great—and, because I wanted to work with her outside the orbit of her mother, who, when she called the first time, said she'd prefer to give me details about her daughter in person. At our first session she'd done just that, with Harriet sitting next to her and objecting to almost everything she said.

"I've had to call the police 10 times in the last 34 months," the mother said. "When Harriet gets angry, she's out of control—"

"I am not," Harriet said.

"—and I'm worried she's going to hurt—"

"That's not true! I'm a good girl!"

"—me. When she was younger, I could physically manage her, but she's gotten much too big now—"

"I'm not big! I'm not! I'm not!"

"Harriet, I'm talking to Mr. Bernstein. You're interrupting."

This was a loaded situation. I could have asked Harriet to wait outside but then it would appear that I was colluding with her mother, an impression I was loath to make. My first loyalty is to the client, not the parent. Whenever possible, I prefer to err on the side of transparency, especially when the child is on the cusp of adulthood, as Harriet was. "What sorts of things happen when you get angry, Harriet?" I asked.

"She pushes me, she hits me," the mother answered. "She once picked up a lamp and threatened to throw it. It got so bad, the EMTs had to sedate her and wheel her out on a gurney." A wrenching cycle of emergency room visits, admissions for psychiatric consults, and next-day releases ensued, with Harriet's anger and her mother's angst and anxiety increasing as time went on.

"It doesn't matter what I do," the mother said. "Harriet blames me for everything, all the time. All I'm trying to do is what's best for her. I arranged for her to visit a girl in her class, but she refused. I want to take her shopping for clothes, but she refused that, too. I just want her to be happy. That's all I want." I didn't doubt it; the woman meant well. I turned to Harriet, who was busy studying her lap.

"Harriet, what do you think about what your mother just said?" Silence.

"Harriet, Mr. Bernstein is talking to you. Answer him, please." More silence.

"It's okay," I said. "I'd really like to hear from you, Harriet. Do you want to say anything?" She shook her head without looking up. We left that first session agreeing that my work with Harriet should focus on defusing her anger so she might be able to get along with others and enjoy her life a bit more.

Now we sat in a restaurant a week later and she still wouldn't look at me. Then Sal, the owner, came over. A garrulous fellow, he's got a soft spot for young people and a gift for sussing out their moods. He asked Harriet's name, and she answered, eyes downcast. After some pleasantries, he turned to her.

"So, Harriet," he said, "you like ice cream?" Now he had her attention. She looked up.

"Yes."

"What kind?"

"Strawberry ice cream with sprinkles."

"What kind of sprinkles? Chocolate or rainbow?" Her eyes glowed.

"Rainbow."

"Okay. After you eat your pizza, go up to the counter and tell them that Sal said to please give you strawberry ice cream with rainbow sprinkles. No charge—free. That's my gift to you." He smiled warmly. There was a palpable pause while Harriet stared at him. Then Sal turned and left. I turned to Harriet.

"What do you think?" She met my eyes.

"He's nice."

"Why do you think he's nice?"

"Because he's giving me ice cream." She smiled shyly.

"It's good that you appreciate Sal's generosity," I said. I then told her a story about a boy I used to bring there and how he never showed any appreciation for what Sal gave him. Harriet's eyes widened.

"He didn't say thank you?"

"Nope." I had my opening.

"So, Harriet, I'm wondering why you didn't say thank you to Sal." Her smile vanished and she looked away.

"Because."

"Because … what?"

"Because I'm tired of always doing what my mother says—'What do you say, Harriet? Harriet, what do you say?!' "

I'd found at least one source of Harriet's anger: She felt defined and controlled by her mother, and she hated it.

"You know, Harriet, you don't have to do exactly what your mother says. You can use your own words." She wasn't following. I tried again.

"Do you know what you were feeling when Sal offered you the ice cream?" She shook her head no.

"You said you thought Sal was a nice man. Those were your own words, right?" She looked up and nodded.

"So that's what you can say. You don't have to say what your mother tells you to say. You can say your own words. Does that sound okay to you?" She nodded again.

"Do you feel like telling him now?"

"Now?" Her eyebrows shot up.

"Why not? I bet Sal would love it. Everyone likes to be appreciated." She mulled it over, then slid out of the booth and walked over to where Sal was rolling flatware up in napkins.

"You are a nice man," she said. Sal looked up.

"And you're a terrific girl," he said. Will you come again?" Harriet's face creased in a grin.

"Yes, I will."

"Now, don't forget about the ice cream."

"I won't. Strawberry with rainbow sprinkles."

"You got it, Harriet." I gave Sal a thumbs-up as Harriet returned.

"How'd it go?" I asked.

"I like Sal," she said. It was the first time I'd seen her look truly happy.

On the drive back, we talked about the difference between saying what others want us to and what we want to say for ourselves. We also talked about how being genuine is an issue that all people wrestle with throughout their lives. It seemed that Harriet was beginning to discover where her mother ended and she began.

Talking to strangers. The following week, I took Harriet to a food court in a shopping mall. Carrying our trays, we saw a hulking teenage boy, probably close to Harriet's age, eating by himself. "Ooh, I don't like him," she said.

"I wonder if other people feel the same way you do. He might be lonely." He was wearing camo-patterned jeans, which added to the intimidation factor, but he looked harmless, just a big kid eating a hot dog. I maneuvered us over to an adjacent table, set our trays down, and started chatting with him. After a minute or so, he said his name was Keith, asked Harriet what hers was, and they began to talk. Suddenly desperate for more mustard, I excused myself and dillydallied at the condiment bar. Harriet needed to talk with a peer without a chaperone; any human connections she could make independent of her mother's involvement (or mine) would imbue her with a sense of her own power—which, I believed, would help defuse her rage. When I returned to the table, Harriet and Keith were still talking. I kept quiet. Harriet left to refill her soda cup.

"She's weird," Keith said.

"It's not her fault," I said. "She has a condition called Asperger's syndrome." Keith smiled.

"So do I." (I am not making this up.)

After Keith left, I asked Harriet if they'd exchanged contact information.

"Yes, we're going to friend each other on Facebook." Her face darkened. "But you can't force me to go out with him!" I knew where that was coming from.

"Of course not. You know, Harriet, even if I think it's a good idea for you to go out with someone—and even if your mother does—it's up to you. You know that, right?" She made a –Hmm sound, as if she weren't too sure.

At our next meeting, I broached the subject of the conversation with Keith and that he appeared to have enjoyed her company. Harriet was averse to that avenue of discussion, so I asked what they'd talked about while I was on my condiment quest.

"He had a fight with his mother," Harriet said. "That's why he was alone."

"They had a fight at the mall?"

"No," she said, exasperated. "At home."

"They fought at home, and then he came to the mall?"

"Yes. He walked away." She told me that Keith said he fought a lot with his mother—bad fights, during one of which he pushed her so hard she fell against the open dishwasher door and had to go to the hospital for X-rays. After that, he made a pact with his mother that, when they sensed an argument brewing, they would walk away and cool off before coming to blows.

"Do you think this relates in some way to you and your mom?"

"I don't like being wild."

"I think Keith didn't like being wild, either. But he found a way to control his wildness." I told her that together, we might be able to find a way for her to control the wildness in herself. She nodded; she was willing.

How fortuitous it was to have met Keith that day! The one person Harriet expressed dislike for turned out to be someone whose struggles mirrored her own. It's ironic that we admonish our children never to talk to strangers: We want to keep them safe, but in so doing, we make them vulnerable to loneliness. People on the autism spectrum are notorious for taking things literally: Richard, whom you'll meet later, ate lunch alone every single day in high school because his parents had taught him never to speak to strangers, which is how he perceived all the other kids at school. People with ASD lack much of the social radar that typical people have and are often taken advantage of, especially when they're young and inexperienced. It's eminently logical, then, for their parents to want to protect them. But telling our kids never to speak to strangers makes them wary if not outright suspicious of people they've never met, and this can compound their isolation as they get older.

Table tennis. I run a table tennis therapy program for young adults with high-functioning autism, and I told Harriet's mother I thought she might benefit from a session. "Oh, I don't think so," she said. "Harriet isn't good in groups; she won't be comfortable around kids she doesn't know." Because I'm accustomed to parents trying to dissuade me from exposing their kids to new things, I'm not easily deterred. Harriet's mother was hard to persuade, so convinced was she that an hour of table tennis would be a waste of valuable therapy time. So I told her she didn't have to pay me if the session didn't pay off. She thought I was nuts, which I would have been were I not certain that it would work. In the end she agreed to let Harriet participate if she could come along.

When we got there, I introduced Harriet to a couple of friendly and relatively laid-back kids whom I thought would welcome a newcomer. I instructed them to play for the fun of it without keeping score, hoping to lessen Harriet's anxiety at trying a new sport with new people. I then escorted Harriet's mother to a snack table and sat down with my back to the group.

As we chatted, she became distracted, squinting over my head in the direction of Harriet's group. I became aware of whoops of laughter punctuated by thumps, thuds, and giddy shrieks. "Oh my god," Harriet's mother said. "That's my daughter. That's Harriet." I turned around and saw her jumping gleefully, waving the paddle, bounding from one end of the table to the other as she tried to hit the ball. At one point, she stumbled into a planter and, laughing hysterically, had to be hoisted out by her new friends. Her mother leapt up.

"Oh, no! Should I go over there and tell her to calm down? She's making such a scene—"

"No, no, let her be. She's having a good time." Harriet was boisterous but her joy was contagious: Everyone was laughing along and indulging her. She couldn't play to save her life, but no one seemed to mind. Little by little, she became aware that she was louder than her companions and calmed down a bit. This was a big step for Harriet, regulating her behavior and getting herself under control.

Later, while Harriet was waiting her turn to play, I had her sit next to Daniel, a good-looking 16-year-old with high-functioning autism. Highly observant but limited in speech, Daniel offered, I hoped, a genial contrast to Harriet's newfound vivacity. Harriet began chatting him up immediately, and, although Daniel could barely get a word in edgewise, he was smiling and looked thoroughly engaged.

When Harriet returned for table tennis the following week, I set her and Daniel up to play a game and afterward seated them together on a bench a little bit away from the action. Whenever an errant ball came their way, they took turns retrieving it and tossing it back. Harriet was beaming, hands clasped in her lap and bristling with energy as she plied Daniel with questions: "Do you like pizza?" Daniel nodded. "Maybe you could come over to my house for pizza! Do you like watching *Friends*?"—another nod from Daniel—"Maybe you could come over to my house and watch it! We can ask your mom." By the time they left, Harriet had persuaded her mother to ask Daniel's if he could come over, and she had agreed.

Over the next several months, Daniel came over to Harriet's house for dinner and movie and TV watching. She continued weekly sessions with me, at which her mother reported that Harriet's anger was abating, and, when tempers did start to flare, they would both walk away until they cooled off. I continued to take Harriet on field trips to encourage interactions with new people. We talked about her friendship with Daniel as well as her improving relationship with her mother. I pointed out how generous her mother was, inviting Daniel over so frequently. "Your mother doesn't want to fight with you, Harriet," I told her. "She's just trying to get through her day. And when she comes home, she welcomes your friend to share dinner with you. I think that's nice."

"Yeah, that's what Daniel says. He says my mom is nice, too." Harriet said she was able to control herself better when Daniel was around, and had figured out a way to do it even when he wasn't. "I just pretend he's in the other room and that he would hear me if I got mad," she said. "That way, I can usually calm down."

Harriet marshals her inner strength. One day, Harriet's mother told me that they hadn't seen Daniel in 3 weeks. "Harriet's upset," she said. "She's invited him over a number of times but he keeps having reasons he can't come. And guess whose fault it is? Mine." This may have been bad for Harriet but it was a good moment therapeutically, and I grabbed it as soon as her mother left.

"Harriet, your mother just told me that Daniel hasn't come over in a long time." She ignored me. I pressed on. "What would happen if Daniel didn't want to visit you anymore?" She turned her back on me: She was ticked. After 7 months working with Harriet, I wasn't surprised. I modified my approach.

"If it weren't for me, you would never have met Daniel." She couldn't argue with that. "So if he stopped coming over, would you be angry at me?" No answer.

"Harriet, I'd like you to answer my question. If Daniel stopped coming over, would you be angry at me?" Without turning around, she mumbled no.

"Would you be angry with your mother? Would that be fair?" She muttered something I couldn't make out and I asked her if she would please repeat it.

"I said I don't want to talk about it." She turned around. "I'm making a change from the inside." That said it all. I let it be.

The following week, Harriet, her mother, and I had lunch at a Mexican restaurant. When the waiter brought Harriet her fajitas, she looked up at him and said, "Thank you." Harriet's mother ended our sessions after 8 months. She said she was satisfied: Harriet's anger had mostly dissipated and their occasional arguments no longer escalated to violence. Best of all, Harriet was happier than she'd ever been, which was what she wanted for her daughter. I would have liked to have had more time with Harriet; I think she could have progressed further. Still, she made great strides, and I made my peace with that.

THINGS TO WORK ON AND THINK ABOUT.

• *Yes, you know your child, but she or he may still surprise you.* Harriet's mother was sure her daughter couldn't abide groups, but when Harriet took the racket in her hand, she was transformed into an unselfconscious engine of joy. Her mother was taken aback; this was a side of Harriet she hadn't seen. Don't make assumptions: If you limit the scope of children's experiences, you stymie their development. Don't decide what they like and don't like; that's for them to determine. Remember that your child is constantly maturing and evolving, as will his or her interests and capacities. There are depths of potential down there—urge your child to dive in.

- *Are you over-managing your child?* Many children with ASD require vigilant supervision when they're very young: Ill-equipped to interpret social cues and confounded by expectations, they need loving adults to translate the world into terms they can understand and guide them as they make their way through it. But if we try to over-manage these kids, they will respond with the same resentment as their neurotypical peers. In the pizza place, I resisted my own reflexive urge to coax Harriet into thanking Sal for offering her ice cream because I knew it would infuriate her. Moreover, I wanted her to express herself in a genuine way, which she eventually did. Think about how you intervene in your child's interactions with the world. Do you give her space to come to her own decisions or press her into making what you believe are the right ones? Are you standing by to guide him through awkward situations or leaping into the fray so he can avoid them? Resist as best you can the impulse to over-manage your child.

KEN, 16

**High-functioning; socially awkward;
anxious; obsessive.**

"**H**e has no friends, not one," Ken's mother told me. "I can understand why: He can't focus long enough to have a conversation,
he blames other people for stuff he does wrong, and once he gets something
in his head, he's stuck there obsessively. Oh, and when he's happy, he flaps
his arms like Big Bird. The other kids all think he's weird, which I guess
he is." A visit to Ken's school confirmed his mother's description. The other
kids—special ed. students, as he was—didn't include him in conversation;
even at lunch, he sat alone. Worse, his eccentric behaviors led teachers to
underestimate his intellectual potential, and the work they gave him wasn't
challenging. As a sophomore in high school, he had only a few years left
to break away from the vocational path he was on. Or is on, I should say:
Ken is a current client; we've been working together for about five months
as I write this.

Ken's mother wanted him to become "more normal socially," as she
put it. Ken lived alone with her and I inferred they were each other's sole
source of companionship—not a healthy situation for either of them. My
goal, then, would be to help Ken develop the skills he needed to make and
keep a friend and start working toward independence.

For the first 2 months, I took Ken out for pizza, ice cream, tacos,
you name it (I'm blessed with speedy metabolism so I can eat a lot).

Verbal exchanges consisted mostly of him peppering me with questions on whether I had ever played whichever video game he was into that week. When I'd start a conversation about something else—a presidential primary debate, say, or the latest film in the Bourne or Bond franchise—Ken would focus only long enough to say whether or not he'd seen it or wanted to see it before pulling out his cell phone and tapping madly away. It wasn't until we went to a fast food restaurant that inspiration hit.

Music therapy. Ken loves fried chicken and flapped his arms across the parking lot and into the store, where we placed our order and moved aside to wait. Someone's boom box was thumping away, and Ken began moving his arms in a sort of funky chicken dance. He wasn't aware of what he was doing, nor did he see anything odd about flitting out of the store before our food came up (I guided him back inside). But his physical response to the throbbing bass line made me think that Ken might be a candidate for music therapy.

The following week, Talia was already in my office when Ken arrived. Like Sasha, the music therapist I hired to work with Freya (p. 135), Talia is starting out in her career and wants experience working with people with autism. She arrayed her collection of sand blocks, rhythm sticks, and shakers, as well as a tambourine and xylophone on a table, and greeted Ken, who declined to look up from his cell phone. "I don't think he likes me," Talia whispered. I told her this was pretty typical of kids with autism and not to take it personally.

Ken did look up when she addressed him again and asked him to select an instrument and start tapping out a rhythm. He chose the tambourine and began smacking it against his leg; Talia used the sand blocks to follow Ken's beat. After a few minutes, she asked him to stop to allow her to establish a rhythm that he could follow. Ken ignored her, banging the tambourine and bobbing his head. She let him continue to play on his own, watching as he switched instruments and periodically repeating her request. After an emphatic request from me that he stop and let Talia lead off a new rhythm, he stopped, listened, and took turns responding to her beats. They were conversing, she with the shuush-shuush of sand blocks and he pounding on the xylophone. It was as if she were speaking in a normal tone of voice and he were shouting.

"Ken, could you try playing softly now?" Talia asked. But he continued pounding, either unable or unwilling to modulate his volume. She began chanting in time to the music they were making—Glad to see you; keep on playing—and I joined in with the rhythm sticks, chanting my own thoughts—Thanks for coming, making music—until a raucous, rhythmic cacophony filled the room.

Then, as Ken banged on the xylophone, one of the mallets flew out of his hand, hit the wall, and its spherical head popped off. As he scampered to retrieve the pieces, I remembered his mother saying he never took responsibility for his actions. I seized the moment and said, "You broke my mallet." Frantically pressing the pieces together, Ken said, "I fixed it! I fixed it!" And he had. But I wanted him to acknowledge that he'd broken it.

"Yes, but you were banging it so hard that it broke."

"I didn't, I didn't, I didn't, I didn't."

"But you did, Ken." I spoke gently and smiled.

"I'm sorry! I'm sorry! I'm sorry! I'm sorry!" The words were appropriate but the delivery was mechanical. I wanted him to connect both with me and the reality of the moment.

"Ken, ask Talia if she thinks you broke the mallet."

"I fixed it!" he shouted. He kept repeating that he'd fixed it, and I calmly repeated, "Ask Talia and see what she says." He was angry and beginning to shout.

I was wondering if Ken were going to storm out when he grabbed a mallet in each hand and began pummeling the xylophone, drowning me out. There was a rhythm to his rage, and I began chanting what I imagined was going through his mind: I told you that I fixed it! I fixed the stupid mallet! Why won't you listen to me? I don't want to talk to Talia! Stop it, stop it, stop it! It was my first therapeutic rap. After a few minutes, Ken's force abated and his playing slowed. I gently took the xylophone from his lap and said, "Ask Talia if she thinks you broke the mallet."

"Talia, do you think I broke the mallet?" he asked, subdued.

"You did break it but you fixed it, and everything's okay." Ken's face relaxed.

This was a provocative intervention but an effective one, as it got Ken to express his feelings through music rather than fleeing the scene. I wanted Ken to take responsibility for his actions and understand that even though he broke the mallet, it was okay—not only because he fixed it, but because people usually forgive you when you admit you made a mistake. In so doing,

I caused him to get riled, but it was worth it: We all have to learn to deal with anger and our own fallibility. Moreover, we have to learn that our actions have consequences. Ken was surprised when I told him that Talia thought he didn't like her. I explained that it was because he never looked up from his phone when she greeted him, and asked what he'd do next time they met. He promised to say hello.

Music and beyond. When Ken arrived the following week, he responded to Talia's greeting and smiled. She said she wanted him to assign instruments to the three of us that day. "Me choose?" he asked. "Yes," Talia replied. "Choose for everyone?" "Yes, Ken. You choose for everyone." He handed us each an instrument and then went on to tell Talia and me who should start and who should follow. In 2½ months with Ken, it was the first time I'd seen him assert his preferences rather than be merely reactive.

The following week, I invited Talia to join Ken and me on a trip to a nearby farm and produce stand. Talia wanted to participate in sessions even if they didn't involve music, which worked well: Three people create a more complex dynamic than two, and I wanted Ken to become comfortable in groups. I hoped the trip might spark some fruitful interactions, but the most productive ones happened before we even left the office.

They had to do with Ken's cell phone, to which he's overly attached (who isn't?). I'd asked his mother not to admonish him to put it away when he arrived, as she usually did. In fact, she often coached Ken on what to say and do, urging him to stand up, shake hands, say hello and goodbye. He had always needed her to direct him so he could function in social situations. This dynamic often comes to define the parent-child relationship, as was the case with Harriet and her mother. I believe it's my job to interrupt this pattern so my ASD clients learn more typical social behaviors from the inside out. Only then can they cultivate and maintain friendships.

Now I stood before Ken in the waiting room, waiting for him to notice me. He eventually looked up, saw me, looked at his mother, looked back at me, and then turned to his mother.

"Aren't you going to ask me something?" he said.

"What should I ask you?" Ken looked confused.

"Aren't you going to ask me something." This time it was a statement. When she didn't answer, he spoke again. "Aren't you going to ask me to put my cell phone away?"

"What do you think you should do?" she asked. After a moment, he handed her the cell phone. This was significant: Ken decided to leave the phone behind without being pressured. Perhaps assigning the instruments the week before had given him a pleasing taste of agency.

Things got more interesting when he came into the office. Talia was there, and after some words of greeting, I suggested we leave for the farm, at which point Ken went out to the waiting room to get his phone. Talia and I followed him, whereupon the conversation became surreal.

"Ken, are you thinking of taking your phone?" I asked.

"Yes. I want to take my phone." This was maybe two minutes after he'd left it behind; he was back on automatic pilot. Then he surprised me.

"Talia," he said, "what do you think?"

"I think it would take away from our time with one another."

"Okay. I'll leave it behind."

"All right," I said. "And why are you leaving it behind?"

"Because my mother doesn't want me to take it." His mother had nothing to do with it, of course; it was he who decided not to take it. I wanted to shake him loose from the habit of always hearing his mother's voice in his head. As we were leaving the office, I pushed the issue.

"So Ken, why did you leave your cell phone behind?" He was silent. "Was it because your mother forced you to?" Ken stopped and thought.

"No. It's because of what Talia said." Yes!

"What's that?"

"She said it would be distracting." Now, this was progress. Distracting was Ken's word, not Talia's.

"What will you do next time?" I asked.

"Not bring the cell phone," he said.

What a terrific exchange! It was as self-revealing a conversation as Ken had ever had with me, maybe with anyone. More importantly, he had left his phone behind because he decided to, not because anyone had admonished him to do so. It was an act of self-direction and the beginning of Ken asserting control over his life. The following week, the three of us decided to go out for ice cream and I noticed Ken's phone in his pocket. I casually reminded him that he'd had a reason for leaving it behind last time. "Oh, yeah, it's a distraction," he said, handing it to his mother. As we walked to the parking garage, I asked if he wanted to take his phone along, and he answered with a resolute no. Ken had made an independent decision without going on automatic pilot.

Two steps forward, one step back, three steps forward. Ken's forays into conversation grew. In the car one day, I mentioned that Talia had grown up in Italy. Ken came alive. "Have you ever seen the Leaning Tower of Pisa? How was it built? Did they make it lean on purpose? Who invented pasta?" When I answered that the Chinese invented pasta, he was flabbergasted. "Really? How come? I thought pasta came from Italy! How do you say pizza in Italian? How do you say pizza in Chinese?" You might associate this level of inquiry with a much younger person, but it was a major accomplishment for Ken, whose conversation had previously strayed no further than factoids about video games. But there was still work to do: When I revived the topic with his mother later on, he was unable to focus on our conversation and piped up twice with irrelevant remarks before gluing himself to his phone. Still, I knew he was capable of responding relevantly to a conversation: He had done it that day in the car, and several weeks earlier through music.

Ken continued to blossom and surprise me. At a hot dog stand one day, I mentioned that I liked ketchup on my French fries, and he got me some. Later, he offered to get mustard for me, and, when I said I was thirsty, poured half his cola into my cup. He seemed pleased to help, which was great: Taking pleasure in helping someone is fundamental to friendship, and helping Ken make a friend is our priority. I thanked him every time he helped me without making a big a deal out of it, because I wanted my responses to resemble those a friend might make. On the ride home, I told him that I thought he'd behaved differently than usual and asked him what he thought. "Was I considerate?" he asked. Wanting to steer him away from needing me to define him, I asked what he meant. "I got you ketchup and I got you mustard. And I shared my soda with you. Is that what you mean?" I said it was, and asked him how he felt about doing those things. "I feel good," he said. The following week, he took me aside and said he wanted us to surprise Talia and take her to the ice cream parlor. "That's a good idea," I said. "Would you call that being considerate?" He said he thought it was, and I agreed with him, reminding him of his thoughtful condiment runs and noting that these were things he wouldn't have done before. If Ken became aware of how much he was evolving and how good it felt, the behaviors would be reinforced.

Donut dilemma. Ken was beginning to respond to social cues, a crucial element of forming a friendship. I told Talia I wanted to begin the next session with us making music and having Ken respond. I began a percussive rhythm on the tambourine, then stopped; Talia responded on the xylophone and stopped; then we looked at Ken, who took up the rhythm on the wood block. As we continued taking up and creating variations on each other's rhythms, a gentle smile softened Ken's face: He was relaxing, losing himself in the music. A minute later, he made an announcement.

"This is boring."

"Boring?" I asked. "But you're smiling. You look happy."

"I'm bored." I suggested that what he called boredom might actually be serenity, a new sensation for him. "Whatever," he said. "Let's get donuts."

As the three of us were leaving the waiting room, Ken asked his mother if he could please have two donuts instead of one.

"No, one's enough," she said.

"But I want two!"

"No, Ken. One donut."

"But, I said please! Why can't I have two?" I love the logic here: I said please, so I'm entitled to whatever I want. Actually, no: Asking politely is still asking. We need to start training kids, typical and atypical alike, that when they ask for something, no is still a possible outcome. In a couple of years, Ken would be asking for a car or two; then what? I told Ken that he could stay and argue with his mother but that Talia and I were leaving, and we did. He ran after us.

At the shop, the young woman took Ken's order for a strawberry frosted sprinkle donut and then—I'm not making this up—told him she liked his face and gave him a second one, on the house. Now we had a problem.

"What do I do? Can I eat both?" he asked.

"I'm not sure."

"Why not? It didn't cost anything."

"It's not the cost. It's that your mother said she wanted you to eat only one."

"But she's not here and you are. What should I do?" The step forward was that Ken was conversing with and not shouting at me; the step back was that he still needed to take orders from an adult. I suggested he eat one and ask his mother about the other one.

Walking back to the office, there were more forward steps: Ken thanked me for taking him for donuts and didn't obsess about the second one. Upon returning, he told his mother that he'd had a good time, that the woman in the shop liked him, and that she had given him a second donut free. Only then did he ask if he could eat it. When his mother said he could have it after dinner, he didn't argue. She later told me he forgot about it until the following morning—a sign that his obsessiveness was waning.

An unexpected outcome. Encouraged by Ken's response to music therapy, I invested in a guitar and some small drums. Talia and I improvise ways of getting Ken to connect with us through music, and it's working: Learning to respond to us musically has eased Ken into the realm of responding to other people. He is also modulating his emotions more effectively, which I think is a result of modulating his music making in our sessions. His obsessiveness is diminishing, if not gone: After freaking out about not getting a perfect score on a math test, he came home from school the following week and told his mother that he'd gotten two tests back—88% and 99%—and, although he was disappointed, he'd try to do better next time. Ken is developing more realistic expectations of himself and learning to defuse inflammatory situations by thinking and acting reasonably.

Music is also reducing his anxiety, which we learned in an unexpected way.

One day, Talia invited Ken to hum along as she strummed the guitar. He declined. She began humming quietly and singing a phrase here and there. Ken began sagging in his chair; eventually, he walked out to the waiting room, lay down on the sofa, and fell asleep for the rest of the session. His mother was convinced he was ill. I didn't know what to think until that evening when she called to tell me that, for the rest of the day, Ken had been agreeable, easygoing, and had not flapped his arms once. "It's the strangest thing," she said. "It was like he was a normal kid."

Talia and I were eager to reproduce the experience the following week but Ken resolutely stayed awake; such are the vagaries of therapy. But three sessions later, Ken surprised us again. The three of us took up our instruments and began playing, responding to one another, taking turns taking the lead. Talia and I introduced rhythmic variations and Ken followed along, sometimes creating his own. We changed instruments, trading among one another and sometimes playing two at once.

We then had a spirited conversation about religion and Italian culture. His creative juices were flowing and we followed his lead until he stopped talking and started playing the ocean drum, a shallow circular vessel containing hundreds of pellets that, when you tilt it gently, sound like the ebb and flow of surf. Ken did this for a while before carrying the drum out to the waiting room, where he lay down on the sofa. Talia followed with the guitar and began to sing, incorporating language from the conversation we'd just had and murmuring his name from time to time. Ken put the drum on the floor, closed his eyes, and fell asleep for 20 minutes as his mother looked on in disbelief. A few hours later she texted me: "Wow. Incredible. Ate fish tonight for the first time in his life. Did his homework and finished in less than an hour. Seems happy, no anxiety."

The next time we met, Ken grabbed the ocean drum, sat in a chair, and began to play. Talia and I joined in. Ten minutes later he slid to the floor, lay down, and played there. His rhythm gradually slowed until he fell asleep. Was he anticipating that the music would relax him? Had he willed his mind to relinquish obsessive thoughts and allow a natural flow to prevail? Did he know at some level what he needed to do to comfort himself and ease his anxiety?

At our most recent session, Ken took the guitar into his lap and began sweeping his hand across the strings. Talia took up his rhythm on wood blocks, and Ken startled her by looking directly in her eyes and holding her gaze as she played. When I joined in on tambourine, he turned and locked eyes with me. It was no accident: When Talia started a new rhythm soon after, Ken turned away from me and resumed eye contact with her. For the rest of the session, Ken deliberately connected with each of us, gazing into our eyes. It was an intimate connection that ebbed and flowed between us, much like the connection linking jazz musicians as they take solo riffs in the midst of a tune. Did he know he was doing it? Will he do it again?

We're still working on it. As is his mother, who's taking guitar lessons.

THINGS TO WORK ON AND THINK ABOUT.

• *Are you your child's only friend?* Parents who bring their kids for therapy have various dreams for them, and I have one, too: to help each and every one develop the social skills and emotional capacity to make a genuine friend. It is through friendships that children build confidence, self-worth, and an idea of how they appear to others. The insular nature of Ken's home life—he lives alone with his mother—encourages his dependency on adult guidance. Is there a similar dynamic in your family? Are the adults in your child's life his or her primary companions? If so, you might want to think about how you can wean your child away from dependency on adults and toward companions his or her own age. It's not abdicating your responsibility; quite the opposite: It's helping your child grow into a self-sufficient, competent adult.

• *Speech is one language; music is another.* Many people with autism spectrum disorder exhibit a heightened sensitivity to music. Bestselling author and autism advocate John Elder Robison writes eloquently that his great success as a sound engineer for rock bands derived from his high-functioning autism.[4] Music therapy has been shown to help persons with ASD reduce perseveration and other self-stimulating behaviors in favor of those that foster engagement with people.[5] In my own practice, it helped Freya, a nonverbal child, begin to speak, and prompted Ken, a highly verbal, intelligent teenager, to respond more typically to others. It might help your child, too.

KAITLYN, 16

> Perseverative; nonverbal; physically aggressive.

Kaitlyn's mother told me her daughter was diagnosed with autism a decade earlier, had been in special education classes all her life, and never acquired language. But the main thing she wanted to know was how to cope with her daughter's aggressiveness. "She's bigger than I am," she said, "and I don't know what to do when she gets mad, which is often. She was never an angry person, but more and more, she's getting into these states where she yells and bangs on the table and throws things. She's even hit her sister a few times. Maya was the best friend she had, but now even she's backed off." I said it was possible, even likely, that Kaitlyn's outbursts were manifestations of her frustration at not being able to speak, and asked her to bring her in.

A week later, she sat in my office trying to force a jigsaw puzzle piece into a spot where it clearly didn't belong. "It's not going to be able to go there, Kait," I said calmly one, two, five, seven times. Still, she pressed on; it was as if I were speaking Mandarin, so oblivious was she to my words. After a while she began to whine, making sounds that vaguely resembled words, then arose angrily and strode to the corner of the room, where she stood with her arms crossed over her chest. Her mother witnessed the scene and said it was typical, only at home she might have swept the puzzle onto the floor.

Kaitlyn communicated by using her body, not words: When she was hungry or thirsty, she pulled her mother toward the refrigerator; at school, she pointed to a sign with the toilet logo when she needed the bathroom. School itself was less than stimulating for Kaitlyn: Enrolled in a task-oriented vocational program, she spent her day learning to count out small items—screws and washers, nuts and bolts—into plastic bags, or arranging canned goods into displays like those in supermarkets. Her mother acknowledged that Kaitlyn's intelligence was probably average at best, but was determined to help her evolve into a functioning adult who could express and look out for herself.

Kaitlyn's perseverative nature prevented her from conceptualizing even basic elements of daily life. I brought out a xylophone and played "Mary Had a Little Lamb"—a basic melody comprising only four notes— several times, then handed her the mallet. Kaitlyn was unable to play even the first note and instead pounded the instrument with neither intention nor thought. She seemed not to notice that striking different bars created different sounds, nor that not striking them punctuated the racket with silence. She just banged away until she grew tired of it.

Abandoning the xylophone, she pointed to a stuffed green fabric alligator about eighteen inches long. As I handed it to her, she grabbed a tissue and began rubbing it rhythmically in the alligator's mouth, as if cleaning its teeth. Her movements appeared as mindless as they had with the xylophone, devoid of attention to what she was doing. Her obsessive focus on the puzzle piece and mindless repetition with the alligator and xylophone were perseverative behaviors that I believed comforted her.

I learned a lot that day: Not only did Kaitlyn have a perseverative mentality, her mind had never forged a connection between language and meaning, something that happens for typical children between the ages of 1 and 2. After observing her obsessiveness, I tested her understanding of big and small by handing her a red M&M and a Wiffle ball and asking her to point to the larger one. She couldn't do it, even after I rephrased the question several times. But when I handed her the spindle toy and asked her to apply the rings in size order, she was able to do it by trial and error, placing and removing and replacing the rings until she got it right. This showed me that she could discern small from large if she worked with concrete objects and exhausted all the options. But she could not think abstractly; she was not able to conceptualize the words big and small, larger and smaller as describing the relationship between the objects in her hands.

Getting Kaitlyn to speak. Kaitlyn needed to forge a connection between the concrete world, her actions in it, and the concept that words could be used to describe them. If I could get her to connect emotionally to something she were doing, language might erupt and take hold. I handed her a ball, backed up two feet, held out my hands, and said, "Kait, throw the ball," which she did. Tossing it back, I said, "Kait, catch the ball." And so it went with me narrating until she started telling me to catch and throw the ball when it was my turn. All well and good—but I wanted to make sure she wasn't merely mimicking what she'd been hearing. So when I caught the ball, I held it and asked, "What should I do?" until Kaitlyn told me to throw it. This established a new pattern of Kaitlyn responding to a direct query, something most of us learn at a very young age.

I began using the exercise in different contexts—watering the plant; feeding the fish; building with plastic bricks; drawing—and describing in words what we were doing while asking Kaitlyn simple questions. But whereas she was able to answer them, her voice was flat and monotonous. She still wasn't feeling what she was talking about.

***Getting to* up.** Up is one of the first words young children say because they associate it viscerally with action—when they stretch out their arms to be hoisted aloft—and hear adults use it in a variety of contexts: Look up at the sky! Come on, stand up! Time to wake up! I began a remediation program with Kaitlyn, asking her to pick up a book, jump up from her chair, and, most effectively, to look up and see the alligator that I'd placed atop a cabinet, which I then urged her to retrieve by using a stepstool. When she did, I tossed the alligator back up, verbalizing my actions, and we climbed up together to retrieve it. We repeated this five, six, seven times, because I hoped that Kaitlyn would utter up on her own. She did not that day. But over the next few sessions, she did.

A tilting turning point. About two months into our sessions, I took Kaitlyn on a field trip to a carnival. Her mother warned me that she would be too scared to go on any rides, but gave me the OK and asked if she might come separately, in her own car, and lag behind us to observe, which was fine with me.

PART 4: ADOLESCENCE (Kaitlyn, 16)

Kaitlyn pointed to the Tilt-A-Whirl™ and walked toward it. I asked if she wanted to go on and she kept on walking, mounting the steps to the boarding platform. I spoke to the young man operating the ride and told him my companion might get frightened and need to bail; he said that was no problem. I told Kait that the man promised to stop the ride whenever she wanted to get off, and we quickly practiced getting into the car, gripping the hand rail, saying off!, and exiting the car. The ride started slowly and the car spun gently a bit to the left and then to the right. Kait was fine. Then, as it sped up, I saw her hands tighten on the rail. I kept up a running commentary, talking about how the car was moving, smiling and relaxing into the seat, never taking my eyes off her. Now the ride was in full spin and Kait's face stiffened. A moment later, she said Off!—the first word she had ever spontaneously uttered to communicate something she felt in the moment. Both affect and meaning were there; it was as if she were experimenting to see if this word stuff really worked. I immediately signaled the operator, he stopped the ride, and we got off.

Later, Kait wanted to go back on the ride. I looked over to where her mother was lurking; she shrugged and smiled, which I took as a yes. As Kait and I mounted the steps to the platform, I asked her if she wanted to go up onto the ride, or off, to which she vigorously shook her head no. I repeated the question several times and every time she shook her head no to getting off. We ascended the steps and she pulled me toward an empty car, at which point she locked eyes with her mother, who now was standing nearby. "Mommy!" she cried, pointing to the car. Kaitlyn's mother clambered up the steps, hugged her daughter, and settled into the car with her as

I sidled off (and gave the ride operator a nice tip for letting us schlep on and off). It was the only time I ever expect to see a grown woman weep at the prospect of riding the Tilt-A-Whirl. And they stayed on for the whole ride.

Next came bumper cars, with Kaitlyn and me in one car and her mother in another. Kaitlyn was driving and had a big grin on her face as she rammed her mother's car. "Hit mommy!" I shouted, and my client obliged, crying, "Hit mommy!" over and over with force and commitment as her mother smiled gamely and tried not to sustain whiplash. As we were leaving, Kaitlyn pointed to a concession stand and said, "Drink water." At home several days later, she said, "Open bottle." The dam had broken. Kaitlyn had begun to speak.

Old behaviors abate. At the next session, when Kaitlyn began to perseverate with a shape sorter, rubbing one piece rhythmically over another, I asked, "Kait, do you want to rub the pieces together or do you want to put the circle where it should go?" She did not quite understand the question, but she did stop rubbing and, after a brief pause, resumed sorting the shapes. This was progress, even if she didn't answer verbally, as Kaitlyn would never have stopped perseverating in response to speech before. I had faith that, just as with younger children on the spectrum, Kaitlyn would stop perseverating when she realized she could control her behavior and, to a great extent, her world. It would just take time.

The following week, standing with Kaitlyn at the fish tank, I lifted out a cardinal tetra in the net. Kaitlyn was distressed. "Where should I put the fish?" I asked. "In water," she replied. "Should I eat the fish?" I asked.

"Don't ... fish," she said, meaning I should not eat the fish. I lowered the fish into the water. "Shall we feed the fish?" I asked. Kaitlyn fetched the jar of food and, when she couldn't get it open, handed it to me and said, "Open bottle."

Around this time, Kaitlyn's mother reported that her hitting had stopped, her yelling and perseveration had subsided, and she was using about a dozen two-word sentences at home to express her needs: More meat, thirsty now, wear dress, not hungry were becoming commonplace utterances, along with Maya mean! when her sister declined to do her bidding. In my office one day, she pretended to cut up an apple and, taking the fruit in her hand, waved it around as if it were on an airplane before delivering it to my mouth. When I took the apple and paused, she said, "Eat it," which, of course, I did. I had no doubt that the de-escalation of Kaitlyn's aggression was connected to her burgeoning use of language to express her needs. Her frustration had not evaporated—whose ever does?—but it was lessening.

Homework. About four months in, Kaitlyn's mother asked to attend sessions so she could see what I was doing and reproduce it at home. We began working as a team, each building on the other's work to intensify Kaitlyn's exposure to language anchored in meaning. We made it fun. I'd open a bag of Oreos and say, "Kait, give mommy a cookie." That was easy. Then I'd make it harder and say, "Now tell mommy to give a cookie to Rob," which she was eventually able to do. Then I might tell her to ask mommy to give her, Kaitlyn, a cookie, and so on.

These were simple, everyday verbal exchanges that imbued Kaitlyn's awareness with new meaning. Watching a child use language in new ways for the first time is a moving experience, especially when the child is on the cusp of adulthood.

The mother's efforts paid off: One day, Kaitlyn walked into the office and announced, "Uncle Steve drove me today." A five-word sentence! I controlled my impulse to turn a somersault and smiled instead.

"Uncle Steve? Who's he?" I asked.

"Uncle Steve! He's my favorite."

"He's your favorite uncle?"

"Yeah, my favorite uncle."

"Why is he your favorite?"

"We laugh. He's funny. He takes me places."

"He takes you places? Where does he take you?"

"Here." She thought a moment. "And the museum. And ice cream." And so it went. I asked about Uncle Steve and heard he was her mother's brother, had a dog named Bongo, and a black car with a top that went up and down. Her sentences were short and lucid, and they flowed logically. In 8 months, Kaitlyn had gone from using virtually no meaningful language to expressing herself in simple sentences. It was a dazzling progression for which her mother deserves much of the credit. When other parents might have given up, this woman found the time and energy to learn what she needed to do to help her daughter.

Kaitlyn left my practice soon after when her father, who was divorced from her mother, agreed to pay for her to attend a residential program.

PART 4: ADOLESCENCE (Kaitlyn, 16)

When her mother last contacted me, she said that Kaitlyn was adjusting to living away from home and had made friends at her new school.

THINGS TO WORK ON AND THINK ABOUT.

- *Persevere: You never know when your child's mind will ignite.* That day at the carnival when Kaitlyn understood that saying off could bring everything to a halt, a tiny spark lit her mind: If I make this sound in just this way, I can make the world stop! It's something most of us take for granted, but it's a revelation for someone with autism. Whereas I may have gotten Kaitlyn started, her mother gets kudos for urging her on and persevering. I cannot emphasize enough the power that parents have to enhance their child's development. Once a spark is struck, a parent's consistent care and attention can kindle it into a steady flame.

- *Nurture trust: When your child starts to speak, respect what she or he says.* When Kaitlyn said off to let me know she'd had enough of the Tilt-A-Whirl, it was crucial that I keep my promise and stop the ride immediately. That moment taught her that speech had power, that she could rescue herself from discomfort with one word. And it was that knowledge that empowered her to risk going back on the ride. Had I tried to coax her to stay on longer when she said off, I would have destroyed the trust she placed in me, and probably dissuaded her from risking another spin. Using words for the first time requires a leap of faith. Parents can help their children take that leap by respecting their fledgling forays into language.

MARTY, 16

Highly intelligent; gifted artist; perfectionistic;
acts in memorized preset patterns.

Arriving for his first session, Marty ambled into my office holding a sheaf of paper and a charcoal pencil, sat down, and began to draw. One by one, an array of eccentric sea creatures emerged that turned out to be the cast of SpongeBob SquarePants. Marty also could recite from memory the dialogue of entire episodes. Week after week, he set about painstakingly drawing the inhabitants of Bikini Bottom, telling me their names and describing salient aspects of their characters, crossing out those he deemed imperfect and redoing them until he was satisfied. When I commented on his powerful recall of all things SpongeBob, he proceeded to write down the lyrics to 17 songs from the series.

Left to his artistic devices, Marty was a happy fellow. But his prodigious capacity for memorization and repetition masked an inability to think things through in the moment. One clue was the perfection with which he approached his artwork. Many times he would labor over a drawing, repeatedly tweaking the angle of a fin or the arch of an eyebrow, only to find it imperfect, scribble it over, and start again. If he couldn't produce a SpongeBob character precisely as he recalled it, it was a failure. He allowed no room for artistic license. There would be no variations, only the theme, which was ironic: Here Marty was, a talented artist who was comfortable only when reproducing other people's art.

First impression. Tall, lanky, and unusually bright, Marty had been in special ed. programs since kindergarten. Like many teens with high-functioning autism, he was exceptionally knowledgeable in one specific area, a characteristic that Hans Asperger dubbed the little professor syndrome. One summer decades ago, my family was in a New Hampshire store that had an old rifle suspended from the ceiling. Jed and Dylan, who were about 7 and 10 at the time, were standing beneath it, transfixed, when a boy of about 14 came over and launched into an exegesis about the rifle—who manufactured it and when, how it worked, what kind of ammunition it took, what it was likely used for—you name it, he knew it. We tried to ask him questions but couldn't get a word in edgewise, so intent was he on telling us everything he knew. And he knew it all, just as Marty knew everything about SpongeBob and his pals.

It was this obsessive memorization of details that prompted Marty's parents to bring him in for therapy. "He's very smart—he's been tested, so we know—but he's having serious trouble at school," they said. "Now he's started walking out of the classroom several times a day. He just gets up and leaves, and they find him out in the hall, walking around. He's not trying to run away, but his teacher's getting pretty fed up." I was reminded of Nate, the camper from years ago who would flee the classroom to ease his stress. They were concerned that, despite his intellectual and artistic gifts, he would end up ill-prepared to do anything but a menial job after high school. They wanted me to help Marty focus on his schoolwork so he might fulfill his potential. At least they saw his potential; this augured well.

After watching him draw for a while, I asked Marty if he could multiply six times four. He answered quickly and correctly. But when I asked him what six times four-and-a-half was, he was stumped. Memorizing multiplication tables was easy for Marty, but conceptualizing what multiplication meant was not. Moreover, he wouldn't try to reason his way through a problem: Rather than risk taking a wrong turn and sounding unintelligent, he would shake his head and repeat, "I don't know. I don't know." His responses were consistently evasive. When I asked him what a cubic inch was, he replied, "An inch of measuring cubic," offering a semantic runaround rather than admitting he didn't know. Concepts eluded him. His class was learning geometry, an understanding of which requires an ability to grasp concepts such as the Pythagorean theorem, which Marty recited verbatim: "The square of the hypotenuse of a right triangle is equal to the sum of the squares of its other two sides"—so far, so good. But when I asked him what it meant, he couldn't describe a right triangle or a hypotenuse, let alone the relationship among them.

Marty's extraordinary memory had enabled him to survive academically and even impress people, including me. During a discussion of ancient Egypt, he once said, "*Tutankhamun* means 'living image of Amun.' His last name is *Nebkheperure*, which means 'Lord or possessor of forms of Re.'" I had recently attended the King Tut exhibit at the Metropolitan Museum of Art and bought the accompanying book, which I later scoured unsuccessfully for this factoid. But now, well into his sophomore year of high school, he was required to reason as well as memorize, and he was unaccustomed to thinking about the ideas underlying issues in history, government, social studies, and the novels he read in English class. He could recite names and dates of important events but could grasp neither their causes nor significance. With this in mind, I asked why he was walking out of class so often.

"I get tired," he said.

"Well," I said, "if you ever get tired while you're here with me, let me know and we'll do something else."

"Really?"

"Yes, really."

"Wow. That's, like, great." My guess was that Marty was feeling overwhelmed, not fatigued, and that's what was driving him from the classroom.

At his mother's request, I contacted Marty's teacher, who agreed to send me copies of his curriculum, handouts, and homework assignments. I began helping Marty with his schoolwork, prodding him to reason his way though problems, step by fumbling step. Starting small, I asked him to calculate the area of a rectangle that was 4 inches long and 2 inches high. He recited the formula—length times width equals area—and I asked him what the area would be. "Eight inches of square," he said. I asked him what that meant and he repeated his answer but could not explain it. So I drew a 4- by 2-inch rectangle and divided it into 1-inch squares. We counted 8 of them, determined that each square measured 1 inch per side, used the formula to arrive at an area of 1 square inch each, and then counted up to eight: 8 square inches. When Marty had a visual representation of the formula, he grasped its logic; he was able to think through the formula rather than merely memorize it.

But old habits die hard, and Marty wasn't leaping onto the logic band-wagon. One day I lit a match, blew it out, and watched the wisp of vapor curl upward.

"Boy," I said, "I'd be in big trouble if I set off the smoke alarm. What do you think would happen to the computer if there was water everywhere?" Marty knitted his brow and pondered the question—for nearly 3 minutes.

"I know," he said. "It would not be good." This was a safe response and also a vague and disconnected one: There was no way that blowing out a match would trigger a smoke alarm. I pressed him to be more specific, whereupon he deduced that the computer would get wet and be of no fur-ther use.

"What do you think would happen to the printer?" I asked. Marty ru-minated again.

"It would not be good." Loath to risk a wrong answer, Marty again retreated to a safe and obvious one. To him, reasoning was fraught with peril, so he chose not to think rather than risk facing ridicule. My mission was to help build confidence in his ability to think rationally and effectively.

Coaxing Marty to think. I began by doing a classic card trick in which I fanned out the deck face down, asked him to choose four specific cards one at a time, and then shocked him by showing him he'd picked the very cards I'd asked for. It's a simple trick (you can watch it demonstrated on YouTube) and, when you first see it, mystifying. I asked Marty how he thought I did it.

"I don't know."

"Think about it, Marty. How could I have gotten you to select certain cards when they were face down?"

"I don't know. I give up."

"Marty, if you think about this for a while, you'll figure it out." We worked through the trick slowly and calmly and when he figured it out, Marty was ecstatic. This was the sort of small success he needed to prove he was capable of reasoning.

Next, I presented Marty with a seriation challenge, in which he had to put in order a set of cards that illustrated the stages of a balloon being gradually inflated until it popped. Spreading the cards out before him, he began perspiring and ordering the cards randomly. I reminded him that he could use his brain to think it through, that he didn't have to make wild guesses and risk being wrong. He calmed down and began to reason his way through the task until he completed it, on his own, with no coaching from me. Next I gave Marty another seriation task: to order a set of cards illustrating the steps involved in writing and mailing a letter. Once again he panicked, resorting to random arrangements of cards in hopes of hitting on the right one. Then, after calming himself and approaching the challenge anew, he was able to figure it out.

For Marty, as for many people with high-functioning autism, two fundamental elements would comprise the remediation process: First, he needed to break out of his rigidity and perfectionism; second, he needed to find and embrace new ways to make his life easier. To address his rigidity, I began with his drawing, which was how he started every session. When he insisted that he needed to draw, then spent 20 minutes making art, and then ripped up pages of drawings and began redoing them, I did what most parents and teachers learn quickly: I distracted him.

"Let's do homework," I suggested. "I'll work with you." He looked up at me, pencil still, and considered the offer. He had to do the assignments; maybe they'd be less onerous if he did them with me. So he set his drawing aside for a while. It was a hairline crack in his edifice of sameness; in time, the small cracks would form a big one and the edifice would shatter. Marty's confidence would grow as he continued to take on and successfully cope with the unknown. Eventually, he would do it without me.

Engaging Marty's teacher in challenging his mind. It became increasingly clear that the curriculum at Marty's school wasn't helping matters. Every day, he received a social studies handout requiring him to read a paragraph about an event in American history and then to fill in a blank with a sentence almost identical to one from the paragraph. So mindless was the task, you could complete it almost without being able to read or understand the material, let alone analyze the event it described. This distressed me mightily, as Marty was a highly intelligent kid who was being taught to approach challenges in a rote, mindless manner. Marty never minded doing the assignment, but when I tried to challenge him by asking questions of my own about the material, he resisted: Why should he exert himself when the assignment did not require it?

I could see his point, which illustrated my objection to the assignment: If you make something so easy that it requires no effort from students, they will sink to the occasion. It happens all the time, especially in special education curriculums, which tend to break material down into tiny, digestible bites. But breaking things down doesn't necessarily make them easier to learn; it can make learning harder, because you don't recognize what you're dealing with. If I grilled you a glorious rib-eye steak and then thrashed it in a blender, it would still be steak when you drank it, but how would you know? The context of the meat—its look, aroma, sizzle, chewiness—would be gone, its steak-ness obliterated. So it is when schools break down material into miniscule steps, which make the learning process more mechanical. It perpetuates a rote mentality, which is the opposite of what young minds, especially those on the autism spectrum, really need.

I once conducted a two-hour reading lesson with an ASD child in which we read a short story about an errant cat. The child kept trying to sound out words, to no avail. He would look at cat, make a *k* sound, then make a separate *uh* sound, then a hissing sound for the t, but was unable to put them together. There was no context, no sense of what the word signified. So I talked with him about the story itself: A housecat jumps out a second-story window into a tree, neighbors gather and mobilize to get her down, all is well in the end. He knew what a cat was, of course, and that they were good jumpers. When he understood the concept that printed letters and words are meant to be strung together and that they should make sense, he started to think in full sentences, which he had never done before. For him, it was like realizing that those breadcrumbs on the forest floor weren't strewn randomly but deliberately, and that they—miraculously—actually led somewhere (courtesy of *Hansel and Gretel*). He began talking about the plot in full sentences—short ones, but sentences nonetheless—that matched up pretty well with those on the page. By the end of the session, the child was reading more or less efficiently—not because I taught him to read in one session, but because he was able to change his thinking process to encompass deriving not mere random words, but meaning from a printed page.

When I connected this to Marty's quandary, a solution emerged: Marty needed academic assignments that required him to think, just as I was pressing him to do in our sessions. I conferred with his teacher, with whom I explained the techniques I was using and whom I invited to call me with updates on Marty's progress. To her great credit, she was open to working with me and started phoning after school several times a week. She reported on Marty's strides and occasional setbacks, and even asked him to help her carry heavy textbooks from her car to the classroom, which made him feel special and improved their rapport.

This was no small thing: Teachers are overworked and underpaid, and this one had many other students besides Marty to think about. Also, she was constrained by a syllabus replete with fill-in-the-blank exercises that encouraged rote responses rather than thought-out ones. Still, she was invested in Marty's progress and went out of her way to ensure it would happen, both academically and socially.

A subtle but significant sign of growth came one day when we played Connect Four, a three-dimensional version of checkers that we'd been playing for several months. Marty claimed the red discs went first and, as soon as the game came out of the box, would seize them. This particular day, Marty held out a red disc to me, an unprecedented act of courtesy. I thanked him for his graciousness, went first, and said how good it made me feel to know he had thought about being fair. When I relayed this story to his teacher, she said that Marty had become more considerate of his class-mates and that his excursions out of the classroom had become rare.

A whopping sign of progress came a few weeks later, when Marty an-nounced he had been assigned a science report. I asked what he might want to write about.

"I've already decided," he said. "I'm going to write about sea turtles." Not only that: He asked both his mother and me for advice on how he might best approach the topic, and accepted our suggestions. He planned and researched the report himself. He did ask for help on occasion, but it was only for those tasks that were genuinely beyond his reach. It was a sublime assignment, when you think about it: He'd gone from drawing underwater cartoon characters to drawing his own conclusions about real sea creatures.

I worked with Marty for 11 months. His parents were pleased when he began working independently and his schoolwork improved, and they terminated therapy. At that point, Marty still loved to draw, but was able to channel his desire for independence into his schoolwork as well.

THINGS TO WORK ON AND THINK ABOUT.

• *Does everything need to be broken down for these kids? I think not.* All too often, children are being taught to memorize information rath-er than how to think. Rote learning is not useful, and breaking down concepts into baby steps can, paradoxically, make them harder to grasp, especially for ASD kids. Children sometimes learn more effectively if the material is presented to them in its original state, even if we think it's too complex for them to grasp. It's not limited to academics, either: Parents often oversimplify things for ASD children when giving it to them straight would be better. If your instinct is always to make things simpler for your ASD child, try refraining from doing so. The goal is to create new thinking patterns, so it makes sense to expose your child to more complex ways of connecting thoughts. If you think the school curriculum is oversimplified, speak up. Connect with the teachers. They may not be uniformly cooperative, but when they are, the kids progress.

- *When you find people who understand your kid, keep them involved.* Teachers invest their hearts, minds, and souls in their students, and care about them long after they've moved on. Our son Dylan's second-grade teacher was a deeply empathetic woman who understood and advocated for him when he was in her class. When he hit a rough patch in school a few years later, we asked this teacher if she would speak with his current one, which helped resolve the conflict. Assistants, aides, babysitters, therapists, and family members have unique relationships with your child and are valuable resources you can call upon for support. The formula for significant change is simple: Understand what your child needs and get as many people doing the right thing as possible.

NED, 17

**High-functioning; intelligent;
unable to think spontaneously.**

I stepped out to meet my new client, who sat with his mother in the waiting room. "Hello," I said. "You must be Ned." He leapt to his feet.

"There are exactly 7 minutes until our appointment, Mr. Bernstein," he boomed. "Our appointment is for eleven o'clock and it is currently ten fifty-three. We can start right away if you'd like to, Mr. Bernstein, or we can stay right here in the waiting room until eleven o'clock, which is—" he jerked his wrist up to check his watch—"currently 6 minutes from now. It's up to you, Mr. Bernstein." His mother looked on in silence; she had been there, heard that many, many times.

And so I made the acquaintance of Ned, or Ned the Announcer, as I came to think of him. His stentorian delivery heralded every interaction I hoped to have with him, a cascade of verbiage drowning any possibility of meaningful connection.

"Exactly 19 days until the opening of *Ocean's Thirteen*, Mr. Bernstein," he bellowed as he entered my office. "That movie features an all-star cast, including Brad Pitt, Matt Damon, Al Pacino, Ellen Barkin, Bernie Mac, Andy Garcia, Don Cheadle, and George Clooney, who has also starred in *Ocean's Twelve, Ocean's Eleven, O Brother, Where Art Thou?, Solaris,* and *The Perfect Storm,* among many others ..." And he would have named many others had I not managed to distract him with the offer of a drink.

Diagnosed with high-functioning autism in his early teens, Ned was a good-looking, energetic fellow who had cultivated a spokesman persona to mask his difficulty relating to others. Superficially, it worked: You'd never mistake him for a regular guy, but his mannered, self-conscious delivery amused people while discouraging them from responding. It was like sitting in the first row at a club: You could see the comic up close and look him in the eye, but you weren't expected to do anything more than laugh. In fact, doing more would be awkward. There was a distance between you that you weren't supposed to breach. And so it was with Ned. It was his show, and your role was to sit back and take it in.

I wouldn't have problems getting Ned to talk; the problem would be getting him to talk to me rather than at me. Irony abounded: After spending most of my career getting kids to use language to connect with people, now I had a kid who used language to keep people away.

Early sessions. Ned functioned smoothly as long as he was in situations that harmonized with his habits. When I pointed out my overflowing trashcan and asked him what we might do about it, he promptly said we should empty it. But when I asked if we should check its contents for recyclables, he stared at me blankly. "Here," I said, "go through and pull out the paper, plastic, and metal stuff, okay?" He looked at me, then at the trash, and walked away. The concept of sorting the trash was as remote to him as calculating the mass of a muon would be to me.

Ned's autism limited his academic potential as well as his social life. Despite his native intelligence, he attended special ed. classes at a public high school along with kids with learning disabilities and Down syndrome. It seemed like a waste. Here was a young man who could reel off vast amounts of information; if he could learn to interpret information as well as a memorize it, he could tap into his intellectual potential as well as his reservoir of normalcy.

"This is the last time in November I'll see you, Mr. Bernstein," Ned loudly announced the following week. "Our next appointment will be on December 3rd and then on December 10th, 17th, 24th, and 31st." He repeated this several times during the session, including the fact that January 7th was the season premiere of *The Apprentice*.

"December 31st is New Year's Eve," I said as he was preparing to leave. "We may need to reschedule." Ned looked baffled. "New Year's Eve is a major holiday," I added.

"We'd better reschedule the 24th, too," his mother said. "It's Christmas Eve and I'll be at the airport picking up Auntie June." Poor Ned looked as if his head were about to explode. The orderliness of the calendar made sense to him, its column of Thursdays whose numbered dates increased by seven every row, on each of which he would come to my office, where we would sit and talk and do other things. But the context of those meetings—the work we were doing and how it might be affected by the Christmas and New Year's holidays—eluded him, and the idea that sessions could be rearranged flummoxed him utterly.

Observing Ned's thinking process. Ned's biggest obstacle was his inability to deal with disruptions to his thinking patterns. I came up with some activities that would do just that so I could observe how he coped.

I presented Ned with a heap of cubes and asked him to sort them into four bins by color. Reprising my color-coding maneuver, I designated two bins as yellow, leaving one for red, one for green, and no bin for blue. Rather than do the exercise, Ned started talking a mile a minute.

"If you put yellow with blue, Mr. Bernstein, you get green. If you mix yellow with red, you get orange, Mr. Bernstein. But if you put blue with red, Mr. Bernstein, you get purple," and on and on and on. It was as I imagined: Seeing no bin for blues, Ned launched into announcer mode to divert attention from his inability to complete the task. It didn't occur to him to remove one of the yellow cubes and re-designate the bin for blues. Ned's mind took things literally: However they appeared, that's how they were, period.

Next, I rolled some modeling compound into two balls of equal size. I asked Ned which ball comprised more.

"That's easy, Mr. Bernstein. They're the same, exactly the same."

"You're saying there's the same amount of clay in these two balls?"

"Yes, Mr. Bernstein. I'm saying there's the same amount of clay in those two balls."

"All right, then," I said, flattening one of them with my hand. "Now, Ned, which has more?" He glazed over. Flattening the ball didn't change how much clay it comprised, of course, but Ned couldn't make the leap. The ability to know that a set amount will remain constant despite changes in its appearance is called conservation. According to psychologist Jean Piaget, who championed the concept, this ability develops in children between the ages of 7 and 11; Ned was 17. Next I counted out 50 pennies and stacked them in two equal columns. I asked Ned which stack had more pennies, and he dutifully replied that they held 25 pennies each. Was he sure? Yes, he was. I then knocked over one of the stacks, spreading the pennies across the table. When I asked Ned which held more pennies, he was befuddled again. I rephrased the question and asked again several times, to no avail. "I don't know, I don't know, I don't know," he kept repeating, becoming distressed and agitated.

What was underlying Ned's inability to think abstractly? He was clear about there being 25 pennies in each stack; he'd counted them out with me. Why was he agitated and repeating he didn't know how many pennies there were when just moments ago he'd been so sure? All that was required was some basic organized thinking. Why could his mind store prodigious amounts of minutiae, yet freeze when asked to think?

Resisting Ned's spiel. At the next session, I brought out my trusty xylophone and played "Mary Had a Little Lamb," one of three songs in my repertoire (the other two being "Twinkle, Twinkle Little Star" and "Three Blind Mice." I have almost mastered "Baa Baa Black Sheep," probably because it's exactly the same tune as "Twinkle, Twinkle," something I noticed only recently. Piaget might cite conversion issues).

"Mary" comprises four notes: E, D, C, and G, in the xylophone's key of C major. It's a simple tune, and, after playing it several times, I asked Ned to give it a try.

"Hello, folks! Time to play *Name That Tune!*" he boomed.

"Come on, Ned, try to play the song."

"Mr. Bernstein, Canadian recording artist Avril Lavigne just released her third album, *The Best Damn Thing*, which debuted at number one on the U.S. Billboard 200, following her second album, *Under My Skin*—"

"Ned." I was smiling but firm. "Ned, I want you to try and play 'Mary Had a Little Lamb' on the xylophone." Ned looked panicked but, after some coaxing, took the mallet and started to play. He struggled with the first three notes—E, D, C, in downward sequence—and, after several tries, he got it. But when he got to "little lamb," where the E note repeats three times, he hit an impasse. Until now, the melody flowed from one note to another, but now three notes had to be repeated, and Ned's mind couldn't adjust. He started to perspire. "I don't know, I don't know, I don't know," he said again and again. Seeing his distress, I suggested we do something else.

Now I knew how to proceed. Ned's mind could function only within the security of a rote system; anything breaking the patterns he'd learned caused his mind to freeze. He had to develop flexibility to adapt to the disruptions of everyday life. Conversing embodied such a disruption, as it required Ned to respond spontaneously to whatever another person said. By spouting floods of minutiae, memorized by rote, Ned had cleverly avoided having to interact with others. It had worked in social situations and also at school, where his tirades were perceived as entertaining rather than disruptive. Had he been spouting invective, the behavior would undoubtedly have been seen as a problem. But because he spewed facts and figures rather than offensive language, the behavior had gone unchecked.

Getting Ned to improvise. Anyone who has done improv knows how scary it can be: You're in front of an audience, making it up as you go along without a safety net—which is exactly what life is like. For someone like Ned, conducting a casual conversation was doing improv, only with an audience of one. To combat the anxiety this produced, he memorized information as if it were a script, which he then declaimed. To break this pattern, I would have to involve Ned in situations that required him to respond spontaneously rather than revert to his script; I'd have to get him to improvise.

We got our chance when my cell phone rang during the session. I usually ignore calls at work but when I saw it was Rachel, I did some improv myself.

"Excuse me, but I need to take this. It's my wife," I said. After 30 seconds, I ended the call and turned back to Ned.

"Did I know the person on the phone?" I asked.

"I don't know, Mr. Bernstein."

"Think about it, Ned. Did I know the person on the phone?"

"No, Mr. Bernstein."

"No? Really? Think. When the phone rang, who did I say was calling?"

"Your wife." Progress! The bombast was temporarily derailed. We chatted for a few minutes about wives and husbands, a concept he understood.

"So, did I know the person on the phone?" I asked.

"No." he responded automatically. I cocked my head and gazed at him. After a moment's reflection, he said, "Yes." More progress—he'd broken his automatic scripting.

"How do you know?"

"Because she's your wife and you know your wife."

"Great! Do you know the person I spoke with?" We talked about what knowing a person means. Ned concluded that when you know someone, you know things such as where she lives, what kind of car she has, what she likes to eat, and what she doesn't like.

"So, do you know the person I spoke with?"

"Her name is Mrs. Bernstein." He still hadn't answered the question. And he was wrong.

"That's a bit presumptuous, Ned."

"What's presumptuous?" he asked. I said sometimes you need to ask a person's name, not presume you know it.

"As a matter of fact, her name is not Mrs. Bernstein, even though she is my wife." I explained that some women choose not to take their husbands' last names, that some add their husbands' names to their own, and that some men choose to take their wives' last names. He looked baffled but didn't argue.

"So," I said, "do I know the person on the phone?"

"Yes, because it was your wife, and husbands and wives know each other."

"Yes, that's right. Do you know the person on the phone?"

"No, because I never met the person, but I know that she's your wife."

"Right again. Do you know her name?" He hesitated.

"Her name is not Mrs. Bernstein. No, I don't know her name."

"Excellent!" Ned had abandoned his script and responded to the exigencies of the moment—a breakthrough. And he had spoken in a moderate tone of voice: In the past, when I asked if he could lower his voice, he whispered; for Ned, there was no in-between. But now there was.

I asked Ned if he'd like to share a snack with me and he eagerly agreed. I handed him a bag of chips and, as he opened it, launched into a monologue:

"Thank you, Mr. Bernstein, for offering to share a bag of Sun Chips with me. These are Harvest Cheddar flavor, and the others in the basket are—" he twisted in his chair—"French Onion, Garden, Salsa, and Original flavor. Sharing with a friend is much better than not sharing, Mr. Bernstein, and I am glad to have the opportunity to share these Harvest Cheddar Sun Chips with you today ..."—and on he went, extolling the virtues of sharing until he'd eaten every chip in the bag. We clearly had more work to do.

Family matters. As I got to know Ned's family, it became clear that creating typical interactions in our sessions could only do so much. Ned lived with his mother and two unemployed cousins (his father died long ago), and it sounded as if the four of them spent most of their time together, watching movies and talking loudly at, not to, one another. I caught a glimpse of this when the cousins, two men in their 40s or 50s, accompanied Ned and his mother to the office and came in after the session. A conversation about Ned's activities that day quickly devolved into a free-for-all, with the four of them interrupting one another at a decibel level that soon became uncomfortable.

"Wow," I said, trying to restore order. "Do you always talk this way?"

"Hah!" Ned's mother erupted. "You should hear us when we get mad!" Ned later confirmed that there was a lot of fighting at home. Breaking the habit of bellowing rather than speaking would not be easy for him.

At the next session, I gave Ned a short story to read about a young man whose first day as a tour bus driver involves a snowstorm, skidding, and a coach full of screaming passengers whose cries are silenced when his mother awakens him from the nightmare he's having prior to his first day on the job. When he finished, I asked what the story was about.

"It's about people on a train, Mr. Bernstein."

"Are you sure? Why don't you read the first line again." I didn't mention the illustration of a bus that headed the page.

"Oh, I see. It's about people on a bus."

"Right! What did you do differently with your mind that time?"

"I don't know."

"Think about it, Ned. When I asked the second time, you knew right away. What did you do that was different?"

"It just came into my mind."

"Well, maybe you can make things come into your mind that way again." He allowed as maybe it was possible. My hope was that Ned was starting to feel the difference between thinking in the moment and the anxiety-wracked rote behaviors he typically resorted to. I had chosen the bus driver story because the surprise ending entailed a shift in perspective, from dream to reality. Ned needed practice seeing things from different perspectives so he could relinquish his need to control interactions, and I knew his social skills would improve exponentially when he could do this. As it turned out, the ending didn't spark his progress that day as much as his shift from automatically picturing a train rather than the bus he'd actually read about. You don't always know where the next step is coming from. What matters is recognizing when it happens.

The following week, I gave Ned another simple story designed to spark creative thinking. It was about two girls who are close friends and visit each other's house several times a week. On a snow day, they meet to go sledding and each of them is wearing one red mitten and one blue mitten.

"That's strange," I said. "Neither of them has a matching set." He brooded for a while, then lit up.

"No, Mr. Bernstein, they do. They just got mixed up when they were visiting. When Gail left Helen's house, she grabbed one of each color instead of two red ones because her father was honking the horn and she was in a rush." This was creative thinking, a major stride for Ned. He had been able to break up sets of red and blue mittens, envision that they might exist separately, and reconstitute them into two mismatched pairs. And he had told me about it without shouting.

Ned surprised us all when he asked a young woman out on a date, and she accepted. We devoted a session to talking about what this meant: He would have to confer with her on what movie she wanted to see, what kind of food she might want to eat, and what time she had to be home, as well as consider her wishes when making plans. The following week, Ned said the date went okay and declined to elaborate.

Mining Ned's potential. Ned was midway through high school and I was concerned about his future. Working against him were his unconventional family's combative communication style and the fact that, despite his obvious intelligence, he'd been funneled into a special ed. curriculum—a trajectory that would, I was certain, thrust him into a vocational program for a job to which I feared he would be ill-suited. Complicating matters was his mother's complacency: She seemed content to accept such a future for her son. But I wasn't: I knew Ned was capable of connecting with others, and I hated to think of him isolated in a cubby counting out bolts all day.

I was convinced he could do more and finagled a part-time position for him at a nursing home where he escorted residents to activities and medical appointments, and served as an all-around helper and companion. They loved him: Most of the residents were hard of hearing and all of them craved conversation, which Ned was happy to provide. And something else happened: Ned befriended one of the residents, 87-year-old Mrs. Bishop, a former teacher who said Ned reminded her of her son who had died many years earlier. Her tenderness weakened Ned's spiky verbal defenses (her background as an educator didn't hurt, either). He began listening to her—something Ned had seldom done—and, to satisfy her desire to know more about him, made a strenuous effort to gather his thoughts before responding to her queries. His impersonal, announcer-like speaking style gradually softened into something approximating typical speech.

I worked with Ned for about sixteen months. He lived nearly ninety minutes away by car, in upstate New York, and his mother told me he'd gotten a job at a retirement community close to their home. She said they were crazy about Ned and had offered to find a full-time position for him once he graduated from high school. I said I hoped Ned might find a way to attend college one day. Most of all, I hope he's happy.

THINGS TO WORK ON AND THINK ABOUT.

- *Cultivate your child's potential; don't sell him or her short.* Ned lived with his mother and two cousins in a cramped and stress-wracked household. His mother's interest in Ned's education was limited to whether he'd graduate from high school equipped to ply a trade. What Ned needed is what every atypical child needs: someone to dig beneath the superficial oddities of the disorder and seek the soul and gifts of the person within. Had anyone ever approached Ned with patience, warmth, and forbearance? Mrs. Bishop did; perhaps because unlike Ned's beleaguered mother, her vision of him wasn't limited by ideas of what he couldn't do. If familiarity breeds contempt, it also creates complacency. Don't be lulled into believing that your atypical child has fulfilled his or her potential: Like any other child, he or she is a work in progress.

- *Learning awaits in unplanned moments.* When my cell phone rang that day, I didn't know a 30-second call would yield a mother lode of learning, but it did. No planned curriculum could have topped the spontaneous learning that happened when Ned and I discussed my wife's name. You don't need a standardized methodology or plan to help your atypical child: No one method will work for everyone. Instead, transform everyday occurrences into opportunities to interact spontaneously with your child.

High-functioning; has trouble thinking sequentially; ate alone every day in high school.

Richard, a lanky, nice-looking teenager, was accompanied to his first session by his mother, a prosperous entrepreneur, who got straight to the point. "Richard is leaving for college in 6 weeks and needs to learn how to make friends. That's what his father and I want most for him." She smiled at her son. "Oh, and I should mention that I'll be paying you in cash. I'd just as soon my husband not know Richard is coming here. He doesn't think anything's wrong and just wants Richard to work harder." The only child of Asian-born parents, Richard felt pressured to further his family's standing in their community. I asked what his goals were.

"I want to write science fiction."

"It's great that you know what career you want. But I'd like to know what your goals are for our work over the next 6 weeks." He looked away, then down.

"Like she said, make friends." After his mother left the room, Richard was more forthcoming.

"Making friends, yeah. And ... um ... I can't talk to girls."

"Have you ever tried?"

"Tried what?"

"Talking to a girl." He looked at me as if I were insane.

"No."

"Why not?"

"I don't know any girls."

"Did you go to an all-boys school?"

"No."

"You had girls in your classes, right?"

"What?"

"You had girls in your classes, right?"

"Yeah."

"So you do know some girls."

"No. They were in my class. I didn't know them."

"Well, Richard, if you'd talk to them, then you'd know them."

"There's no talking in class."

"Well, what about lunch? You could talk in the cafeteria, couldn't you?"

"I didn't eat in the cafeteria."

"Where did you eat lunch, then?"

"Huh?" What?"

"I asked you where you ate lunch."

"Computer room."

"How often?"

"Every day."

"How long?"

"Forty minutes."

"No, I mean, how long did you eat by yourself? Senior year? Junior year?"

"Every year."

"You never ate lunch with the other kids?"

"Once."

"What happened?"

Richard told me that he'd pointed to a sign listing the lunch du jour as Mexican tacos and asked the other kids if they thought that was the kind of food they had in Mexico. The table went wild, and Richard never went back. Thereafter, he never initiated a conversation with someone he didn't know, which fortified his conviction that he should always eat alone. I said that surely there must be someone with whom he'd interacted over the last 3 years and he said yes, there were two guys that were sort of friends. When I pressed Richard, he said a few weeks earlier, they'd invited him to a party and suggested he pick them up in his car. When Richard pulled up to the party house, they jumped out and told him he could come in if he wanted to but shouldn't try to hang out with them. He drove home, where his parents peppered him with questions about why he'd left the party so soon, adding to his feeling of humiliation.

This is both sad and typical of many ostensible friendships of ASD teenagers. They pal around with kids who seem friendly but who are as likely as not goofing on the kid with autism, who's unaware that he or she has inspired the merriment. This goes on until something happens that can't be construed as anything but a rejection, and reality sets in. Richard was painfully aware that these kids didn't really like him but persisted in calling them friends, as they were the only ones who talked to him.

I asked Richard about his writing and he came to life. He was passionate about science fiction and had even self-published a novel in the genre. Yet, when I asked him to summarize the plot, he responded vaguely, "There's this kid, he's alone, everyone else is dead; you know." My theory was that, like many people with high-functioning autism, Richard had trouble thinking sequentially. This was borne out when I asked him to multiply 10 times 10 and he came up quickly with 100, but was unable to describe how he arrived at the answer. He agreed that it was hard for him to think in order and said that he had trouble staying organized, pointing to his backpack and saying there were about a hundred papers crammed inside because he couldn't remember to extract and go through them. He had been accepted to college on an early-decision basis and managed to keep his GPA above the minimum required to insure his admission, but was worried about how he'd manage when he got there. He had trouble focusing in class and completing assignments; he didn't do well on tests, was incapable of delivering oral reports, and felt awkward working in groups. Most of all, he didn't know how to interact with new people, and, without his parents there to provide companionship, was afraid he'd spend the next 4 years even more isolated than he'd spent the last 4. He wanted me to help him learn to focus, become more organized, and develop social skills, all in 6 weeks. We'd have to work fast.

Facing down his fears. Richard was an ideal candidate for in vivo therapy, a cognitive-behavioral technique in which a person desensitizes him- or herself to anxiety-provoking situations by participating in them. With the cooperation of a Korean fellow I know who owns a local bagel shop (this is New York, remember), I got Richard a temporary job behind the counter where he'd have to take orders, learn to execute a perfect schmear, and say, "Hello, may I help you?" to every man, woman, and ear-budded teenager who came through the door. It was perfect.

Richard wasn't so sure. When greeting a customer, he could barely mumble "hello." He had to learn to make coffee in three sizes with seven kinds of sweeteners and creamers, and dispense iced tea, sweetened or unsweetened, plain or flavored with Peachy Keene, Vanilla Ice, or Hazel Nutcase. He had to memorize scores of prices, including spreads by the quarter-pound, bagels by the dozen, and four different sizes of bottled orange juice. He would have to make tuna, turkey, and chicken salad sandwiches; crack, fry, and scramble eggs and ease them onto bagels and bialys—round baked rolls that he first had to slice in half—and master the technique of cutting a whitefish-salad-on-bagel sandwich without letting the fish squish out—no easy feat, as the veterans behind the counter made clear. Sothy was from Cambodia and Minh from Vietnam; between the two of them, they'd been working at the shop for 31 years. Both could slice a bagel in 3 seconds flat.

Richard came for a session after his first day at work. "It was really hard," he said, "and a lady got mad at me."

"Why?" I asked.

"She said I made her the wrong thing."

"What'd you make her?"

"Mustard and butter on a sesame."

"Mustard and butter? Who eats mustard and butter?" Richard shrugged.

"Richard, no one eats a mustard and butter sandwich."

"But they do! They order weird stuff." It turned out she'd ordered tuna and tomato on an everything bagel. I never found out how that transmogrified into mustard and butter, but I did tell Richard that he should always repeat orders back to customers to make sure he knew what they wanted.

This was a real challenge for Richard. It took him a week to raise his voice so people could hear him above the morning rush din. I asked the owner to explain to Richard why greeting customers and bidding them some sort of farewell was an important part of the job. It took Richard 3 weeks to smile at a customer; soon after, he was saying "Hello" and "Have a nice day," albeit in a monotone.

One of his earliest lessons was in how to cut a bagel in half, demonstrated with dazzling panache by Sothy and Minh. Everyone does it differently but there's one basic requirement: You start by positioning the knife blade on the one-inch flat section of the bagel's curved circumference. That's all I can say; the rest is top secret. But I can tell you this: Bagels are chewy and you have to exert significant pressure on the knife to make it move, which gets tricky when you reach the uncut edge on the opposite side and the blade suddenly saws through it and into your palm if you're not careful. That wasn't the only difficulty for Richard; the other was inserting the sandwich in the small plastic bag the shop used. Sothy practiced the shake-and-slip-in-the-bagel technique, whereas Minh deployed the lift-the-top-flap-with-bag-on-table maneuver—what finesse these guys had! Poor Richard's fledgling attempts usually smeared the bag with chicken or tuna salad, so, for his next office session, I brought in a dozen bagels, sandwich bags, and a bread knife. We spent 10 minutes slicing bagels in half and an additional 20 exploring bagging techniques until Richard found his way. The key was to first open the bag and then, nestling the cut edge of the bagel deep in his palm, use the slip-and-shake method—an original and impressive solution. When Richard demonstrated this at work the next day, the old-timers approved.

I began visiting the bagel shop an hour before lunchtime and watching Richard as he finished the morning shift. I'd sit away from the counter but in view and earshot of what he was doing and saying. When he took a break, I'd tell him what I'd observed, noting his accomplishments and suggesting ways he might make things easier on himself. Richard began mustering a smile for customers around three weeks in, a good sign. One day, when he joined me on his break, he told me that he had waited on four people that morning whom he knew.

"That's great!" I said. "Did you say hello?"

"No."

"No? Why not?"

"Because we don't talk." I almost lost it.

"Richard! If you don't talk to people you know, how are you ever going to be able to talk to people you don't know?" At our office session that week, I had him stand behind my desk while I walked up, placed an order, and waited for him to acknowledge my presence with eye contact and a greeting. If he balked, I said, "Wait—don't I know you from somewhere?" and prodded him into responding. Richard had complained that he didn't like the robotic nature of calling out Have a nice day!, so role-playing gave him practice at imbuing his remarks with genuine feeling. The next day, I watched as he tried connecting with customers, especially a few he knew from outside the store. And a funny thing happened: When he spoke to someone in a warm, connected way, they began talking to him, asking how long he'd worked there, if he'd graduated yet, what his plans were for the following year. He started saying things such as, "Oh, hi—I had you for English," and "Hi, I think I know you from church." Everyone he spoke to responded warmly, which reassured and encouraged him.

Talking to a stranger. One day as Richard and I were eating lunch, I noticed an elderly woman sitting alone at the table next to ours. I turned to her, smiled, and said hi. "Do I know you?" she asked. I said we'd never met but that I just wanted to introduce myself. Her name was Millie, and we started chatting about how she comes in every day for a vanilla yogurt and onion bagel, the tai-chi class she takes at the senior center, and how different the neighborhood is from what it was 30 years ago when she first moved there. When she began rummaging in her purse, I turned to Richard.

"See, it's not hard to talk to someone," I said. He didn't bother looking up.

"She thinks you're weird."

"Why do you say that?"

"Because no one just starts talking to someone they don't know. She thinks you're, like, totally weird."

"She does not think I'm weird," I said, with conviction. "How about if I ask her if she thought I was weird when I said hi?" Richard's head snapped up.

"Absolutely not!" he hissed. "That would be even more weird." He turned back to his shrimp salad on jalapeño bagel. I turned to Millie, who was getting up to leave, and decided to ask her anyway. There was a chance that Richard might flee in embarrassment, but he had two hours to go before his shift ended. The odds were on my side.

"Millie, may I ask you something? Did you think it was weird that I said hello to you, even though we didn't know each other?"

"Not at all."

"Well," I continued, "this is my friend Richard, and he thinks you thought it was weird." Millie turned to him.

"Oh, no, Richard," she said, smiling warmly. He looked up cautiously. "I did not think he was weird. Just the opposite! I live alone and I come here to have lunch around other people. It's nice to talk to someone you don't know, because then they're not a stranger any more. It's friendly; it's normal."

I could have hugged her—normal was the absolute best word she could have used. We'd hit the jackpot. As she walked away, Richard spoke.

"Well, I guess it's okay to say hi to an old lady who's sitting by herself." He'd opened the door a crack. Now I'd jam my foot in.

"So," I said, "you agree that Millie didn't think it was weird that I said hello to her?"

"Yeah, but that's only true for old ladies sitting alone."

"Why? What makes it different from a young person sitting alone, or for that matter, two or three people sitting together? The key is knowing what to say to engage them. If you know what to say, they don't think it's weird. This doesn't mean that everyone's going to want to talk to you, or to me; it means that people don't think it's weird when someone says hello. Can you agree with that, at least?" Richard nodded.

If you're a parent, you know that you can lecture your kids until you're hoarse but it doesn't sink in until they experience the change for themselves, by themselves. Likewise, I could have asserted to Richard the naturalness of greeting a stranger a million times, but he would never have believed it until he witnessed it for himself.

Richard, untethered. "There's this girl who comes in. She's cute." It was Tuesday of Richard's next-to-last week of work, and we were sitting in the shop.

"Really? What's she like?"

"I don't know … blonde. Pretty."

"When does she come in?" He thought for a moment.

"Morning, usually."

"So tell me about her."

He said she had come in that day and asked if they had chocolate cream cheese. Richard asked Minh if they had such a thing and Minh replied that yes, they did. She said she really wanted to try the chocolate but decided to go with plain cream cheese. Richard said that after she left, he regretted not getting her number. I told him that he needed to talk to her first and establish some sort of relationship before asking for her contact information.

"How do you do that?" he asked.

"You have a conversation."

"What about?"

"Girls like guys who are considerate. If she comes in again, you could start a conversation and show how considerate you are by letting her sample some chocolate cream cheese. You can just give her a taste."

"Would they allow that? A free spoonful?"

"We can ask the owner, but I think he'll say yes." (He did.)

By Friday, she still hadn't shown up. Richard came to my table, dejected.

"Look," I said, "maybe she'll come in on Monday."

"Next week will be too late. The moment is gone."

"No, it isn't. In fact, it's better if more time passes because it shows that you remember her and what she wanted. It shows how considerate you are."

Monday came and went but she didn't show. Nor did she appear on Tuesday or Wednesday. Now it was Thursday and tomorrow would be Richard's last day of work.

"Why is she not showing up?" he asked.

"Who knows? Maybe she's away on vacation. Or maybe she lives somewhere else and was just visiting here." Richard looked glum.

The next day, I watched as Richard completed his final shift. And wouldn't you know it—in walks a young woman with blonde hair up in a twist and a large fringed shoulder bag. Richard shot me a look of disbelief. As she approached the counter, he said, "Hi! Can I get you some of that chocolate cream cheese?" She smiled broadly.

"Indeed." (That was indeed her word.) I watched as she took a taste and nodded. I heard her say, "Okay—I'll have chocolate cream cheese on a plain bagel, please." And then, "I'm sure I'll see you again." Richard shook his head.

"Maybe not. I'm leaving for college next week."

"Oh! Where are you going?"

He answered and she said she knew someone who went there and loved it. Richard's eyes lit up; he was in a state of bliss. Six weeks earlier, he couldn't conceive of saying hello to a woman; now he was conversing with one he found attractive and hoped to see again. He had made friends with a stranger. They agreed to be Facebook friends, and Richard said he hoped they might see each other when he came home for a visit. The following week, he emailed me to say he was heading off to school.

Three weeks later, Richard returned for Labor Day weekend and we met at my office. I asked him if he had initiated any conversations at college and he said he had. Not only that, he had made two sets of friends: a nerdy set who studied together in the library, and another set who liked to party. And, he was happy to tell me that he ate lunch with one or the other group every day.

"Also," he said, "I talked with this freshman girl for 10 minutes, and she didn't even realize that I was weird."

"Richard, you're wrong about that," I replied. "She didn't know that you used to be weird. You're not like that any more. Years from now, you'll look back and think, 'Yeah, I used to be weird in high school.' You're different now."

"You're right," he said. "This is the new Richard."

Update. As I was finishing this manuscript, I dropped by the bagel shop where Richard worked and spoke with the owner, who told me he'd heard that Richard had graduated from college, was working in Manhattan, and was engaged to be married.

SOMETHING TO WORK ON
AND THINK ABOUT.

• *Don't relegate your ASD child's treatment to the therapist's office:* Lure him or her outside and into the orbits of other people. The mundane activities of everyday life provide a vast laboratory for experimenting with new behaviors: Get out there and use them. Talking to a bank teller (before they're all replaced with ATMs), ordering a meal in a restaurant, and telling the barber how long you want your sideburns to be are occasions for connecting with people. Pay attention to how you interact in these situations. Does your manner invite cordial interaction? Do you look restaurant servers in the eye when you order? When you pay for your groceries, do you greet the cashier? The bagger? Your children are watching (when they're not glued to their mobile phones, that is). Demonstrate how natural it is to interact with another human being. Show them how it's done—unless you're glued to your mobile phone.

Part 5

**High-functioning; college graduate;
yearns for girlfriend.**

"T he thing is," Adam began, "I don't want to lose everything that makes me different. Not that I'm perfect. But there are parts of me that I want to keep. Like my writing—I don't want to change the writing part of me. My mother told you I'm a writer, right?"

"Yes."

"So you know that writing is my life. I'm in the middle of a story, maybe a novel, but at the moment it's a story because I'm still working out the idea, but it's about a guy, sort of like me, who wakes up one day and he's different from the way he used to be but it's really everyone else who's different, which makes him feel different even though he's actually the way he always was …" Ten minutes later, Adam was still explaining the intricacies of the plot, never looking me in the eye or otherwise connecting. If I'd closed my eyes, I don't think he would have noticed.

This isn't an exaggeration: His mother told me that she once walked into Adam's room as he regaled his sister with details of his writing, unaware that she had dozed off. So obsessive was Adam, he often came home at dinnertime, strode past his family as they gathered in the kitchen, and went straight to his room to write down an idea that couldn't wait. He sometimes stayed upstairs for hours, refusing to come down to eat. His parents were concerned that Adam's writing was intensifying his isolation:

Now that he had graduated from college, the only people he met were at his mother's jewelry design business, where he worked part-time fulfilling Internet orders. He had participated in several interpersonal skills workshops led by social workers and speech therapists, but was unable to apply to everyday life what he'd learned. His parents wanted him to make friends and be socially adept, but most of all, they wanted Adam to relate better to his sister Taryn, who had all but written him off. I met with Taryn at the office early on to learn her perceptions of her brother. "He has no interest in me or anything I'm doing—zip, zero, nada. He'll come into my room and jabber about whatever he's into—his awesome writing, or some girl at work he's got a crush on—and doesn't even notice that I'm busy. It's like, Ta-da! I'm here! Stop everything while I talk about myself! You know, I'm leaving for college at the end of the summer, and I don't care if I ever see him again." Later, I asked Adam his side of the story. "Yeah. She's right," he said. When I asked Adam which relationships were important to him, he didn't mention his sister. What he really wanted was to have a girlfriend, but said he was realistic and, at that point, would be happy if he could learn to speak comfortably to a woman for 5 minutes.

Our work was clear from the first session onward: If Adam wanted to have a girlfriend, that would be our priority. When meeting new clients, I've learned it's best to start with what they want, and for Adam, it was learning to relate to women his age. Trying to force him to cultivate a relationship with his sister—which was important to his parents but not to him—would have alienated him and been ultimately futile. Besides, I knew we would get there in time.

One in-office session with Adam was enough to evaluate his strengths and vulnerabilities. He was very intelligent, highly articulate, and unusually good-looking. He could express his thoughts in fluent speech, but was unable to make the casual conversation that kindles connections with others. His problem was obliviousness to the needs of other people and the many cues they offered to clue him in. So focused was he on his own passions, he neglected to acknowledge the existence of similar feelings in others. Like many people on the autism spectrum, he was unaware that his self-absorption was undermining his ability to cultivate friendships, let alone romance.

Young adults with high-functioning autism must be made aware of their egocentrism and how it hampers relationships. But in order for them to do this, someone they trust must meet them where they are, not where I, their families, or anyone else wants them to be. It is critically important that I listen to and be guided by what my young adult clients value. For them, I am a trusted guide who helps them navigate the world according to their needs and desires, not those of their parents, even though it's their parents who are paying me. It is my obligation to advocate for my clients, just as you must do for the ASD person in your life.

This doesn't always ingratiate me to the parents. Years ago, my phone rang close to midnight and I picked up to a woman shouting, "I've had it—I'm done! He kicked me, knocked me down—I'm taking him straight to the ER and they'll put him away! You hear that?—" she turned away from the phone—"I hate you, you lunatic! I wish you'd never been born!" I told her I was coming over and hung up. I glanced at Caller ID, grabbed my car keys, told Rachel I had an emergency, and jumped in the car. If I drove fast, I could get there before they left.

This mother had spoken before about committing her high-functioning, bellicose, physically aggressive son to a mental institution and I feared she would succeed. At 15, Hector was too young to challenge her legally, and once he was stuck in an institution, it would be hard for him to get out. I empathized with his mother, who feared for her safety and was lacking in resources. But she was not my priority; Hector was. He was too intelligent and had too much potential to be exiled to an institution.

The apartment door was ajar and no one answered when I knocked, so I walked in and announced myself. There was no sign of the mother but I found Hector pacing furiously in the living room.

"Did you hear what she said?" he cried. "She's crazy!" I nodded. "I mean, she's my mother and she hates me? She wishes I were dead? What kind of mother says shit like that? She should be locked up, not me!" I spoke quietly and deliberately.

"You're right. Your mother should go to the hospital, Hector, not you. She should be sedated, not you." Mirroring his perspective was my only hope of getting through to him. He stopped and looked up, tears flooding his eyes.

"Hector, your mother's in a terrible state and doesn't know what she's saying or doing. That's why you have to be the adult right now."

"But I'm not an adult; she's the adult! She's the one with the problem!"

"Yes, she's the one with the problem, but you're the one going into a mental institution." That got his attention. "If you don't want that to happen, you have to be more grown up than your mom." I told him that kicking his mother was wrong, that no matter how angry a man gets, he has to control himself, and that he had to apologize. He wasn't crazy about the idea but came to understand that part of being an adult meant doing the right thing even when you felt the other person was wrong. He said that he would apologize to his mother. I asked if he knew where she was.

"I'm right here." She appeared from behind the bathroom door and glared at me. I told her that Hector had something to say to her. He apologized and she accepted. I said I'd like to see them both in the office the following day; the mother said she would call me in the morning. When she assured me she wouldn't bring Hector to the hospital before then, I left.

When they arrived the next day, the mother closed the door so we were alone in the office. "I really didn't like what you said last night. I'm not sure I want to continue." I told her I understood why she felt that way, and explained my reasons for speaking as I did. In the end, Hector continued with therapy and his mother abandoned her threat.

Hector's mother was different from Adam's parents, whose desire for their kids to get along made perfect sense. That said, Adam had other priorities. I told Adam I understood how much he wanted a girlfriend, then proposed his making a real friend as the first step. I would introduce the idea of rapprochement with his sister later, when I thought he might be open to it.

Friendship 101. The first step toward helping Adam find a friend was suggesting he attend a meetup group—an Internet-driven, actual gathering of people who share a common interest. The informal rhythm of interactions in meetups works well for people with high-functioning autism, many of whom attend them. Adam told me when we met that his modus operandi in groups was to stand on the periphery and duck out when he thought no one was looking. When I told him I'd accompany him to a meetup, he agreed to give it a try.

We scoured the Internet for local meetups that focused on Adam's three passions: writing, animé, and computers. He found an animé group convening several nights later at a local diner and we showed up looking like a father-and-son duo. Several tables had been pushed together with close to 20 young people talking, eating, and changing seats. We grabbed chairs and began listening. It was an eclectic group comprising some professionals in business clothes, teenagers in Pokémon T-shirts, and bohemian-looking 20- and 30-somethings chatting in, well, animated fashion. It had a sophisticated vibe—the kind of group you could feel good being part of—which made it easier for Adam to stick around. We ordered food, waited for it, and ate. Adam just listened at first, but after twenty minutes or so, a debate arose about the relative merits of animé and manga, and he made a comment. The others responded amiably, which lifted Adam's spirits and made him feel comfortable enough to stay until the group dispersed. Afterward, in the car, we talked about what it had taken for Adam to speak up, how he felt about the group's response, and why he'd spoken only once. "What else could I say?" he asked, at which point we talked about the advantages of having more than one thing to talk about. As I drove, I engaged him in a faux conversation in which I posed as a young woman he fancied. I had him start with "Hi," to which I responded with a hi of my own. When he got stuck, I mentioned some things people are commonly interested in, and several emerged that appealed to him, including visiting a comedy club, taking a yoga class, and jogging. As we wended our way through thickets of conversation, Adam was surprised to find that he was open to pursuing new interests, which made him perceive himself differently. I gently pointed out how much more appealing he would be to a new acquaintance if he could converse about more than writing and computers; that having varied interests makes a person not only a better conversationalist, but raises the odds of finding something in common with another person—the foundation of many relationships.

At subsequent animé meetups, Adam met and conversed with new people successfully when he remembered to talk about more than computers and writing. Then, one evening, I struck up a conversation with a young man named Gavin, whom I thought was a potential friend for Adam. He spoke as if animé interested rather than obsessed him and sounded like a balanced, happy fellow with a job and interests similar to Adam's. And he mentioned having a girlfriend, which made him seem like a regular guy whose social life transcended the group—whose members, truth be told, were more than a little eccentric. Half of them behaved as if they might be on the spectrum, so obsessed were they with all things animé and manga. I didn't want Adam to befriend another obsessive, ASD guy—not now, anyway. Most importantly, Gavin seemed kind and patient, and perhaps willing to give Adam a chance.

After our conversation, Gavin excused himself and moseyed to the other end of the table. I told Adam that I thought Gavin was someone he might like, and that now was a good time for him to go over and say hello. Mingling is normal and expected behavior in meetup groups, but Adam wasn't sold. "No," he said. "He's talking to other people."

"Adam, a minute ago he was talking to me. Really, now is the perfect time." He hesitated. I told him to go for it. Adam wanted me to follow but I hung back. A few moments later, Adam got up and walked over. As I'd hoped, Gavin invited him to sit down. No matter how the encounter turned out, I knew it was right for Adam to engage with Gavin. And I was right. On the ride back, Adam exulted in how good he felt when Gavin asked him to join him. They hit it off and Adam spoke of the warm surprise he felt at being accepted just as he was. Adam said that in 4 years of college, he had been invited only twice to do anything with anyone, both times by the same person. Like Richard, who ate lunch alone throughout high school (p. 305), Adam was starved for the camaraderie that gives young people a sense of belonging and worth. That night, he felt he belonged, and his morale soared. He said he even initiated a conversation with a woman at the table, and kept it going by listening closely and responding to what she said.

That night, Adam and Gavin exchanged contact information, and a few weeks later, they met for a movie with others from the group. Adam told me later that people scattered after the movie, but that he and Gavin hung out for 4 hours more. Adam confided his difficulty meeting women and outed me as his social coach, to which Gavin responded, "Whoa, that's cool," and offered to be Adam's wingman and help him meet women. "And it's already starting," Adam said. "I got Bronwyn's number and I called her last night."

Decoding dating behaviors. "Good work, Adam," I said. "What happened?"

"We're going to go out sometime."

"Wow, that's great! When are you getting together?"

"Don't know yet. I'm going to call her back in a few months."

"A few months? Why? Is she going away?"

"I don't think so."

"I don't understand. Did you ask her out?"

"Yeah. I asked if she'd like to go to a movie with me."

"What did she say?"

"She said she would like to go but she couldn't because she had a lot of work to do and would continue to have a lot of work to do for a long time to come. So I'm gong to call her back in a few months when she's not so busy."

"Adam, I think you were taking her too literally."

"What do you mean?"

"I mean that I think she might have been trying to tell you politely that she doesn't really want to go to the movies."

"No. She said she did."

"Yes, I know she said those words. But when a woman tells you she's busy and she's going to be busy for a long time, it's a way of saying no."

"So why didn't she just say no?" He sounded cross.

"Because she didn't want to hurt your feelings. Saying no to your face would have felt awkward, so she made an excuse that would let both of you off the hook."

"But how am I supposed to know? Why can't people just say what they mean?" He had a point.

"I agree with you; it would be clearer if people said what they meant. But sometimes speaking directly embarrasses other people, or we think it will. So to avoid that, we sometimes speak in a sort of code."

"Yeah, well, I don't know that code."

"I know. But you can learn it. We'll work on it together, okay?" He looked skeptical, but agreed to try.

We began by going places where young people congregated and a mature fellow like me wouldn't look out of place. At subsequent meetup gatherings, standing in line at coffee shops, and browsing in bookstores, I watched as Adam conversed with young women whom he saw as dating prospects. I observed his inability to perceive that a young woman facing him squarely was interested in him, whereas one angling her body away from him was not. I pointed this out to him and explained the difference. Once he understood that he needed to be conscious of this, I would ask him questions about subsequent encounters, such as, "Did you notice that when she was turned away from you she wasn't making a lot of eye contact? What do you think that might have meant?" Or, "Do you remember how she looked steadily in your eyes while you chatted? Why do you think she did that?"

Waiting on line at a cafeteria, a young woman in front of us noticed Adam, who was behind me. She pivoted out of line and casually squeezed in between Adam and me, positioning herself close to him. He was oblivious to this maneuver. I brought it to his attention in a whisper and suggested that he invite her to sit with him. He expressed disbelief but, after I pressed him, asked her if she'd like to share a table. They ate and talked for 45 minutes, after which the woman arose, smiled, shook Adam's hand, and left. He bounded over to where I was sitting, said it was the longest conversation he had ever had with a woman, and that he made a concerted effort throughout to be aware of her body language. Still, he'd been too excited by the encounter to remember to ask her for her number. He wanted to kick himself.

In time, Adam learned to connect feelings to the body language he was observing. He began to see that a woman looking at him directly with a relaxed posture, animated gestures, and bright eyes was showing interest, and that those conversations lasted longer than ones where a woman seemed to be looking beyond him, fidgeting, or yawning. Adam's initial desire for a mechanical approach—needing to be conscious of how someone was or was not facing him—eventually evolved into his being able to fill gaps in his understanding about the way people communicate with their bodies.

On the way to and from these excursions, I'd coach Adam on different ways to make himself sound both interesting to and interested in other people. I asked him to come up with at least five things that he might express curiosity about when speaking with a new acquaintance. When he didn't reply, I said, "How about music? Or stand-up comedy? Or the theater? Or a dance recital?"

"I don't know much about that stuff."

"Well, would you be open to attending a concert? Or going to a comedy club, or seeing a play, or the ballet?"

"I guess. But how do I say it?"

"When someone asks you what kinds of things you do for fun, you might say, 'Well, I've never been to a dance recital but I'd like to go to one.' If a woman says she loves soccer, you could ask her if she plays the sport. If she says yes, you could ask her what it's like to play and why she enjoys it; if she says no, you could ask which teams she follows." These sorts of verbal forays feel natural to most of us but are foreign territory to most young people on the spectrum, who typically view conversation as a way to exchange information rather than a means of connecting. Adam had to train himself to reframe his understanding of what it meant to talk to people.

And as we all know, appearance counts. Adam was interested in meeting women, but that didn't mean he always combed his hair or even washed it. But once he started talking to people and seeing how they looked and dressed, he not only became conscious of maintaining good grooming, he asked his mother (who nearly fell over) if she would go shopping with him and help pick out new clothes to wear when he went out.

Jumping in the dating pool. Adam was emerging from his cocoon, reaching out to women, and encountering a bewildering array of signals. He met someone he liked in a class he was taking, who told him she was new to New York City, had not yet visited the Museum of Modern Art, and would love to go. Adam replied that he'd gone there when he was a kid and remembered it as a great museum. He told me later he liked this young woman and felt bad that the conversation had fizzled. I said I thought he hadn't realized that the young woman was trying to tell him that she wanted Adam to invite her to go to the museum with him.

"Well, if that's what she wanted, why didn't she just say it?"

"Actually, she did, but she used different words. By letting you know she wanted to go to the museum, she was giving you an opportunity to invite her to go there with you. It's similar to what happened when Bronwyn told you she'd be busy for a long time; it's a sort of code. Bronwyn didn't want to seem unkind, so she didn't say no to your face. This young woman didn't want to seem aggressive, so she was trying to get you to ask her out."

There were other missed opportunities. Adam met a woman at another course he was taking and when she asked him for his contact information, he provided it. But he didn't ask for hers, which would have been the natural thing to do when she requested his. Adam could not bring himself to do it; as he told me later, he thought it would have been risky because she might have said no. The possibility of such a rejection felt overwhelming to him.

Familiarity didn't automatically confer understanding. After Adam had several dates with a woman named Sally, he came in one day and told me he was going to see her the following night.

"She called me today to confirm," he said, "and to ask me to bring my laptop when I come to pick her up."

"Hmm, that's interesting," I said. "What do you think she meant?"

"What do you mean? She wants to see my writing."

"Okay. But do you think she might have another motive?"

"What other motive? I told her I'm a writer. She likes to read and wants to see my writing. What else?"

"She might be thinking that the two of you could have a more intimate connection if you started the date at her apartment reading some of your work. Maybe then you'd decide to bring in take-out for dinner, and stay in instead." He looked at me as if I were from another planet.

"No. She wants to see my writing. That's what she said." To Adam, there were no undercurrents, no subtext. If it wasn't floating on the surface, it didn't exist.

These examples reflect a pattern common to individuals with high-functioning ASD. At the core is their egocentricity: They tend to be very limited in their ability to see things from other people's viewpoints. Those of us who live with, teach, or work with people on the spectrum know that they tend to take things literally and often do not perceive underlying meanings. They are often oblivious to subtleties of social interactions and miss tones of voice, puns, double entendres, sarcasm, and other nuances of humor. They react only to what is forthrightly presented and not to what is implied, and miss opportunities to react to the feelings behind the words.

Young people with ASD also need to understand the need for clarity in speech. In setting up a date, for example, a young woman told Adam she was free the following weekend, to which he replied, "Great, see you then," and hung up. It never occurred to him that, to most people, a weekend comprises 2 days and 3 nights, any one of which represented a chance to get together. To him, next weekend meant Saturday night, period. He needed to grasp that other people didn't know what he was thinking, and that he had to be clear and specific. If he meant Saturday night, he needed to specify Saturday night, not to mention place, time, and the rest of it.

Sisters and other women. It was only now, 3 months into my work with Adam, that I thought he might be ready to entertain the idea of a better relationship with Taryn. I suggested that he invite her out to lunch, and urged him to try to have the kind of deep, engaged conversation with her that he was having with other women. I suggested he treat Taryn like a woman he had just met, and said he might be surprised by what happened.

After their lunch, Taryn told me that she noticed a change in her brother, which changed her attitude toward him. She said that for the first time in memory, Adam made eye contact and focused his attention on her. He listened closely to what she said and suggested solutions to some problems she mentioned. Taryn was surprised at how much Adam had changed and said she wished he could have been this way years earlier, saying, "He's acting like a real brother just in time for me to leave."

At the risk of being redundant, I'll be redundant: It is critically important for someone with high-functioning autism to develop a healthy, balanced relationship with another person, which in turn will improve relationships at home. Adam's friendship with Gavin and the women he began dating served as a springboard toward improving his relationship with his sister. This is easier said than done: As parents, teachers, and therapists, we know it's hard to help someone else, even a beloved child, and foster a friendship. But although we can't control how other people will feel about or act toward our ASD person, we can help him or her learn to be as appealing as possible. Coaching an ASD teen or young adult on the importance of cleanliness and grooming and how to express interest in other people and keep a conversation going are basic skills that we are in a good position to teach.

And the telephone—we must teach young people not to be intimidated by the exigencies of real-time communication. Texting and email are the preferred communication modes for most young people, especially those with ASD. Digital messaging gives you time to think, absorb, and discuss what a message might mean, and to vet your response before you fire it off. But telephones are not yet obsolete, and it's crucial for people with ASD to become comfortable using the phone and learn to interpret nuances of other people's voices, as well as the dynamism of typical conversation. The Adams of the world need to learn to extract meaning from a disembodied voice's tone, laughter, hesitations, and pauses.

To coach ASD young adults in phone conversation, you'll need to be patient and willing to let them stammer, flounder, and even fail before they get better at it. Rehearsing, role-playing, and advising them about how things might go are not nearly as effective as experiencing the real thing. Let your ASD person have privacy when calling someone he or she is interested in. Don't hover nearby; leave the room and close the door behind you. At completion, have him or her tell you what the other person said. Be gentle but firm in your request for details: You need specifics of the conversation to offer a neutral perspective on what took place because your young person's impression may be based on the literal meaning of what the other person said, with no inkling of context.

PART 5: YOUNG ADULTHOOD & BEYOND (Adam, 22)

In establishing relationships with friends or lovers and strengthening those with siblings and other family members, young persons with high-functioning autism will begin to recognize changes within themselves. The young man who progresses from being unable to talk with a woman to conversing for 5 minutes, to 10 minutes, to hours at a time is doing something that was within his power all along. And new qualities appear: As Adam became more practiced at interacting with women, his natural wit emerged. Before, it had usually manifested as cutting, sarcastic remarks speared at his parents. Now he used his sense of humor with charm, first with women he was meeting, and later, with his parents, too.

As young persons with autism improve their social skills, we must assure them that they are not losing their essential selves and morphing into someone else. You may recall reading about Samantha, who didn't want to stop her mind from flitting about because she liked herself (p. 185). When she was persuaded that calming her mind wouldn't change who she was, she embraced the concept. As parents, teachers, and therapists, we must remind young adults that we all evolve and change as we experience new things, and that in doing so, we begin to see ourselves differently: as more capable, more competent, funnier, stronger. As young persons with ASD evolve, personality traits surface that liberate them from the isolation that has come to feel like home, albeit a lonely one.*

---

* *Many young adults with high-functioning ASD do not want to change. Aspies for Freedom, an organization founded in 2004, rejects the idea that high-functioning autism, or Asperger's syndrome, is a disability, and advocates for acceptance of persons with autism rather than trying to change them. This book is intended for those who believe that cultivating flexibility and connectedness enhances the potential for living a fulfilling life with autism, and does not in any way diminish a person's dignity, integrity, or uniqueness.*

Self-awareness is required, not optional. Adam had to acknowledge his limitations and transcend them before he could have a solid relationship with a woman. This wasn't easy. He so strongly valued his orderly, mechanized way of thinking that he clung to it even when it sabotaged his attempts at romance.

He came to the office one day brimming with excitement over a young woman he had met. He described her as his ideal of beauty, and said they conversed with relaxed yet animated body language (his description), laughed a lot, and that she told him she had nothing to do that evening. I asked Adam if he had asked her to dinner.

"Of course, not," he said. "Beautiful girls always have something to do."

"Adam, come on. She told you she had nothing to do."

"Well then, she must have been lying."

Adam's mechanical thinking stopped him from living in the moment and asking out this woman, even though she practically begged him to do it. His inflexible thought pattern, stiffened by a lack of confidence typical of people with ASD, probably went something like this:

1. Beautiful women always have something to do, no matter what they say;

2. Even if she were free, no woman that beautiful would want to have dinner with me;

3. Even if she were free and wanted to have dinner with me, I'd have to ask her out according to a formula: First I'd have to get her phone number, then wait a certain amount of time, then call her. Only then may I ask her out.

When I gently said that he might have missed an opportunity with this woman, Adam was adamant: What I was saying was impossible. When I highlighted the evidence that she showed him, through actions and words, that she found him attractive and that she'd made a point of saying she was free that evening, he shook his head and reiterated the misperceptions that forced his thinking into a circle (and a vicious one at that). He fiercely rejected any interpretation that differed from his own.

Like someone assembling a bookcase from IKEA, Adam wanted a foolproof series of steps to construct a relationship because he couldn't put together the emotional components on his own. You can't provide instructions to successful social interactions, nor can you rewire a mechanized mind. But you can use it to help an ASD young adult identify patterns of social behavior and learn to act appropriately. Adam's initial strategy, like that of many young people with little or no experience of typical social dynamics, was to expect unpredictable, nuanced human interactions to conform to an explicit regimen that would yield the desired results. If your ASD young adult initially needs a mechanical "just tell me what to do" solution to making conversation, you might suggest the following:

- If a woman tells an ASD man that she goes to college, he could ask her the name of the school, what year she is in, what her major is, what courses she is taking, whether or not she likes the school, and so on.

- If a man asks an ASD woman where she works, she could tell him and then ask him where he works, if he likes his job, how long he's been there, and so on.

The key element in these scenarios is listening. When an ASD person starts to really listen to what other people are saying, the compulsion to think mechanically dissipates.

Emphasize that paying attention to body language is a form of listening. If an ASD man's date puts her hand on the armrest between them at the movies, he can ask her if it's okay to take her hand, and, if she says yes, do it. (There's no rule that says a woman can't make the same request.) He should then be aware of her response: Is she returning the pressure and holding onto his hand, or letting it lie limply in his? Does she keep removing her hand to reach for the popcorn, even though her other hand is available? Or is she reaching awkwardly for the popcorn with her free hand to avoid breaking contact? Mention that even though he may feel as if he's acting mechanically, he should still try to think about how he feels right before he asks to take his date's hand, and then urge him to act on that feeling. Being conscious of his own energy and that of his date before, during, and after handholding or other romantic interactions is an important step in connecting the ASD person to his feelings.

Speaking of feelings, I can't tell you how many times I've heard someone say that the ASD person in their life doesn't have any. No, I tell them; that isn't true. People with autism most certainly do have feelings; they are just disconnected from them. And with practice and help, they can and will connect with them. It took Adam a long time to connect to both his feelings and those of other people. But little by little, it happened. He developed empathy as he began to be able to link other people's tones of voice and body language to what they were probably feeling; he started to see how his own ways of expressing himself affected other people's responses to him; and, finally, he began to act on his own feelings. He may not have perceived the myriad subtleties and underlying meanings of other people's communication, but he became aware enough to react in the moment to forthright expressions of emotion. As I was Adam's social coach, so can you be for the young person in your life. Our job as coaches is to help young adults with high-functioning autism tap into and embrace the feeling part of themselves, and let them know that it is safe to acknowledge both to themselves and to others that they're attracted to someone. Then the coach helps the person connect those feelings to socially acceptable behaviors, which in turn will eventually yield successful interactions.

I worked with Adam for about a year and a half, and suggested we end therapy when it was clear that he was connecting socially on his own. At that point, he was working full-time for his mother's company and training for a management position that would require him to travel overseas, meet vendors, and negotiate contracts.

THINGS TO WORK ON AND THINK ABOUT.

• *You never know how someone will react to your young person with ASD, and it is inevitable that he or she will sometimes meet with failure.* It takes courage on your kid's part to try again and perhaps deal with rejection, and on yours to maintain an encouraging attitude. Parents, siblings, and other trusted advisors of a high-functioning ASD person must assess, as best they can, people who might respond well to their loved one. Even if the potential new friend isn't receptive, the ASD person may have done everything right, should be assured of that, and encouraged to try again. He or she needs to understand that rejection is part of life: It happens to everyone, whether or not they're on the spectrum. When rejection happens, as it surely will, you can help by gently and tactfully pointing out how she or he might handle things differently next time. You can also examine how you respond to your kid's rejection: Are you being overprotective and discouraging your son from reaching out again? Are you empathizing so much with your daughter's disappointment that you unconsciously validate her belief that risking rejection again isn't worth it? Are you elevating the hurt of rejection to a trauma from which it's difficult or impossible to recover? If any of these scenarios sounds familiar, don't berate yourself; instead, rethink your responses and change them.

• *Think of yourself as a social coach.* We all had to learn how to shake hands, introduce ourselves, establish and maintain eye contact, make conversation, and proffer an invitation. The next time you do these things, pay attention to the thoughts and feelings that accompany the event. Notice how your thoughts affect your feelings and vice-versa, as well as how they inspire and determine what you say and do. Notice as well how others respond to you—what you said that made them smile or stiffen, nod, or nod off. Then, use your new awareness to coach your ASD person in similar social interactions. Explain how you knew it was time to broach an issue, change the subject, or end the discussion. Play the role of a prospective friend and improvise conversation. Practice shaking hands, advising on how hard to squeeze and on how long to hold. Rehearse ways of answering queries such as, "What do you do for fun?; What are your plans for after graduation?; and, Why do you still live with your parents?"

- *The challenges facing neurotypical siblings of people with ASD are often underestimated, and even ignored.* Neurotypical children might love and protect siblings with autism, but may also feel resentful about the amount of their parents' time and energy these siblings consume, the absence of normal sibling affection, and limitations these siblings' difficulties impose on family activities—not to mention the guilt and anger they direct at themselves for resenting difficult brothers and sisters who can't help being the way they are.

- *Become your child's strongest advocate, if you aren't already.* Before young adults with autism can revise their understanding of the world and their place in it, they must have at least one person they trust with whom they can share, without fear of judgment or rebuke, their wishes, goals, and anxieties. This does not mean that you don't hold up the mirror of reality when they persist in behaviors such as magical thinking (confabulating scenarios that bear little resemblance to reality, as in, "The woman I've had a secret crush on since fifth grade—and to whom I've never spoken a word—secretly loves me, and when I ask her on a date, will leap with joy!"); and locked-in thinking (having unreasonable expectations of others' abilities to intuit what she means, even if she doesn't express herself clearly, as in, "No, that's not what I said, but he should have understood what I meant"). But when you hold up the mirror, be tactful, be gentle, and be kind.

ALEX, 24

High-functioning; college graduate; distrustful; lonely; can't make decisions.

Diagnosed with high-functioning autism when he was 6, Alex was tall and nice looking. He told me at our first meeting that he had recently graduated from college and had 310 friends, whom I soon learned existed solely on Facebook; Alex had never met any of them, nor did he have any intention of doing so. He lived in Manhattan with his parents, two brothers, and a half sister who had some issues of her own. Home life was stressful: Alex's father was chronically depressed and emotionally distant, and Alex barely related to his siblings, all of whom were younger than he. He was aggressive with his mother, who was concerned about her son's isolation and chronic hostility, which sometimes erupted in rages so threatening, she had to call the police to calm him down. I asked Alex about his anger and was startled when he expressed empathy for the Virginia Tech shooter. "If he had had even one friend, it wouldn't have happened," Alex said. "I know that feeling, where no one knows you or cares about you, and you just want to show everyone that you don't give a damn about them, either." I asked Alex if he could see himself going on a similar rampage. He looked at me as if I were insane. "Hell no, I'm not a murderer," he said. "I'm just saying I know how he must have felt." I was relieved for society, if not for Alex.

Alex yearned to live on his own but hadn't the interpersonal skills to interview for a job, let alone hold onto one. His utter lack of social intelligence was evidenced in his strategy for meeting people, which was to spend hours in Washington Square Park in Greenwich Village imitating a chicken in the hopes that someone, anyone, would compliment his technique and strike up a conversation. (No, I am not kidding.) So far, his efforts had produced only two encounters, both with older men who invited him back to their nearby apartments, where they importuned him for sex. "I'm not gay, but they were nice to me and we had coffee. But that's all," he said. (His parents knew nothing about this.) Like many young people with autism, Alex's loneliness made him vulnerable to exploitation by those whose overtures felt friendly but were anything but.

Poultry impressions aside, Alex spent much of his time alone in his room, drawing elaborate maps of train systems he dreamed up. Still, Alex said that the most important thing I could do for him was to help him initiate conversations with other people. The next most important thing was to help him get a job. "My parents give me spending money but it's no good anymore," he said. "I've got to get out of there. It's driving me crazy."

It's common to find educated young people with high-functioning autism who are unable to live independently. They emerge from the cocoon of college into a world that lacks the support system they'd come to rely on and are soon overwhelmed. They retreat to their parents' homes and there they often remain, because they can't keep a job (even if they are fortunate enough to get one) and can't manage the complexities of living alone or the social interactions of living successfully with a roommate. Eventually, both young person and parents chafe under the arrangement and frustrations mount. Alex's parents were buckling under the stress of having three kids at home in addition to Alex. As for Alex, I don't think he smiled once during the first session. So, how to begin?

When in doubt, order pizza. I had a professor at Columbia who said you could learn more about how people think by observing how they make a peanut butter and jelly sandwich than by putting them through a battery of psychological tests. When I opened my own practice, I learned how right she was. I've been taking her advice for years, only with clients age 12 and over, I use pizza ordering rather than PB&J construction. Here's how it went with Alex and me at his first session.

"Alex, I'm going to order a pizza. What kind do you want?"

"Plain."

"I'm going to have mushroom. How many slices do you want?"

"One."

"Okay. I'll order a mushroom pie with a couple of plain slices."

"Mushroom is good. I could eat mushroom."

"Well, which do you like better—mushroom or plain?"

"Actually, my favorite is pepperoni."

"Pepperoni's your favorite? Why didn't you say so?"

"I don't have to have pepperoni all the time." This sort of waffling is typical of many people with high-functioning autism: Attached more to thoughts than feelings, they often cling to their most recent idea. My job was to keep Alex connected to his feelings, so I intentionally ignored his stated preference.

"So, I'll order all mushroom."

He looked down and said nothing. I decided to press him.

"Alex, if I asked you again, what would you order now?"

Silence. Then, "I guess I would have pepperoni."

"So why did you say plain? And then mushroom?"

"Because plain popped into my mind first, then mushroom."

"Okay, but you just told me you prefer pepperoni. Why didn't you speak up when I said I was ordering mushroom?"

"When I say something, I stick with it no matter what."

"That must cause you a lot of problems." His eyes lit up.

"It does, it does! I often buy things I don't want because when I get an impulse to do something, I have to stick with it."

"Why don't you just think before giving an answer or making a decision? Just now, you could have thought about what kind of pizza you liked, and come up with the answer that felt right." He thought for a moment.

"When I think about something, other thoughts come into my mind, like a tidal wave. I can't think straight."

"Do you lose track of the original question?"

"Yes, exactly. So I just go with whatever pops into my mind and stick with that."

"If I can get you to think in a way that enables you to actually make a decision you're happy with, would that be good?"

"Yeah. That would be good."

"Alex, the first step is tapping into the feeling part of yourself—the part that tells you that you feel like having pepperoni—rather than letting your mind make the decision."

"No. In order to make a good decision, you need to know everything about a situation. Knowing happens in your mind. Feelings are something else."

So ended the pizza exercise, along with a half-mushroom, half-pepperoni order. I'd learned a lot. First, Alex didn't trust himself to make decisions on his own, even something as personal as which kind of pizza he preferred. His refusal to state his preference might have been interpreted as politeness, but his unfamiliarity with the precepts of etiquette ruled that out. Second, he spoke of being overwhelmed by thoughts. What did that mean, and how did it work? Was there a specific sort of thought that brought on the tidal wave, or did thinking in general do it?

After ordering the pizza, I returned to Alex's theory of what comprises a good decision.

"How about relationships? Some people get married without knowing everything about the person they're marrying."

"That's stupid," Alex said. "What happens if the person isn't telling you the truth? My rule is you don't trust anyone."

"Wow! You must miss out on a lot."

"When you trust someone, it ends in disaster. It's not worth it."

"You don't think a good relationship with someone is worth trusting them? It's a good feeling, you know."

"Don't trust anyone—it ends up in disaster!"

"Alex, do you know what love is?"

"What do you mean?"

"I could be wrong, but I don't think you've experienced love."

"I don't want to experience love."

"Would you want to experience a loving, trusting relationship, if I could help you have one?"

"No! Absolutely not." He theatrically raised a forefinger and declaimed, "Note to self: Never love. Never, ever, ever."

So ended our first session. Some of Alex's issues were clear: He lived in perpetual isolation because he refused to trust anyone, and he was alienated from his feelings, which made it difficult if not impossible for him to make decisions. When I spoke to his mother that night, she said that Alex was willing to come back: "He seems to trust you," she said. High praise, indeed.

At our second session, I saw that for Alex, a drive for gain—monetary or otherwise—had supplanted his capacity for trust, wellbeing, even happiness. We were talking about sports and Alex told me he especially liked basketball. I reached into a drawer and handed him a collectible player card with Michael Jordan on it (I buy such cards when I find them and keep a supply on hand).

"This could be worth, like a hundred dollars," he said. When I didn't respond, he added, "I can sell it on eBay." I remained silent.

"You're tricking me, right?" he said.

"What do you mean?"

"You're gonna take it back. You wanted to see what I would do, and now you're gonna take it back."

"No. I don't want it back."

"What if it's worth something and I sell it? Do I have to give you half the money, or all of it?" I smiled.

"No. I'm giving you the card. It's yours. You can do whatever you want with it." He watched me as he put the card in his shirt pocket, waiting for me to demand its return. Was it worth 100 bucks? Maybe. To me, it was worth a lot more to see Alex's reaction to receiving it.

"Why did you do that? Give me something worth good money?"

"You told me you like basketball, so I thought you'd enjoy having the card."

"Yeah, but it could be valuable."

"So what? Giving it to you made me happy. Giving people things they like makes you feel good. You could give someone a pencil and feel good about it."

"But that's different. Giving a pencil is easy to feel good about because it's not worth anything. It's cheap."

"So you can't feel good about giving something that costs a lot?"

"Kinda."

"What about birthday presents and Christmas presents? You don't give those?"

"I do give those, to certain people. But I do it because then they won't ask me for anything else." For Alex, there was only one reason to give a gift: to avoid further contact and future obligation.

GOAL NUMBER ONE:

Replace chaotic thoughts with orderly thinking

My plan was to start by helping Alex recognize when he lost control of this thinking, then steer him toward focusing it. We set out for that versatile laboratory of psychological phenomena, a gaming arcade. Alex espied the skee-ball tables and headed toward them, but on the way stopped at a video game and declared he wanted to play that instead.

"What about skee ball?" I asked

"Now I want to play this." I pointed in the direction of a raucous cheer.

"What about air hockey? That sounds like fun, too."

"Yeah—let's go there."

"Hold on, Alex. That's three different games you just picked as your first choice. You're going with whatever pops into your head."

"I am?"

"Yes, you are. And you said that gives you trouble. Let's work on changing it." I insisted that he rank the games in order of preference and that we play them in that order. This was a verbal version of when I physically restrained Daisy from descending the slide ladder when she wanted to run off to the swings (p. 151). Both she and Alex were in thrall to their impulses. By preventing them from flitting from one impulse to the next, I forced them to exert control over their actions and gain confidence in their ability to see an intention through to a completed action. As Alex was an adult, I trusted he would soon see how exerting control over his actions led to clearer thinking. This would make him feel good, which would in turn prod him toward connecting with his feelings.

GOAL NUMBER TWO:

Help Alex develop and maintain healthy relationships

This would be more challenging, as it involved interacting genuinely with strangers—something Alex was loath to do. So far, he did not have the confidence to speak to women; thus, the chicken imitations, which were amusing to contemplate until it hit you: This intelligent young man had distorted reality enough to imagine that such bizarre behaviors would induce women to approach him as a romantic prospect. When I asked him what was stopping him from making even a forthright coffee date with someone, he had an excuse: "What if I wake up that morning and don't feel well?" He also envisioned relationships mechanically, as was evidenced when I asked if he would invite someone to accompany him to his cousin's upcoming wedding: "No. You need at least a year to get to know someone and the wedding's next month. There isn't time." Clearly, he hadn't a clue about how to connect with others. Here's what we did to get him started.

Watching people's behaviors. I asked Alex if he liked observing people and, when he said no, suggested that we do it together. We met at Chelsea Piers, a gargantuan sports and health club complex on the Hudson River in Manhattan. It's usually teeming with people, most of them young, and offers countless opportunities for spontaneous conversation and casual mingling. By observing people, he might see the logic in their actions and realize that most of us don't act on impulse most of the time. Sipping overpriced, under-brewed coffee, we sat and watched a woman walking a few steps ahead of a child of around seven.

"Alex, do you think she's going to look back?"

"How would I know?"

"Well, think about it. I think she will." Seconds later, the woman looked back, which Alex grudgingly admitted made sense. Next, I pointed out a fellow ordering ice cream from a vendor while holding his mobile phone.

"I bet he puts his phone into one pocket and reaches into another," I said.

"No one can predict the future, Rob, not even you." Ten seconds later, the guy stashed his phone in his jacket pocket and extracted his wallet from his jeans.

"See? I can predict the future, and so can you—to a point. If you watch what people are doing, you can see a logic to their actions. Most of the time, they're focused on completing an action—say, ordering ice cream and then paying for it. They're not jumping from one action to another." By repeating this exercise, which Alex enjoyed, he saw how thoughts and actions could be logical, continuous, sensible, and predictable. One obsession was broken.

Getting a temp job. Even a basic-skills temporary job demands organized thinking, continuity of thought, and a firm connection to reality, all of which Alex needed to work on. I proposed he apply to give away free samples in a department store, which would force him to interact with people, observe their reactions, and see that it was safe to give things away and not expect anything in return (my son Dylan did this one summer and it made him much more comfortable approaching people, so I knew its therapeutic potential). Alex's response was impulsive and predictable.

"I wouldn't do that."

"Why not?"

"It's stupid. People take stuff because it's free, not because they're going to buy the product. I'd be helping people rip off the company."

"But the company wants people to take the samples."

"Only if it makes them buy the product. And they won't buy it."

"How do you know?"

"Because I take free samples and I never buy the product."

"So you're ripping off the company when you take a sample?"

"Yeah."

"Why is that okay?"

"Because I'm not working for the company when I take something. If I am working for the company and giving stuff away, I'm ripping them off."

This was a classic example of how Alex's thinking got hijacked by his impulses—in this case, his excitement at getting something free. The only way he could see the job was from his perspective as a consumer, from which he derived pleasure at getting something for nothing. He could not imagine that the company might have a different perspective. I pointed out that if people took multiple samples, they might eventually try the product, and that seeing people do this might persuade an onlooker to try one, too, which could eventually result in a sale. After a lengthy debate, Alex allowed as perhaps he didn't know more about marketing than a multimillion dollar corporation, that they wouldn't continue to give out free stuff if it lost them money, and, most importantly, that when you work for someone, you have to do the job their way and trust they know what they're doing. He agreed to apply for the job and give it a chance, which was good. What was even better was that he acknowledged how good it felt to complete a logical thought process (albeit a circuitous one) and reclaim deliberate thought from the chaos of impulsivity.

Chatting up a stranger. Around this time, Alex's mother told me he'd bought his half sister some earbuds to replace a set she'd lost, and they were getting along much better. They'd even gone out to dinner, just the two of them. This was probably one of Alex's first experiences conducting conversation with a woman, and I wanted him to build on it.

We returned to Chelsea Piers. Alex noticed a woman in her early 20s who was looking uptown as if she might be waiting for someone. I encouraged him to approach her but he refused, so we walked over together and I struck up a conversation. She quickly noticed Alex and made eye contact with him as we spoke. She said she was waiting for a friend, that they were going to France in 3 weeks, and were heading off to buy a book of French phrases for tourists. Alex reacted sociably to what she said and added a comment here and there. I busied myself with my phone and drifted away so the two of them could talk. The young woman's eyes were bright and she was smiling, and I heard her say that she saw her friend coming, which Alex took as a sign to end the conversation. A moment later he was at my side.

"That's the longest I've ever talked with a girl!"

"Great! Why'd you stop?"

"She said her friend was coming."

"So?"

"So, what do you mean?"

"You could have kept talking."

"What would I do when her friend got there?"

"You could talk to her friend, too."

"No. I ran out of things to say." To prolong the conversation, I suggested he might have mentioned his recent trip to Europe when she mentioned her upcoming one. I told Alex he needed to both listen and keep in mind what to say next. He didn't even think of exchanging contact information, and her first name wasn't enough to find her on Facebook. Nevertheless, Alex's confidence got a boost, which was critically important.

Chatting up two strangers. On an excursion to a marina, we were admiring a boat when a man and woman appeared from below decks. "Nice boat," Alex said.

"Thanks," the man said. "We just got it. We're very excited."

"Do you sleep on it?" Alex asked.

"Sometimes. Hey, would you like a look around?" They invited us aboard and we visited with them for about fifteen minutes. We bid our goodbyes and left feeling exhilarated. I told Alex this adventure was all thanks to his having the courage to strike up a conversation with the boat owners, and that they'd enjoyed the visit as much as we did. I told Alex he'd given them a gift and made them happy, and it hadn't cost him a nickel. "The gift was your appreciation of their new boat. And they repaid you by giving us a tour. How did it feel?" Alex said it felt good.

Joining a group. Buoyed by success, Alex was eager to meet new people. He said he'd always been curious about acting, so we found a basic class for him at a small studio. It worked well: Not only was Alex participating in acting exercises, he was interacting socially with the other students, who were (not surprisingly) outgoing and accepting. After several sessions, he said he wanted to ask out his scene partner but didn't know where to start. We brainstormed and he decided he would ask if he could walk her to the subway after class—a big leap for him. He came up with the idea himself but needed input on what words to use when he asked her, and, assuming she assented, how to say good-bye once they got to the subway entrance. He even proposed riding with her to Brooklyn to avoid having to say good-bye at the subway entrance—"She'll just jump off at her stop"—but we came up with phrases he felt comfortable using whether he got to walk with her or not.

About five months into treatment, we were at Chelsea Piers when we saw two women ambling toward us, checking Alex out. He mustered up the courage to say hi when we passed one another and—lo and behold!—they introduced themselves. Enthusiastic conversation ensued, which ran rings around the sort you make in a social skills group because it was risky and real. Vera, the one that Alex seemed drawn to, seemed to like him as well, and after about fifteen minutes, she linked her arm with his and suggested all four of us decamp for a nearby restaurant and gaming parlor. My job was to talk with her friend, who was gracious enough to put up with a companion easily old enough to be her father. As Alex and Vera walked ahead of us, I caught glimpses of his face, which was animated and expressive. His eyes gleamed; he was in the moment. Alex and Vera exchanged information and saw each other several times over the next few months. He said they were friends and didn't elaborate. But now Alex could talk to women.

A real job. Alex was ready for another leap: financial independence. I encouraged him to take the civil service exam and we studied for it together. I asked him which job he'd most like to have; he didn't know. We discussed this over several weeks and requirements eventually surfaced: The job couldn't be in an office; it should involve walking and maybe traveling; and most importantly, it should enable Alex to work on his own. I was stumped. Then, it hit me: Alex could be the guy who walks around the park with a pointy stick, spearing papers. There's no pressure; he'd be outdoors, no one would be looking over his shoulder, and he might get to travel to different parks. It wasn't the ideal job for a college graduate, but it was a start, which was what Alex needed. He'd have to show up on time, wear a uniform, and perform simple, prescribed tasks. He'd be around people all day but have no obligation to interact with them. Best of all, he'd be making some money of his own. When I mentioned this job to Alex, he liked the idea.

Alex passed the civil service exam, applied for a job as a park maintenance worker, and got it. His parents were delighted and offered to help him pay the rent on his own apartment. (It costs a lot to live in New York City.) Alex was happy to accept their largesse and moved to an apartment in Queens.

Alex and I worked together for 7 months. He ended therapy when he started the parks job. He'd come full circle, in a way, from acting bizarrely in one park to becoming gainfully employed in another.

THINGS TO WORK ON AND THINK ABOUT.

- *Are you expecting enough of your child?* If you had a son or daughter like Alex, you might be tempted to leave well enough alone: He made it through college, after all, and sometimes spent time in a park where other young people hung out. But you might not know that he was imitating a chicken there in hopes of connecting with people, and those with whom he'd connected had something other than friendship in mind. If you are the parent of a young adult who spends days playing video games in his room, you might feel justified in leaving him to his own electronic devices. But I urge you to confront your anxiety and avoidance and prod him into relating to a living, breathing, non-virtual person. Alex's mother did it by persuading him to work with me. Our relationship led to him initiating other relationships on his own.

- *Are you expecting too much?* If you'd witnessed Alex's progress from distrustful misanthrope to acting student, you might think he'd have no trouble asking out his scene partner. But it's important to remember that even though Alex had become more adept socially, he still needed coaching to get to the next step, and the next. Do expect enough of your ASD person to get him or her out in the world, and acknowledge the progress she or he makes. But keep in mind the need for patient, consistent support. Help your child find the words and the wherewith-al to throw his or her lot in with the rest of us.

* *Encourage your child to risk getting real.* A social skills group provides a safe space in which to practice conversing and interacting with others. But there's nothing like the edginess of a real conversation in real time to learn how to be spontaneous. Great conversationalists are made, not born; they listen energetically, can talk about a variety of subjects, and are passionate about connecting—and they practice constantly by chatting with people they've just met. Alex was talking comfortably with me after two sessions; after that, I had to coax him farther afield to build his skills. Urge your child to venture into the wilds of the natural social world. It's scarier out there, but that's the point.

* *Let your kid know you see improvement.* Once kids grow up, there's not much you can do to influence them—typical and atypical alike (I should know: I've got one of each). But when an adult child feels moved to seek help for a problem, parents can still play a significant role in his or her progress. If your grown ASD child is making an effort to work through his difficulties, let him know you see improvement, however small. Tact is paramount. There's a big difference between *(a)* "Gee, you sounded almost normal last weekend" and *(b)* "Uncle John told me he really enjoyed talking with you at the reception." Go with *(b)*.

**Highly intelligent; lives independently;
has test-taking anxiety.**

J ordan knew exactly what he wanted from me. An Ivy League graduate and veteran of 2 years of coursework toward a Ph.D. in psychology, he had now earned a master's degree from a highly regarded social work program but twice flunked the licensure exam—the only graduate of the school to hold this dubious distinction. His parents were baffled; after sailing through the GREs and completing his doctoral course work, Jordan had become overwhelmed and abandoned the degree. Why would someone so academically inclined fail a standardized exam not once, but twice? Jordan heard about me from his father's sister, a college classmate of mine with whom I kept in touch. "She says you're a learning specialist who can help me improve my test-taking skills," he said. His delivery was flat and deliberate, and, viewed with his awkwardness when we first shook hands, seemed characteristic of someone with high-functioning autism. Still, as we talked, he made no mention of ever having been tested or even suspected of having the disorder. This wasn't shocking, as Jordan entered the school system before awareness of and screening for autism was standard among young children. Had he been born 10 years later, he would probably have been diagnosed in elementary school. The one piece that surprised me was that neither of his parents had been sufficiently troubled by Jordan's eccentricities to investigate further.

When I proposed doing an evaluation to uncover possible underlying problems, Jordan declined, saying he didn't have the time and insisting his problem was test taking, end of story. I extolled, to no avail, the advantages of delving deeper, but Jordan was desperate to pass the social work exam and saw no need for anything more. Had he been willing to invest in three to five sessions to undergo a thorough evaluation, we could have identified his disorder and avoided spending 3 months on exhaustive test review. He would still have had to brush up for the exam, but could have used test-taking strategies more effectively by understanding how his way of thinking both underlay and undercut his ability to do well.

Why Jordan couldn't pass the test, and how he eventually did. Over 27 sessions, we painstakingly went over old copies of the exam, and Jordan's problem emerged: Despite his mastery of the material, his literal way of considering the questions prevented him from answering them correctly. He overthought multiple choice questions, burying his original, correct response under layers of rationalization; he couldn't distinguish between questions that required precise calculations and those that demanded a grasp of a bigger picture. There were fill-in-the-blanks, long texts to read closely and interpret, short texts to read and answer quickly, and multiple choice questions offering an array of possibilities. But Jordan was unable to perceive differences between the categories and approached every question the same way: He overthought it to death. His thinking reminded me of pointillist paintings, where images comprise tiny dots of color: When you get up close, all you can see are the dots, and the literal bigger picture is invisible.

I worked with Jordan on viewing the exam from afar so he could discern patterns of inquiry, avoid traps, and consider the questions less literally to assess what was really being asked. We analyzed different kinds of questions and developed strategies he could use to answer them correctly:

- *Multiple-choice questions,* which required choosing among several plausible options. As is common among people with ASD, Jordan created a scenario that would validate each available choice, which in turn neutralized his certainty about the right answer and convinced him to choose the wrong one. I proposed a radical strategy: that Jordan read the question while covering all the choices with his hand, and come up with the answer on his own. Only then could he view the choices. If he saw one that matched his answer, he had to choose that one without considering the others. This method contradicts conventional wisdom, which says you're supposed to read all the choices, eliminate two straight off, and then choose the better of the remaining two. The cover-up strategy worked for Jordan because it prevented him from dreaming up possibilities irrelevant to the heart of the question. And it saved time.

- *Judgment call questions.* These often presented a critical situation—what to do on a home visit when encountering possibly abusive parents, for instance—and asked, "If you were the social worker, what would you do?" Given four choices, Jordan would typically choose the most reactive option, which prescribed acting immediately without taking the whole picture into account. The strategy we developed was to rank the four choices using a commonsense approach and making client safety the paramount concern.

- *Case history questions.* These presented detailed narratives followed by multiple choice questions. Even though Jordan knew the content cold, he ignored critical information that pointed to the correct answers. Sometimes glossing over a single word in a description of a client's psychological or medical condition made the difference between getting an answer right or wrong in how to handle the case. I taught Jordan that he needed to read the case histories very carefully, attending to each and every word. When he didn't, he chose answers that were almost correct but not quite, because they described protocols that were very similar to those outlined in the correct choice. After many cursory readings, Jordan was persuaded that knowing the right answer was simply a matter of paying attention to what he was reading.

After meeting twice a week for over 3 months, Jordan took the licensure exam again. This time, he passed. He thanked me and we parted ways.

But that's not the end of the story. A year later, Jordan called to say he'd been fired from three social work positions. His colleagues thought he was weird, he said; he'd repeat their requests back to them three times before attempting to carry them out; he had trouble multitasking; he mixed up notes, files, even clients. Now he was on his fourth job, and had recently been approached by his supervisor.

"She said she could tell I was working harder and really trying," he said, "and that my work had improved." I suspected that the supervisor was making a show of being encouraging and supportive, which is often required before terminating an employee.

"Are you doing anything differently?" I asked. "Do you think your work has improved?"

"No, I haven't changed anything. I always work hard."

"In that case, I think you're going to be fired again, unless we make some changes." I was blunt but got through. Jordan agreed to undergo a thorough evaluation and we set up a session for the following week. Sure enough, the night before, he called to say he'd been fired again—his fourth termination in a year. I advised him not to seek another social work position until we could get a handle on his problem.

Over the next month of sessions, I administered an informal evaluation to observe how Jordan perceived problems: Could he think, reflect, deduce? I gained insight into his defensive thinking when he told me he'd taken a job as a dog walker and lasted less than a week. It wasn't fair, he said; after fetching five dogs from different homes for a group walk, he'd returned two to the wrong owners. "All these dogs look alike," he said, having confused a schnoodle with a maltipoo. "What's the big deal? No one got hurt." Maybe not, but they did get angry, and Jordan got fired.

The same issues that impeded Jordan's social work skills surfaced as I evaluated him: his inability to do more than one thing at a time or remember to do more than one task when given verbal instructions; overwhelming anxiety in the face of failure; and countering missteps with lame excuses.

Childhood difficulties foretold his adult ones: In third grade, Jordan struggled with math because of his obsessive need to second-guess every detail of a problem. But it was clear he was highly intelligent and, because his overall performance was good, no one addressed his basic problems. Perhaps if Jordan had struggled more in school, his parents and teachers would have paid more attention. Now he was enslaved to a mental process that meandered down countless irrelevant paths, obsessed with the idea of infinite possibilities and compelled to consider them all.

From dogs to cats, and beyond. Jordan said he sometimes stretched the truth when he wanted to impress someone. A woman he was chatting up in a restaurant mentioned she liked birds, so Jordan told her about Dolly, his pet African grey parrot—except he didn't have a parrot. When I asked what would happen if she came to his apartment and went looking for Dolly, Jordan said he'd just make up another story about the parrot actually belonging to his mother, and that he'd just been bird-sitting. And if it went any further, he would simply say that poor Dolly had died.

Covering up was second nature to Jordan; he couldn't fathom that he might be worthy of someone's interest, respect, and affection. As I got to know him, I saw that he lived in a perpetual fantasy state, protecting himself from reality by pretending to be someone he wasn't. He'd told the pet care agency that he loved dogs and knew just what to do when he'd never even walked a dog, just as he pretended to understand things he didn't at his social work jobs. When he signed up with an online dating Web site, he claimed to be two inches taller and a lot more athletic than he actually was.

So it was a big deal when he met Ellie, a junior high school social studies teacher. I knew we'd have to work overtime to keep Jordan from sabotaging the relationship, and indeed he tried. Ellie walked too slowly and ate too fast; she liked to leave parties too early and stay up too late. He fretted that she wasn't religiously observant when he wasn't, either. And then there was the tarot debacle.

Ellie's roommate read tarot cards, and Ellie asked Jordan if he'd be interested in having a reading.

"Had you ever had a tarot reading before?" I asked.

"No, of course not!" Jordan replied. "It's all bullshit."

"So what did you say?"

"I said I'd love to do it."

"But why? You don't believe in it."

"That's right. I don't."

"So why'd you say you'd love to have a reading?"

"Because it was Ellie's roommate and I could tell Ellie wanted me to do it."

"So what happened?"

"I told her that it was a great idea, and maybe the tarot would tell me whether I should call her again or not."

Uh-oh. Wrong answer.

Ellie was offended. She said she thought Jordan was lying about wanting a reading and was insulted that he would base the future of their relationship on its outcome. His voice shook as he told me the story, so agitated was he at having alienated her.

"I should have told her the truth, that I think card predictions are bogus and I'd never go to someone who did them. That's what I really believe, and that's what I should have said."

Lost and found in translation. For Jordan, navigating a romantic relationship was like living in a foreign country. Imagine yourself in a market in Japan, surrounded by people whose speech you can't understand and items whose labels you can't read. Some of the fruits and vegetables look familiar but you don't know what they're called. You don't know how to count out the money to pay for them. You can't even sound out the meanings of words because the alphabet is completely different. Everyone is bustling about and you feel abashed and incompetent. So you nod and smile too much, emanating goodwill and hoping people don't realize how clueless you are. That's how Jordan must have felt; in fact, I imagine that's how most people with high-functioning autism feel as they attempt to function in the neurotypical world.

The tarot incident was a major therapeutic opportunity. It was imperative that Jordan recognize his autistic thinking patterns: his leaping to extremes, lack of self-awareness, meager ability to empathize with others' feelings, inability to perceive nuances in human interactions. His distress about offending Ellie might be sufficient motivation to do it.

I asked Jordan what he thought had gone wrong. He was bewildered by Ellie's anger. He knew she thought tarot readings were cool, so he hadn't expressed his contempt for them. Quite the contrary—he said he'd trust the reading to determine the future of their relationship! He was showing respect for both Ellie and her roommate—what more could he have done?

"You could have been more truthful."

"Truthful? I should have told her I think tarot is bogus?"

"No. But you went to the other extreme: You pretended you trusted it so much that you'd let it decide the fate of your relationship. That was a lie, and Ellie knew it."

"But I had to lie! I couldn't tell her the truth!"

"You could have been more truthful, Jordan. That is, more truthful, not completely truthful." I explained that Ellie wanted to hear his true feelings, not what he thought she wanted to hear. But the hard part was that he had to find a way to express his feelings while being considerate of hers.

"The idea is to find a way to be both honest about our own feelings and gentle about the other person's. Your feeling that tarot is nonsense is honest but extreme, and saying that would have hurt Ellie. But saying you'd let it decide the relationship was also extreme, not to mention a lie. Ellie knew you were lying, and she was repulsed, not impressed." He looked glum.

"The answer usually lies somewhere in the middle, Jordan, away from either extreme. In this case, a good response lay somewhere between utterly rejecting tarot and embracing it as gospel. What do you think you might have said that was somewhere in the middle?"

After half an hour of ruminating, Jordan arrived at a solution: He could have said he would enjoy having a tarot reading—for fun. Such a response would have honestly suggested his perception of such things while respecting Ellie's appreciation of them (as well as her roommate's). Jordan was comfortable with this compromise: Whereas he wasn't saying he believed in tarot, he was implying that he cared that Ellie believed in it.

This was the beginning of a new era for Jordan. He began reining in impulsive, extreme responses in favor of processing other options before he spoke. His progress was gradual, as such growth tends to be, but he became better at recognizing whether he was representing himself honestly with others or bending the truth to impress them. He saw that when he deceived others, he also deceived himself, such as when he made a show of understanding things that eluded him. He became more honest with himself: If he didn't understand something, he would say so. He spoke of the relief he felt at being more authentic, and the burden of keeping track of the lies, white and otherwise, he had routinely spouted.

Jordan interviewed for a job as a researcher at a social work agency—and got it. He was jubilant: He had his own cubicle and desktop computer, and would be providing colleagues with information they needed to lobby local officials and create new policy. Perhaps best of all was that he'd been honest and told the interviewer that he'd prefer doing research to working with clients. At past interviews, he tried to ingratiate himself with interviewers by claiming he thrived on personal interactions with clients—an act of self-sabotage if ever there was one. By being honest about his genuine needs and desires, Jordan got a job he both wanted and at which he could succeed.

Jordan and Ellie eventually parted ways. But a few months later he met Orna, whom he described as the real thing. He brought her to several sessions so they might work on better understanding each other. She was a school psychologist, familiar with high-functioning autism, and generous in her willingness to accommodate Jordan's eccentricities. He showed his commitment by working mightily to become better at expressing his emotions, which was something Orna said she needed.

After 9 months, Jordan left my practice. A year later, he called to tell me that he and Orna were married, they'd bought a house, and he'd just been promoted to research supervisor.

SOMETHING TO WORK ON AND THINK ABOUT.

• *If you see something, do something.* When I first met Jordan, I was surprised that he was unaware of the depth and nature of his difficulties. He said a psychologist had never evaluated him despite his obsessive overthinking in third-grade math. His parents and teachers knew he was intelligent and understood the concept of numbers; how could they not be curious about this obsessive behavior? Perhaps they were lulled into complacency by his otherwise solid academic performance. Whatever they were thinking (or not), the message is clear: Pay attention to your child's cognitive development. I know how easy it is to be oblivious to your child's foibles: It happened to me. Don't assume that your child's odd ways are manifestations of a quirky personality: If something seems wrong, have him or her evaluated. Even if the problem seems like an isolated issue, it may not be. Jordan was extremely bright; who knows how much heartache he might have been spared had the adults closest to him paid more attention to his intellectual growth? Jordan grew up in the 1970s, when research into ASDs was young; he would not have had access to the interventions and treatment we have today. Still, he would have had years of remediation by the time he reached adulthood, and his self-image would have benefited mightily.

GEORGE, 62

Retired scientist; genius I.Q.; can't remember wife's requests.

I knew George and Ursula by sight and had chatted with them a few times over the years, although in retrospect, I couldn't remember George saying anything. Now they were in my office and Ursula was still doing the talking.

"George finally retired," she said, "and I was looking forward to having some help around the house"—Ursula worked full time as a pharmacist—"but nothing has changed. It's not that he doesn't want to help; he just can't remember what I ask him to do." George sat silently. I asked Ursula for an example.

"Going to the market. Before I leave for work, I tell him we need two or three things. He says okay. I ask if I should write them down. He says no, he'll remember. I tell him he won't remember, but he says he will. I ask him to write them down and he gets annoyed, so I go to work. I get home and guess what? He's bought nothing, because he couldn't remember."

"You didn't remember to go to the store?" I asked. George shrugged.

"I went but when I got there I couldn't remember what to get, so I came home."

"When we went on vacation, he forgot the camera. When I asked him to RSVP to a wedding invitation, he forgot. When I asked him to order tickets for the Monet exhibit, he forgot."

"Is this a recent development?"

"It's been this way for 31 years. I thought things would get better once he retired and wasn't obsessing about work 24/7. Now he has all the time in the world, but it doesn't matter. He still doesn't remember what I ask him to do, and it's frustrating." I asked George how he felt about it.

"How do I feel?" He pondered a moment. "I feel lousy. It's like I have a mental block. I just can't remember certain things."

George was quiet, withdrawn, and awkward; you'd never know he was a distinguished chemist with a dozen patents and a genius I.Q. (170, to be precise. He told me). He and Ursula had been together since they met in graduate school and the marriage was solid: They admired and respected each other's intellect and character, and said they were still in love. Yet they were very different: Whereas Ursula's speech was animated and expressive, George's was slow and deliberate, his voice flat. He avoided eye contact, and took several seconds to respond when you asked him even a simple question.

"We were hoping maybe you could help George with his problem," Ursula said. I turned to George.

"Do you agree? Do you think you're the problem?"

"Absolutely. Yes, I do," he said.

This was rare. Usually when a couple comes in, they say, "We have an issue" or "It's really both of us" even when it's clearly one of them who's at fault. But George and Ursula agreed that it was he, not she, who had the problem. I was inclined to agree. My gut told me that, were George tested today, he would likely be classified as having high-functioning autism.

If you've read this far, you know that I like to engage new clients with a puzzle or problem to figure out how their minds work: something captivating, challenging, and fun—something cool. With George, it wasn't easy.

I started to suggest a darkly volcanic experiment combining sulfuric acid and sugar, but he stopped me cold—duh—the guy's a chemist; what was I thinking? I grabbed a deck of cards to show him a nifty trick but he stopped me again: he hated magic tricks, card tricks in particular. Chess? No way; he'd competed in tournaments when he was younger, so I couldn't stump him there. No matter what I thought of, he'd done it, knew it, mastered it, or disliked it. I'd encountered resistance before: You can't coax adults into doing something they're set against, as you often can with kids. But I'd never before had such a brilliant client. How could I challenge him?

Then it came to me: I would show him the fabled crossword puzzle that appeared in *The New York Times* on November 5, 1996—a presidential Election Day—and stunned the international crossword community by purporting to predict the winner. I figured if maniacal crossword aficionados had a hard time figuring it out, George would, too. I was in luck: He wasn't familiar with it. Best of all, it was awesomely, extravagantly cool.*

I pulled it up on my laptop. The clue for 39 Across (seven letters) was "Lead story in tomorrow's newspaper." Just to its right on the grid was 43 Across, the answer to which was "ELECTED." George immediately said the answer to 39 Across was CLINTON. "But George," I said, "how could the puzzle maker predict who the next president would be? I know for a fact

* *Will Shortz, the* Times's *long-time crosswords editor and a good friend, says that this puzzle, by Jeremiah Farrell (professor emeritus of math at Butler University), is his all-time favorite. The Web features numerous postings about it.*

that the editor would never publish a crossword naming the winner before the election—it would destroy his credibility. Can you figure it out?"

George was perplexed. Accustomed to solving math and science problems at warp speed, he was at sea when it came to anything outside his area of expertise. He was struggling and none too happy about it. He wouldn't even try to solve the puzzle; instead, he tried to cajole me into telling him the answer. It was fascinating to watch how frustrated and grouchy he became: Most of us struggle to figure things out every day. Here was a certifiable genius who, when presented with an intellectual challenge, was acting like an 8-year-old who doesn't want to jog in gym, insisting I spare him the rigors of mental exercise.

Thus, my theory was born: George, whether he knew it or not, divided life into two categories: things that were important, and things that weren't. If he deemed something important, as he had his work throughout his career, he would attend to it with laser-like focus. But if it was unimportant—say, shopping for groceries or solving the mystery of an oracular crossword puzzle—he wouldn't deign to think about it. It was as if he refused to squander his mental energy on anything he judged unworthy of its exertions. George agreed with me, so I set about helping him break the habit of instantly dismissing from his mind whatever he judged unworthy of its focus.

Intelligence gathering. I asked George how he typically responded to obligations such as shopping for clothes ("Hate it; only go when stuff gets holes"); shopping for gifts ("Never do it. I give Ursula a check and she buys what she wants"); household chores ("I try but forget"); family gatherings ("Hate them. Only go to funerals, which I also hate"); and social gatherings ("I go to make Ursula happy but go off by myself once we're there"). Did he like music? ("It's okay"); Theatre? ("Nah"); Museums? ("Depends"); Reading? ("Some journals"). I spoke to a mutual friend, a former colleague of George's, about his perceptions. He said that George usually stayed at work later than everyone else and was sometimes still there the next morning. They'd gone to the movies a few times but no longer went out one-on-one. "I was always calling him, never the other way around," he said, "and, well, it just got dull. We'd go out afterward and I couldn't get him to talk about the film; it was like I was doing a monologue. All George ever wanted to talk about was the project he was working on or the one he was going to work on next. When I go to the movies, I'm trying to get away from work."

Here was a man who had been obsessed with work and took little interest in anything else. But now that he had retired, the structure of his life was gone. He couldn't anchor himself to life's small satisfactions because he'd never thought them important enough to cultivate.

At the end of that first meeting, George said, "People say 'just do it.' Well, I can't. Caring about everyday stuff comes so naturally to everyone else, they just don't get how alien it is to me." I told him it felt alien because of the way his mind worked, and that he certainly could change if he put his first-rate mind to it. "You just have to find a reason to put the time and work in," I told him. That reason was his marriage, George said. "I want to be a better husband to Ursula. She's done so much for me."

"In that case, I will help you change." He looked up.

"Where were you when I was 5 years old?" I smiled.

"In kindergarten, just like you."

"I can do this." I began meeting with George once a week at the office. He began his first solo session by asserting his determination to change, which lasted until I showed him a simple magic trick and asked him to figure it out. "I told you I don't like magic tricks. I don't want to do this," he said. "Fine," I replied. So now you'll do something you don't want to do." He gave me a look but then turned to the trick, which he got in 15 seconds. He said it felt good, like when you stretch a muscle you haven't used in a long time.

I proposed he stretch some more with a visualization exercise. He came up with three items that Ursula might ask him to buy: half a pound of honey-roasted turkey breast, half a gallon of 1% milk, and raisins (golden, not brown). I then asked him to keep these items in mind as he imagined himself walking into his local market.

"Okay, George. What do you see?"

"I'm walking inside, turning right, walking toward—wait—I'm passing the produce section and there're fresh cherries. I love cherries."

"What's happening now?"

"I'm tasting one ..."

"You're getting distracted. What did you come in for?"

"Turkey. Raisins. Milk. Okay. I'm at the deli counter now and I'm taking a number, it's 97, but they're only on 92. It's going to take forever! I'll come back later."

"No, you can't leave until you buy those three things—" He opened his eyes.

"This is a pain. Let's do something else."

"George, no. This is the work. Go back into the store."

"Okay, it's my turn now."

"See how fast that was?"

"Very funny. Okay, I've got the turkey."

"Can I hear you order it?"

"A half. Pound. Of. Honey. Roasted. Turkey."

"Good! Where to next?"

"I don't remember."

"Think, George. It'll come to you." He thought.

"Milk. I'm walking to the dairy case. I got it."

"What did you get?"

"Half a gallon of 1% milk. But there's a problem."

"What's wrong?"

"I didn't get a basket."

"So go get a basket."

"This is so boring! Why do I have to do this?"

"Why do you think? Come on. You've got one thing left."

"I know, I know. Raisins."

"What kind?"

"The yellow ones. I'm not a complete idiot, you know." George wended his way back to the produce section, found the raisins, put them in his basket, and then traipsed to the checkout counter, where he had to wait again.

George hated this exercise but he saw it through. For all his grousing, he admitted that the burden of a boring exercise was less onerous than knowing he was failing his wife. And he felt the grim satisfaction of enduring an ordeal and coming out the better for it. I know he was pleased because a few weeks later, he asked if I would help him work on his relationships.

Small talk and other daunting prospects. Conversation, both intimate and trivial, forms a major part of relationships. George wasn't crazy about either but found small talk particularly tortuous. We discussed its value, including the potential for small talk to grow into something more. Still, George found it intimidating, not least because his membership in a faith community made it impossible to avoid. He didn't attend weekly services as Ursula did, but they both participated in synagogue-sponsored dinner and museum groups, at which George sat silently while his wife held up their end of the conversation. Now he wanted to do more.

Another couple invited him and Ursula to join them for a movie and dinner on a night when Ursula was out of town. She urged him to go without her, which he did. "I liked the movie a lot," George told me later. "No car chases or superheroes, just ordinary people dealing with everyday problems. And I said that at dinner afterward. I almost didn't say anything but that's what I felt, so I said so." George would never have done this in the past. I was impressed, and told him.

The following week, he and Ursula attended a community theater production starring a friend from the congregation. They joined others for a meal afterward, at which George offered several comments and had brief conversations with the people sitting on either side of him. In the past, Ursula would have gone on her own. "She thanked me for coming with her," George said. "The show was not too hot, but hearing that thank-you made it worth it."

The next breakthrough came when George agreed to go out with another couple, something he and Ursula had never done. The four of them took the train into the city on a Friday night and went to the Whitney Museum and dinner afterward. George said that he managed to maintain light conversation with both the wife and husband, whom he was surprised to learn he actually liked.

George and I reviewed each outing, concentrating on the hard parts. For example, he was upset one afternoon because he was supposed to meet someone for lunch and they called to say they'd be 15 minutes late. George got angry and was brusque throughout the meal, which he regretted afterward. Even changes requested in advance upset him—adding another person, switching restaurants, changing the meeting time from noon to one. We talked about what was reasonable and not reasonable when it came to changing plans, and how he could develop emotional flexibility to accommodate reasonable requests for change. He also joked one day about the hazards of post-cinema conversation. "We were out with a group and this woman starts talking to me about her bathroom renovations. On and on she went about brushed nickel versus stainless steel finishes. What could I say?" I told him that had I been on the receiving end of that monologue, I wouldn't know what to say, either.

This led to an epiphany for George: He realized he actually enjoyed going out and doing things, that theater moved him, movies diverted him, music transported him, art exalted him. He saw it was the social interactions attending such activities that he'd dreaded. And he saw something else: that no one is immune to the vicissitudes of social interactions, that even quick-witted people are occasionally tongue-tied, brilliant conversationalists sometimes speechless, and the extravagantly curious now and then struck dumb with boredom. When George believed that the rest of the world struggled as he did from time to time, he no longer felt like an utter misfit.

George progressed rapidly. Ursula told me his only recent shopping mishap was an unsuccessful quest for tahini. And she and George were spending more time together: One evening when she told him she was going out for dessert with friends, George asked if Jerry would be there. "Yes, Jerry'll be there," Ursula said. "Then I'm coming, too," he said.

After 4 months, George asked if he could stop coming weekly and come in for a session whenever he needed a brush-up, which was fine with me. I still see him every few months. He's doing great.

THINGS TO WORK ON AND THINK ABOUT.

- *It's never too late to change.* Like my brother Ben, George lived well into his sixties without knowing the root of his difficulties. Both men were extremely intelligent and sociable enough to get by. But neither man was as happy as he might have been had he been made aware of his problem earlier in life and been able to work on it. Absent-mindedness is one thing; chronic disengagement from broad swaths of life is another. If you're the parent of a highly intelligent, gifted young person whose disengagement betokens more than a wacky personality, don't ignore what you're seeing. Have him or her evaluated. Just because a kid can get by on brains doesn't mean he or she will flourish. And if you're the partner of a disengaged adult, do the same thing. He or she may have been getting by for years, but chances are, they could be a lot happier.

- *Offer subtle support.* When George first began reaching out to people, I suggested to Ursula that she brief a few close friends on how they might support his efforts. If you know a few rules of autism engagement, things will be more comfortable for everyone:
  - When an ASD person makes a remark, make a point of listening and responding. She or he will feel heard and be encouraged to engage further.
  - Don't press an ASD person to interact when conversing, as this will compound his or her stress. Let them contribute or not.
  - When an ASD person takes tentative steps toward socializing, it's helpful if others understand that the mere act of being in their presence is an accomplishment. If your ASD child or adult is beginning to reach out socially, gently ask others to refrain from trying to elicit an opinion or remark. Instead, when a comment is eventually made, ask them to listen and respond thoughtfully.

AFTERWORD

Dylan Bernstein

I want to talk about the adjustments I made to create the life I now enjoy. In my early years, I needed to learn to respond to specific situations. My read of a situation is often different from other people's. I might interpret someone's intentions incorrectly, or take something at face value.

I missed out on the experience of being a kid. I felt isolated: not able to have friends in the ways other kids did, bad in groups, caught like a deer in headlights in group dynamics. I felt like the worst baseball player on the team, constantly striking out and preoccupied thinking about the long term. I didn't do as much carefree play as other kids.

I stuck it out growing up, though, hoping that I would eventually be able to contribute in a unique way by inventing something that could help a lot of people. Being an inventor was my mission. I had confidence growing up that I would be able to be accomplished and successful.

I learned to think about things from other people's perspectives, to try to anticipate what they might be looking for or might be helpful to them. In a business context, I think about what the other party wants to get from a deal or relationship.

In social situations, I learned to look around to see what other people might need. I spend less time in my head now, and more time taking in my surroundings. I feel less vulnerable and more ready to respond to the situation if someone confronts me. I am even able to initiate conversation and small talk based on something I notice in my immediate surroundings. This is one of the most helpful things I have learned.

I have come a long way in relating to others. I have learned to respond when meeting new people and in interview situations. Opening up to people is an important step in forming meaningful relationships. I learned to share more of my thoughts and feelings, even if they may be negative or make me feel vulnerable. Now, when I am one-on-one with a friend trying to build the relationship, I push myself to talk more about how I'm actually feeling and what's on my mind.

In my job as a product manager in a tech company in San Francisco, I am now learning a lot about building products and managing teams. It's fun to reach consensus about a product's direction and then work with various colleagues—engineers, designers, and marketing people—to build it and get an audience.

At my job, I like to take a brief walk on the roof where I can see Twin Peaks. The first three months of the job were the most enjoyable. I attended a 7:00 AM yoga class before work that helped focus my mind. The class focused on breathing, stretching, and meditation, and gave me more control over my thoughts (which still sometimes wander), preventing me from reflecting on the actual situation and from being productive.

I have a wonderful girlfriend with positive energy and clear thinking. We have been together three years now. In our initial conversations, she didn't realize I had Asperger's. I didn't, either, at the time. When she suspected I had it, she gave me a book about it to see if I saw some of myself there, and I did.

I've been able to enjoy hanging out with friends more, so that's something that has gotten better. My girlfriend has been wonderful at hosting small groups, such as other couples and friends: We even saw some friends in New York, including three from childhood, before coming out to California.

It hasn't been easy learning how to live in the world. When I was a kid, there were times I wanted to give up. I'm glad I didn't. It's all been worth it.

REFERENCES

CHAPTER 1: Stranger in the Strangest Land

1. Jeanne Safer, Ph.D., *The Normal One: Life with a Difficult or Damaged Sibling* (New York: The Free Press, 2002).

2. Steve Silberman, *Neurotribes: The Legacy of Autism and the Future of Neurodiversity* (New York: Avery, 2015).

CHAPTER 3: Early Childhood, Ages 2–5

3. Jane Gross, "As Autism Cases Rise, Parents Run Frenzied Race to Get Help," *The New York Times*, January 30, 2004.

CHAPTER 5: Adolescence, Ages 15–18

4. Robison's *Look Me in the Eye: My Life with Asperger's* (New York: Three Rivers Press, 2008) describes his childhood; *Switched On: A Memoir of Brain Change and Emotional Awakening* (New York: Spiegel & Grau, 2016) describes his experiences as a subject in a study of transcranial magnetic stimulation.

5. "Music Therapy as a Treatment Modality for Autism Spectrum Disorders," American Music Therapy Association, www.musictherapy.org/assets/1/7/MT_Autism_2012.pdf, accessed September 21, 2017.

American Book Fest 2017 Best Book Award Winner in the "Health: Psychology/Mental Health" category

ACKNOWLEDGMENTS

Robert J. Bernstein

This book has been percolating for the past 30 years. The person who saw the magic in my work before I did was Yosef Willner, a fellow teacher with whom I worked at a summer camp in Upstate New York for youngsters with autism and disabilities—some of whose stories appear in this book. College students, including Yaakov Weglein, were my dedicated assistants, and my experience that summer catapulted me into private practice, where I have happily worked ever since.

On a recent Sunday evening, I got a call from Colorado with an unfamiliar caller ID that I thought belonged to a telemarketer. I picked up and was shocked to hear the unmistakable voice of Temple Grandin. She called me to say that my book had the potential to change lives, and that parents would find their child in the stories I present. Her words resonated with my whole heart and soul, and my being as an educator. Thank you, Temple, for writing the foreword.

Ram Kairam, M.D., a pediatric neurologist, introduced me to the staff at Columbia Presbyterian Hospital and invited me to give presentations at his New York City clinic and at Bronx Lebanon Hospital. I cannot thank him enough for being a staunch supporter who put his stamp of approval on my work and referred many patients to me.

I especially want to thank Robin Cantor-Cooke, who saw the importance of my work and made my words come alive. She is a true professional whose humor flowed naturally while capturing the essence of my work. She immersed herself in this work just as I have done. This book would not have seen the light of day without her. And thank you to my sister-in-law, Dr. Sarah Krakauer, who introduced me to Robin.

Through the years I have had many writers and editors, including my brother, a university professor, my wife Rachel Gordon Bernstein, Simon Aronin, Sheila Hays, author Stefan Kanfer, and psychologist and author Howard L. Millman, Ph.D. A special thank you to Judy Zendell for her editorial assistance on the first draft of the book and for collaborating with me on the Westchester County conference for first responders learning to deal with people on the autism spectrum. There would be no book without these people.

This book would not have been published without the enthusiastic professionalism of the good people at Future Horizons: John Yacio, designer for both the book and its cover; Rose Heredia-Bechtel, managing editor; Jennifer Gilpin Yacio, president; and Leta Henderson, who has since moved on but whose early embrace of this book persuaded me it had found its true home.

I am grateful to my college buddies Steven Strauss, Jan Benson, Roy Greenberg, and Rob Smith for their thoughts about the book at our annual vacation get-togethers. Each has had his own influence on me, especially Steve, a neurologist and linguist, who shared his ideas about the developing mind. Steve has encouraged me since college to follow my dream without compromise. Thank you also to Rob Smith for his work on designing the book's cover.

Many of us have people we go to when we feel we are at a crossroads in life. Shelly Marder, a rabbi and poet, has been one of those people for me. Steve Zeitlin, Ph.D. often influenced my thinking between points of a table tennis match. Will Shortz, crossword puzzle editor for The New York Times, is the best problem solver I know: Figuring out how a child's mind works with Will as we travel to out-of-state table tennis sites heightens my thought process remarkably.

Simon Aronin knows my work intimately and his guidance is boundless. As my advisor and friend, Simon can speak for me any time. I'm fortunate to have input from Rosie Aronin, as well.

I must thank Dr. Douglas Hudson, a brilliant physician and friend, who is always there to answer medical and drug-related questions. Doug has helped me gain perspective on some of the children whose stories are in the book. For the last 17 years, we have watched the Super Bowl together, and between the commercials, he answers all my medical questions.

The magician who revealed his magic to my clients with autism is Jason Lederman (now an attorney). Jennifer Keluskar, Ph.D, did psychological testing on some of my clients, and Robert Roberts and Rawle Alleyne, of the Westchester Table Tennis Center in Pleasantville, N.Y., encouraged my work with children using the sport. Yoga instructors Angela Alfieri and Maria Maldonado worked with my clients and were helpful to me in my practice. Thanks to Melina Florence Bernardi, a music teacher who understood music's therapeutic value for children on the spectrum. I'm grateful to Vance Austin, Chair, Special Education Department Manhattanville College, who invited me to speak to his inspirational graduate students. Sunil Weerawantry propelled my use of chess therapeutically, and I mustn't forget director and filmmaker Olha Kaly, who so generously consults with me on behalf of youngsters seriously interested in film. All these people contributed to the intensive positive energy needed to continue my work.

My friend Bess Altwerger, Ph.D., first suggested that I write a book of case studies from my practice. Bob Smith and Carol Van Bommel are good friends who have been supportive of my writing habit. I also wish to thank Susan Bonnici, who opened my eyes to how the traditional educational system often fails children with autism.

Greenburgh Town Supervisor Paul Feiner helped me concretize my thoughts by interviewing me regularly on his radio show in New Rochelle, N.Y.

I also want to thank the wonderful-hearted Marcy Wagner who joined me enthusiastically in a behavior intervention program for children with learning issues. Elissa Weindling assisted me many times, especially with one client in this book. Allen Epstein, a wide-ranging thinker, always comes up with new angles during our hours-long discussions, and Christine Tomasino unearthed the title that was used for the book.

My colleagues at United Cerebral Palsy in the Bronx, Howard Milbert and the late Jeannette Rehbock, helped me see the value of visiting typical nursery school kids next door, long before "inclusion" or "mainstreaming" came into fashion. From the first day on my first job, Howard, Jeannette, and I jumpstarted innovative and creative programming that became the basis of my professional life.

Also deserving of thanks are my many colleagues, too numerous to mention here, but several stand out: Professor Maris Krasnow; therapists Carol Dallinga, Mitch Samet, Carolyn Marcus, Alan Kuras, Alan Mohl,

ACKNOWLEDGMENTS

and Jonathan Kleinman; speech pathologist Gloria Lazar; psychologists Marcelo Rubin and Josette Banks; physicians Sheree Krigsman and Cheryl Appel; neuropsychologist Anne Cromwell; radio host Chrissy Thibodeau; geologist Alan Plante; botanist Bill Greiner; renaissance man Dr. Theodore Kazimiroff; friend, colleague, and parent Elyse Braun; executive director of the Rockland County Association for Learning Disabilities Ed Jennings; and naturopathic physician Eugene Zampieron. Marion Anderson, executive director of Heartsong, deserves a special thank-you for involving me with her group and introducing me to Dr. Kairam.

A special thank-you to Frank Donato of Brick Oven Pizza in Dobbs Ferry, who was one of many who enabled me to extend my office into the community.

I would be remiss not to thank my dear mentors and professors: Aaron Lipton of Stony Brook University, who helped me develop educational beliefs that soon were inseparable from myself; and Ignacy Goldberg of Teachers College Columbia University, who demonstrated by example how society can help normalize individuals with disabilities through simple accommodations. My knowledge of behaviorism was augmented by A.O. Ross of Stony Brook. Because of him and others at Stony Brook, I was able to understand behaviorism so I could go beyond it with my cognitive approach. I thank deeply Ioana, Phyllis, Margarita, Margie, Nelcida, Leonard, Elyse, Jennifer, Eileen, Aaron, Crystal, Candice, Bob, Debbie, Marvin, Nicole, Miles, Esther, Leticia, and many other parents who shared their deepest thoughts and feelings of what it's like to have a child on the spectrum. I was touched by the mother who said she feels she has no choice but to outlive her son because he will always need her. Being a parent myself and knowing this is a lifelong adventure drives me more than anything to reach out. I sometimes feel that I am helping the parents more than I am helping the children, especially when the kids become more independent and self-sufficient. And of course, I thank the kids, some of whom still call me with lots of time and space between us.

Bernie Witlieb, Harry Waizer, Aaron Jaffe, and Esther Sloan were always there for any advice I needed relating to the book. My gratitude goes to Benjy Silverman for his professional support and for welcoming me to give the annual orientation to the typical children in his Friendship Circle.

I thank my lifelong partner Rachel Gordon Bernstein, who has encouraged me to live my dream of teaching in all shapes and sizes, whether it was the Special Olympics, job coaching, baseball, chess, ping pong, chemistry, natural history, reading, or math. Somehow these elements all contributed to my work with people on the spectrum. I thank my younger son, Jed, who helped me through the publishing process, and his wife, Zoe, for her constructive criticism.

I am especially grateful to my firstborn son, who contributed the Afterword to this book and understands the truth of the Chinese proverb, "Sometimes one must ride a donkey while looking for a horse." And I thank his "partner in crime", Clare, for just about everything.

And of course, I thank my mother and father, without whom I would be a lot less able to write anything, let alone this book.

ACKNOWLEDGMENTS

Robin Cantor-Cooke

Rob Bernstein, collaborator extraordinaire: your energetic, heartfelt commitment to this project made it a pleasure to go to work every day. Your faith in your clients and dedication to their growth are revelations.

Temple Grandin: I cannot imagine a greater honor than knowing you believe in this book. I hope we meet one day so I can tell you in person.

Rose Heredia-Bechtel and our team at Future Horizons: Your enthusiasm for this book energized and inspired us; and Leta Henderson: Thanks for bringing us home in the first place.

Nathan Arries, researcher: Thank you for your conscientious efforts to find the information I needed and for sharing your thoughts on this subject. Your intelligence and candor enriched and deepened my understanding.

Sarah Krakauer, psychologist and friend: I am grateful for your sensitive reading and astute observations, which provided insights beyond my expertise.

June Cantor, veteran teacher of special needs kids, and my sister: Watching you work with your gloriously eccentric students granted me rare insight into the world of autism. Your endless patience and devotion to these children defies description. You change lives every day.

Bill Cooke, partner in all things that matter and some that don't: Thank you for understanding why I have to spend so much time at my desk. I love you. End of story.

ABOUT THE AUTHORS

ROBERT J. BERNSTEIN

 Rob Bernstein holds a bachelor of arts degree in psychology and education from Stony Brook University and a master of arts from Teachers College Columbia University in special education, focusing on intellectual disabilities. He has devoted his career to improving the lives of children, teenagers, and adults with autism spectrum disorders. He developed his cognitive-based approach over more than 30 years of in-depth, one-on-one work with clients ranging from nonverbal toddlers to high-functioning adults. He has consulted for the pediatric neurology department at Bronx Lebanon Hospital and Pediatrics 2000, a medical clinic in New York City; an educational consultant to the National Council on Alcoholism and Other Drug Dependencies; and has provided expert testimony at hearings on behalf of young people on the autism spectrum. Mr. Bernstein conducts evaluations for neurologists and neuropsychologists around the country, and was coordinator for special education and science for the New York City Department of Education. In addition to his private practice, he conducts workshops, seminars, and support groups for families of persons with autism spectrum disorders, and appears regularly on WVOX radio in New Rochelle. In 2012, he founded the Table Tennis Therapy Program for Asperger's Individuals in Pleasantville, New York, the first program of its kind. He has two grown sons and lives with his wife, artist Rachel Gordon Bernstein, in Ardsley, New York.

ROBIN CANTOR-COOKE

 Robin Cantor-Cooke is the co-author of *One Less Thing to Worry About* (with Jerilyn Ross), *Satisfaction* (with Anita H. Clayton, M.D.), *Thriving with Heart Disease* (with Wayne M. Sotile, Ph.D.), and the ghostwriter of two books, one of them a *New York Times* number one bestseller. She has worked as a writer, editor, scriptwriter, and producer on more than 40 books and tape programs and is an adjunct faculty member at William & Mary. She has two grown sons and lives with her husband in Williamsburg, Virginia.